A Matter of Degree

*To
Guy Cummings
Best Wishes*

[signature]

To
E.E. Cummings
Best Wishes
[signature]

A Matter of Degree

The Hartford Circus Fire
and the Mystery of Little Miss 1565

Don Massey & Rick Davey

WILLOW BROOK PRESS

Copyright © 2001 Willow Brook Press

All rights reserved under International and Pan-American Copyright Conventions. Published in the United States by Willow Brook Press, Simsbury, Connecticut

RINGLING BROS. AND BARNUM & BAILEY® and THE GREATEST SHOW ON EARTH® are federally registered trademarks and service marks of Ringling Bros. and Barnum & Bailey Combined Shows, Inc.

Publisher's Cataloging-in-Publication Data

Massey, Don, 1948-
    A matter of degree: the Hartford Circus Fire and the mystery of Little Miss 1565 / Don Massey & Rick Davey. — 1st ed.
    p. cm.
    Includes index.
    LCCN: 00-130550
    ISBN: 1-930601-24-7 (hbk.)
    ISBN: 1-930601-23-9 (pbk.)

    1. Hartford Circus Fire, Hartford, Conn., 1944. 2. Ringling Brothers Barnum and Bailey Combined Shows—History. 3. Circus—Connecticut—Hartford—History. 4. Fires—Connecticut—Hartford—History. 5. Hartford (Conn.)—History. 6. Dead—Identification. I. Davey, Rick, 1948- II. Title.

F104.H3M37 2001   974.6'3'042
                          QBI00-193

www.hartfordcircusfire.com

Manufactured in the United States of America

First Trade Edition

For

Eleanor Emily Cook

*Fear not, for I have redeemed you.
I have called you by name, and you are mine.
When you pass through the waters, I will be with you,
And through the rivers, they shall not overwhelm you.
When you walk through the fire, you shall not be burned,
And the flame shall not consume you,
For I am the Lord your God.*

Isaiah 43:1-3

PREFACE

First and foremost, *A Matter of Degree* was written to honor the memory of Eleanor Emily Cook, whose identity remained a mystery for nearly fifty years. She and 167 other souls—including 68 children killed in the circus fire—have waited far too long to be memorialized. Other than that which is found in these pages, there is no lasting testament to their existence and their importance to the world from which they were called so soon.

Our second reason for having written this book was the desire to journey across the boundaries of time and space to Hartford in the 1940's, America's most romantic era. It was our hope when we began, and it is our hope now, to honor a ravaged city for its capacity to mobilize itself in the wake of an unexpected disaster, gathering every ounce of communal courage in an effort to heal the wounds inflicted by a fire whose principal victim was cultural innocence.

We were inspired to write a nonfiction work because no definitive history of the Hartford Circus Fire had ever been written. The absence of an accurate portrayal of the tragedy, an intimate portrayal that sought to offer something other than a chronicle of carnage, underscored the importance of such a book as a literary and historical necessity. We believed that the American people—and people around the world—had not been properly informed about a tragedy of astonishing emotional magnitude, a tragedy equal in scope to the Oklahoma City bombing of 1995. There were no video cameras, satellites, or cable news networks in 1944. Had there been a way to transmit images of human sacrifice as they were captured, the impact of that sad summer afternoon would be indelibly imprinted on our nation's memory.

The story of the Hartford circus fire is riveting, both as history and as human drama. Many of the details presented in this book have never been revealed before, despite the extensive international media coverage of Lieutenant Rick Davey's 1991 re-investigation of the Ringling case. By placing his nine-year mission of the heart against the backdrop of a public tragedy, we hope to humanize history, revealing the spiritual bond between a fireman and a little girl he never knew, a lost child who called to him from beyond the grave.

We are deeply indebted to many people whose assistance and support made the publication of this book possible. We extend our gratitude to Attorney Edward Rogin, John Vendetta, Wilson Faude and the Old State House, Greg Parkinson and Circus World Museum, Marianne Curling and the Mark Twain House, Jim and Annie Bissonnette (special thanks for the glorious solitude of a lakeside cabin in New Hampshire), Don and Linda Cook, Lori and David Fagone (for taking the trip before the map was printed), Darryl Spencer Tookes (for the friendship and the music), Tim Philen (a gorgeous cover), India Blue (true photo synthesis), Darryl Greene, Kathy Simpson (for text design consultation), Jeanne Marchand-Massey (for final text design and implementation), Joan Kelley (for infinite patience), Kate and Barry Blackaby, Allen Blagden, Howard McClintic, Jack Wieselman and Chip Houlihan (the law always wins), Miss Demma, Miss Valentine, Carl Radcliff (Columbus County Sheriff), Guy Cline (former Ohio Prosecutor), Mike Simmons (Ohio Fire Marshal's Office), Dr. Eugene Nedelsky, Dr. George North, Ming Fisher, the Ohio Psychological Association, and the Connecticut State Library.

Most of all, we want to thank our families, whose love and faith never wavered, even in the most difficult moments.

INTRODUCTION

A *Matter of Degree* is a work of narrative nonfiction. As such, it seeks the emotional and artistic truth that underlies the tragedy of July 6, 1944. By the time the writing of this book began in 1998, many of the individuals whose names, actions or official positions were important to a thorough understanding of the Hartford circus fire had long since died. Therefore, a large measure of our work was devoted to the reconstruction of the circumstances surrounding the suspicious blaze that claimed 168 lives and virtually destroyed the Ringling Bros. and Barnum & Bailey Circus. By examining the facts as we gathered them, we attempted to comprehend the personal, cultural, legal and political implications of the circus fire and its aftermath.

The names of all individuals cited in the text are real. Wherever possible, we have omitted dialog that was not uttered in our presence or which was not previously made a part of official documents or the published record. While we have occasionally attributed thoughts and dialog to some individuals, the incidents to which those expressions relate were reliably described to us in the course of our research. Descriptions of criminal proceedings and legal inquiries were derived from a review of official court documents and municipal records, all of which were obtained in accordance with Connecticut law.

The published recollection of any tragic event—especially one that has taken on immense personal and historic proportions—must be considered subjective when presented after the passage of fifty years. The account that follows is based on the information that was available to us. While we have exercised some artistic license in describing certain events, every attempt has been made to maintain accuracy and authenticity in the research and writing of this book.

The flame of hope burns within the human heart, lighting the way to the truth we seek. We pray that there will never be another tragedy similar in scope to the Hartford circus fire of 1944. Let us honor those who lost their lives that day by remembering the contributions they made while they lived, rather than by dwelling on the manner in which they died. May their souls rest in peace.

Rick Davey
Don Massey

PART ONE

THE CENTER RING OF HELL

Prologue

May 12, 1987   *1:25 PM*

A silver shield protects a beating heart. Sunlight shatters when it strikes this gleaming barrier, scattering brittle beams in all directions, as if a life force were emanating from the inner chambers of the man behind Badge Number 539. A flag-draped wooden platform, its steps and borders split and fraying from extensive use, rises into a blue sky whose clouds have the appearance of brush strokes on a watercolor canvas. The air carries the sweet scent of early spring in New England. Except for the intermittent chirping of sparrows and jays, there is only silence.

Squads of Hartford firefighters in dark blue uniforms have filed into a semicircle of seats fanning out from the base of the platform. They have come to honor one of their own, a man with unique intuitive gifts, a superior investigator with an unbroken chain of successful arrests and prosecutions. In celebration of his achievements, shining silver bars will be placed on his uniform, enhancing the brilliance of his reputation.

The man behind the badge is young and well-muscled, with piercing brown eyes and a fireman's bushy mustache falling to dagger points beyond the corners of his mouth. The central figure in a long line of highly-decorated officers, he sits rigidly in place, years of military training evident in his bearing. One white-gloved hand is clenched in a tightly-coiled fist, while the other lies open and calm along the arched surface of his leg. The opposing attitude of his hands suggests the vast expanse of his inner terrain, the emotional boundaries of which remain uncharted.

This is a day of celebration, but the demeanor of the man behind the badge suggests discomfort rather than joy. Even in silence, the power of his persona alters the atmosphere of the moment, establishing a mood similar to that of a courtroom in which strangers have gathered for the purpose of weighing evidence and passing judgment. He sees himself as a man on trial, a trial conducted in secret, an inner trial that has continued in full each day for years, recurring and reverberating in his mind, with identical circumstances and identical facts leading to an identical, inevitable result.

He has never told anyone about the voice, the voice of a child, a little girl who died before he was born, a little girl whose spirit called to him, begging to be found, longing to come home. He is infused with her spirit, a spirit that haunts him, but he has never revealed her existence. The man behind the badge is known as a man of the concrete and the absolute, a man with little patience for that which cannot be proven. There would be no way to explain his decision to accept the voice into his life, so he has not tried. Even those closest to him would think he had lost his mind, and his connection to the brotherhood of fire would be severed. Her spirit is a secret he cannot share, a secret that is tearing him apart.

When she called him to a mission of the heart—a mission whose scope and complexity he could never have foreseen—he had answered, just as men of heroic caliber have always done. Setting aside his fear and disbelief, he began a quest that has continued for five years, a quest that has yielded only failure. For a man accustomed to success, failure is never acceptable. This is his own private trial, and he has examined the evidence of his performance, imposing a sentence from within. She is still lost, still calling, and there will be no leniency until he finds her.

For now, he shows no sign of the furious struggle being waged within his heart, the heart beneath the gleaming badge. There is no visible evidence that his spirit is fleeing from this place as silver bars are pinned to his uniform, as a hand is shaken, as a salute is returned. When the moment of celebration is over, the shining shell of the man behind the badge simply drifts from the platform to the rhythmic accompaniment of sustained applause, a sound he cannot hear.

He will return to the mission that has consumed so much of his life, and he will do so without uttering a word about his real purpose. To expose his quest would leave him open to ridicule. He would be unable to explain his commitment to the ghost of a little girl who died alone one summer day, losing her life and her name in the same tragic instant.

Anyone learning of his secret interest in a high-profile case nearly five decades old would assuredly question his motives, even his sanity. Most of all, they would call him obsessed. No one would ever be told that the man behind the badge is driven by a single closely-held belief: in the search for truth, the difference between commitment and obsession is simply a matter of degree.

ONE

July 6, 1944   6:03 AM

A soaking sun rose in the morning sky. Even as the day began, there was no escape from liquid heat as it dripped like candle wax on the city below. Brave souls waded through the thermal tide, certain that this would be a day to remember.

Like most American cities, Hartford had seen its share of suffering by the summer of 1944. Thousands of families had lost loved ones in the years since World War II had begun, but the community was bonded together by a shared sense of purpose, and by the belief that each loss was a contribution to a larger sacrifice, a heroic sacrifice that would surely benefit the world. Mythical as that perception might have been, it served as a unifying principle.

Hartford is a city born of belief. In 1633, Dutch settlers established a trading post on the banks of the Connecticut River. Seeing agrarian symbolism in the lush green landscape and gently rolling hills, they named their new community the "house of hope." Two years later, a splinter group of zealots from the Massachusetts Bay Colony drove the Dutch away and claimed the region as the new home for a restrictive form of religious expression. Once established, the separatist Puritans led by Thomas Hooker paid tribute to their British homeland of Hertfordshire by naming the river settlement Hertford. Hooker's leadership would inspire the creation of the Fundamental Orders, the fledgling democratic nation's first written constitution.

A vibrant port city for the first century of its existence, Hartford—as it came to be called—routinely welcomed heavily-laden sloops and schooners from the Orient and the Indies. After the Revolution, the Puritan leaders abandoned their symbiotic union with the city's fluid border, choosing to bind themselves to the land instead. As tillers of souls and soil, they preferred to cultivate the earth rather than the maritime trade. In the centuries that followed, the growing community expanded west from the river, building a granite-gray future on the foundation of the insurance industry.

The city's arc of glory coincided with the Industrial era. Even as it opened itself to the future, Hartford sustained many of its pastoral qualities. Public landscapes and greenways were strung across the city like an emerald necklace. Elizabeth Park quickly became renowned for its rose gardens. Frederick Olmstead, the widely respected architect of Central Park in New York City, designed Bushnell Park, a rolling campus that flowed like a river from the base of the State Capitol. The burgeoning city offered sophistication, prosperity and beauty, a unique cultural chemistry that attracted new waves of residents, including celebrated icons of American literature. In 1873, Mark Twain built a sprawling Victorian mansion on a knoll called Nook Farm, adjacent to a notch in the course of the Connecticut River. He would describe his adopted hometown as the city he loved above all others, the city where Tom Sawyer and Huckleberry Finn would be born to the world. Twain's Hartford neighbors included Harriet Beecher Stowe and her abolitionist family—until swirling river currents claimed Stowe's youngest son.

After the turn of the century, cargo ships no longer steamed into the shallows of the central Connecticut River. Rails began to replace the docks and river ways as the city's primary means of transport and economic opportunity. Modern industrial advancements would serve as the catalyst for a rising quality of city life that improved steadily in the first half of the twentieth century.

During the 1940's, Hartford was a thriving wartime economic center, with a population that had swelled to a peak of more than 165,000 residents. The city's mood and productivity were stimulated by the abundance of high-tech jobs for a well-trained workforce, and most of those jobs arose from the need for city-built engines, propellers and other aircraft components that were so vital to the American war effort.

Ironically, the post-industrial period would make an economic orphan of Hartford in the decades following World War II. But a thread of courage had been woven deeply into the fabric of the community, and hope would always be the key to survival. Even after the loss of Hartford's pastoral innocence, the spirit of the people would not dissolve. Hope would flow freely through the heart of the city—even in the presence of adversity.

Month-old memories of the D-Day invasion were still fresh on a scorching summer morning in 1944. The Fourth of July holiday, coupled with the prospect of an Allied victory in Europe, placed the people of Hartford in a festive state of mind. They were eager for emotional relief, any brief respite from the punishing realities of life in the shadow of war. In the early afternoon, thousands of residents—most of them women and children—would gather beneath a square mile of canvas to witness a rite of summer entertainment called "the greatest show on earth." They would find the time to follow the rhythms of their hearts, to escape to a netherworld of sad-faced clowns and ferocious animals and dangers on the high wire, a netherworld that promised to reveal its mysteries once the canvas threshold had been crossed.

A revered American institution since the turn of the century, the Ringling Bros. and Barnum & Bailey Circus was known to deliver nonstop action and a level of suspense and excitement that would capture the attention of even the friskiest kids. Still thriving in the romantic 1940's, years before profound cultural competition from television would diminish its value, the Ringling circus attracted enormous audiences in every city on its tour. Hartford was no exception.

Like so many city residents, Mildred Cook had been planning her trip to the circus for months. She had come to Hartford in search of peace, but that was not the way her life would unfold. A tall, tubular woman of 38, Mildred hid the soft beauty of her oval face behind dark horn-rimmed glasses. The more fundamental aspects of her being lay sealed beneath the surface, and were never exposed at all. Those who had gotten to know her in the months since her arrival had learned to accept a warm smile as compensation for cold silence, the customary currency of concealment.

The secrets Mildred guarded so closely were secrets of the heart, truth that demanded release, truth that could only be held in check by self-deception. During rare moments of trust and comfort, Mildred opened herself to other human beings and became an engaging, animated creature. Arms of unusual length, suspended from broad shoulders as if they were tentacles, flailed before her with a sometimes wild and unknown purpose whenever she spoke. Like her spirit, Mildred's body had been stretched to its limits, but true happiness had always remained beyond her grasp.

Southampton, Massachusetts is a rural farming community nestled in the Connecticut River valley. The Parsons clan had lived in town for several generations, sharing the land with many other New England families of Dutch and Anglo-Saxon lineage. Life was often serene and quiet, just as they had always wanted it to be, but there had been a string of devastating events in Mildred's early life. First, her brother and sister died during infancy. A short while later, her mother—who had made an extraordinarily powerful and lasting impression on the four-year-old Mildred—died of cancer. Her father re-married with the hope of providing a proper life for his daughter, but even more tragedy intervened. Both of Mildred's older stepsisters would soon die, one of them after being crippled by polio.

When Mildred was 27, she met the dashing Wesley Cook. He was a handsome young Yankee, and Mildred had fallen in love with him the moment she looked into his deep-set blue eyes. Perhaps in an effort to escape from the home in which so much misery had occurred, she married Wesley after a brief courtship, then she moved out of the Parsons homestead. In a matter of months, however, Wesley's true nature began to reveal itself. He would often drink with a group of friends well into the early-morning hours, returning home long after a drop too much had been taken.

Mildred and Wesley in 1934, one year before their first child was born.

PHOTO COURTESY OF DON COOK

On so many dark nights, Wesley would become hostile and angry for reasons that Mildred never fully understood. Without warning, he would release his ill-conceived aggression on his young wife, leaving her frightened and insecure. After coming to his senses, Wesley would beg her to forgive him, demonstrating the affection that Mildred wanted and needed so badly.

Their volatile emotional chemistry made daily life as dangerous as it was unpredictable. Because of the values with which Mildred had been raised, she remained committed to the marriage, despite the uncertainties that steadily confronted her. Into this environment, three children were born. Donald was the first, in 1935. One year later, the daughter Mildred would nickname "Honey" arrived. Edward, the last of three, was born in 1938.

By the time Edward was five years old, Mildred's marriage had begun to dissolve. She had become unhappy with the fact that her children lacked many basic necessities—including milk to drink, heat during the winter, appropriate clothing and shoes—because of Wesley's inability to earn a decent living. No longer willing or able to withstand her often-absent husband's neglectful behavior, Mildred decided to gather her children and their few belongings and move into her brother's home in Southampton.

The Parsons family was New England born and bred, stoic in the face of adversity. Asking for help from an outsider—even from someone within the same community—would be considered a sign of weakness, so it was never done. Instead, the family had always borne its own burdens, strengthening the bonds between them by caring for their loved ones whenever a crisis arose.

From the moment Mildred and the children arrived, Ted Parsons made it clear to his sister that they would always be welcome in the family home. And for a while, those arrangements were acceptable to Mildred, who went to work to contribute to the cost of raising three children. But she soon realized that more definitive changes would be necessary. Despite Mildred's efforts to avoid conflict with her husband while they were separated, Wesley would make periodic attempts to reconcile, pleading with her to return to him. He would promise a better life, and Mildred would be tempted. Each time, a voice inside her soul would scream a warning that could not be denied.

By the time Mildred came to the conclusion that she would never return to her husband, Wesley had decided to abandon his family forever. Mildred was suddenly faced with the most difficult decision of her life. Just days before Christmas, she brought her concerns to her brother, as she had always done in the past.

During a late-night family meeting, Mildred openly acknowledged that her marriage had crumbled, and that she had decided to build a new life on her own. Mustering the courage to continue, she also acknowledged that she did not have the means to care for her three children properly. As tears welled in her eyes, Mildred forced herself to outline the plan that she had reluctantly developed in the dead of night, a plan that most human beings would find shocking, even unthinkable.

Swallowing her pride, she told Ted that her children had to come first, before any of her own human needs. She wanted them to have a good home, and she recognized that she could not provide one for them. Although she knew that most people would never understand or accept her reasoning, Mildred asked her brother to take Don, Honey and Edward into his home and raise them as if they were his own children—without Mildred in their daily lives.

A 1943 pre-school photo of the Cook children. Honey is holding her kitten, Tea. The family's dog is named Coffee!

PHOTO COURTESY OF DON COOK

Before her brother could answer, Mildred made it known that she was not abandoning her children. Rather, she was asking Ted to provide the kind of environment that Mildred had always dreamed her kids would enjoy. Now that her dream had faded, she would move to Hartford alone to find work in the insurance industry. She would commit to any job that would allow her to pay her own way and make some contribution to the lives of her children.

Mildred's promise to them, and to herself, was that she would see them as often as she could, especially on holidays and weekends. Their familial relationship would continue, even though this new plan would impose intensely emotional changes on all of them. Having thought it through, Mildred asserted that this was her only choice. God willing, she and the children would be united again in the future. For now, though, there were no other options that would leave her dignity—and the quality of her children's lives—intact.

Ted Parsons loved his sister too much to confront her about a decision that he recognized to be both difficult and devastating. This was a choice that no young mother should ever have been forced to make. Knowing Mildred as he did, Ted understood that she was thinking of her children first, and that she wanted only the best for them. So, without speaking a word that would stimulate guilt or suggest repudiation, Ted agreed to his sister's plan.

At that moment, Mildred was overcome by a complex mixture of intense relief and profound remorse. She realized that the effects of her decision would immediately be imposed upon those she loved most. The time had come to tell her children that their lives were about to change. Mildred knew the announcement would be brutally painful. Her only hope was that they would understand.

Two

Mildred made her home in a sparsely-furnished, dimly-lighted space on the third floor of a yellow brick tenement overlooking a concrete courtyard on the west side of Hartford. Soaring summer temperatures were made bearable by dark shade that covered the stone structure like a shroud most of the day. While there, the world could be controlled. While there, the world could be denied. Mildred simply entered the darkness and turned the key, never looking back, never listening too closely because listening could be dangerous.

Although the symbols of her existence suggested an ending rather than a new beginning, Mildred persevered. Despite near poverty, she maintained an elegance of motion and manner that had its origins in a quiet corner of her spirit. From that place, strength rose. In private moments, the still-young woman wondered whether she would ever find love again, a love that did not shout, a love that did not strike. In the absence of a partner on whom she could rely, she would rely on herself—just as she had been taught to do.

Mildred rarely ventured beyond the shaded Marshall Street courtyard except to walk to work at Liberty Mutual, a large insurance company near the center of the city. The two-mile journey was pleasant when there was silence, and excruciatingly painful when the voices of children moved along the sidewalk with her. Their laughter echoed through the streets, bouncing into Mildred's mind despite the strength of the barriers she placed in their path.

When young voices penetrated her consciousness, memories were awakened, each one a reminder of children she once had, children who were still her own, children who would always be with her, even when they were gone. They were voices that cried, voices that longed to be heard, voices that begged for attention that could not be paid. Once inside, those voices moved deeper, forging new pathways through the inner spaces of her soul. In those moments, Mildred would simply close her eyes and surrender, knowing that she was powerless to stem the tide of memories flowing over her. Visions of her children—two sons, one daughter—arrived on a restless current of pain, waves that rose and fell then died away, setting whispered thoughts free, as if they were prayers. *Forever is such a long word. Three young souls cannot be gone forever. That would be impossible to accept, making life impossible to endure.*

Her mind often drifted to the choir loft in the First Congregational Church, where her maturing teenage voice united with the voices of friends. Mildred heard the music vividly, as if the moment had returned and she were alive within it. The memory offered fleeting solace, and she sang the passion inside herself, just as she sang then.

On a random Sunday morning in 1923, Mildred had seen her father fall to the floor of the church. She never fled from the choir loft, never ran to his aid, and she never stopped singing—even as she watched him die. She remembered wanting to sing forever then, never stopping, not even for breath.

Because her mother had taught her that crying was a sign of weakness, Mildred had refused to shed a tear for the man she loved above all other beings, above all other things. On that day, her will was forged and molded and cooled, its shape permanent, its strength certain. From that moment on, there would be no doubt about her capacity to endure suffering, no doubt about her ability to find the means of survival.

Mildred had seen Don, Honey and Edward only rarely in the months since she moved to Hartford. When she left Southampton, she had promised to spend as much time as possible with her children, but the distance that separated them had made weekend visits difficult to arrange. Mildred clung to the hope that she would find the money to bring her family together again, no matter how long that might take. In an effort to compensate for their time apart, she had been planning a Fourth of July holiday surprise, an event that was sure to please the kids.

Her job as a claims clerk paid little more than a subsistence wage, so Mildred had taken a second job in the evenings. Over the last eight weeks, she had set aside some extra money, adding coins to a Mason jar she kept on the kitchen shelf. Each night after work, she sat on her bed and emptied the jar, counting the coins over and over again, eagerly anticipating the moment when she would have enough to buy tickets to the Ringling Brothers circus. She and the kids would be spending four days together during the holiday, a much longer visit than usual, and Mildred hoped an afternoon at the circus would be a very special occasion for all of them, a memory that would linger long after the kids returned to Southampton.

In 1884, five young brothers from Baraboo, Wisconsin pooled their cash, purchased a half dozen horse-drawn wagons, and set out to make their fortune as circus entrepreneurs. Natural showmen, the Ringling brothers crisscrossed the country, promising their mostly rural audiences a new form of entertainment, a public spectacle unlike anything America had ever seen. At a time when audiences were accustomed to single-ring circuses, the Ringlings established their reputation by presenting three rings of exotic entertainment equal in scope to the traveling shows of P. T. Barnum, the business rival they would ultimately vanquish. Ringling shows quickly evolved away from Barnum's known focus on freakish attractions populated by bearded ladies and deformed beings, many of them abandoned—even sold—by their parents and symbolically adopted into the sideshow world. The Ringling circus offered wholesome family-oriented entertainment.

Above all, the Ringlings developed the street parade to the level of high advertising art, a live-event form of self-promotion that quickly became as popular as the traveling shows themselves. Wherever the circus appeared, hundreds of local children were sure to line the streets as the performers and animals made their way to the Big Top, accompanied by the high-pitched strains of a steam calliope, the signature sound of the circus.

The calliope was invented in 1855 in Worcester, Massachusetts. The premiere concert featuring the novel keyboard instrument was performed on July 4 of that year for intrigued Worcester residents who raced to the town green as soon as the first raspy notes filled the air. When Phineas (P. T.) Barnum began his circus career several years later, he decided to make the calliope the sonic centerpiece of his traveling show. Acting on a promotional impulse, he ordered a uniquely ornate version built at the extraordinary cost of $11,000. Barnum's keyboard instrument was trimmed in shining brass, its appearance as shocking as its music was shrill.

Years later, Otto Ringling mounted his show's calliope on a truck and placed the colorful unit in motion, the rolling keyboard signaling the climax of every Ringling street parade. As the performers filed by, the sound of the steam organ held the promise of excitement, sustaining the attention of spectators who followed the music like children answering the Pied Piper's call.

Within two years of their inaugural effort, the Ringling brothers had succeeded beyond their hopes and expectations. By 1907, they had acquired their primary competitors and purchased the famous Barnum & Bailey Circus, toppling the entertainment legend and announcing to the world that the Ringling Brothers Circus had truly become "the greatest show on earth."

In the decades that followed, the Ringling brothers prided themselves on their ability to offer the finest circus talent in the world. The Flying Wallendas, a renowned family of German high-wire daredevils, abandoned a lucrative performing career in Europe in favor of a contract with the Ringling troupe. Continuing a tradition established by the Cirque d'Hiver in France, the Ringlings introduced American audiences to French trapeze artists, Italians who flew through the air from spring-loaded cannons, and African animal acts featuring eighteen snarling lions, leopards and panthers under the command of renowned trainer Alfred Court and May Kovar, the "lion queen" with a leather whip.

But the perennial favorites of young children in every city on the tour were the clowns—especially Emmett Kelly, the sad-faced mime in a bowler hat and floppy shoes. Celebrated by audiences of all ages, Kelly had become one of Ringling's star attractions, the only clown in the company's history to command the center ring as a solo artist. Years later, millions of Americans would watch "Weary Willie" on television as he stood silent and alone on the stage, with a broom as his only prop, making viewers believe he had the power to sweep a playful spotlight beam into the darkness.

Emmett Kelly was a Vandalia, Illinois native who found work in Hollywood as a film cartoonist in the early 20's. The young Kelly was intensely self-conscious, always aware that he had not been blessed with the ruggedly handsome features of a leading man. In 1924, he was invited to demonstrate some of his drawing techniques before a California audience, but he became terrified that they would find his face repugnant. Kelly's fear of appearing before the public became so extreme that he could not find the strength to speak. In an effort to overcome his performance anxiety, he opted to create a new face for himself, sketching the image he envisioned onto his art pad. Then he propped the pad on an easel in front of a mirror and recast his face in the image of a sad hobo, using a makeup brush as if it were a cartoonist's pencil. Kelly's new persona gave him the confidence and freedom to go anywhere, step onto any stage, without being afraid. In the years that followed, he would hone his performance craft, evolving from a nightclub slapstick artist to a mime of international reputation.

Without the makeup, Kelly was "a rosy-cheeked, black-haired Irishman," according to George Brinton Beal, a feature writer for the former *Boston Sunday Post*. Kelly told Beal that clowning was a very personal activity, a form of art that allowed him to project the thoughts and frailties of all humanity. Kelly asserted that it was the recognition of those frailties that made audiences laugh. "We laugh because we see ourselves, and we instinctively think that we are wiser than the poor fool, the clown," Kelly said. "He helps us to feel superior, and people like that."

According to Beal, clowning is an ancient profession that dates to the Talmud. In the biblical text, the prophet Elijah states that clowns are worthy of eternal life because "they cheer the depressed and sorrowful, causing the sufferers to forget their grief." In entertainment history, there were three primary classifications of clowns: the white clown, the august, and the elegant. The white is the classic form, his face done in vivid white makeup with "grotesque designs painted in black and red." This was the domino, or mask, of the Renaissance era, a symbolic shield that gave the performer license to be crude or satirical. The white clown's conduct would have earned an unmasked person scorn or punishment from the royal figure who was often the target of the jester's ridicule. The august clown is the rags-and-patches hobo form, of which Kelly was the premier American version.

Ironically, Kelly entered the circus world as an aerialist, becoming a trapeze performer in the first year of his career. But the competition for flying stardom, coupled with the extreme risk of injury and death, soon drove him back to the sawdust and the safety of clowning. After a stint with the Sells-Floto circus, Kelly joined the Hagenbeck-Wallace troupe, followed by a year of collaboration with clowning icon Otto Griebling in the Cole Brothers Circus. Then he moved to Europe, where he worked the Cirque d'Hiver in France, and the major winter circuses in Germany and England. London critics called his hobo character "the saddest man in the world." Kelly returned to the United States at the start of World War II. He traveled with the Shrine Circus for a short time before joining the Ringling troupe in 1942. He married Mildred Ritchie, a "bally girl" from the aerial ballet, during the Madison Square Garden stand in 1943. That same year, Kelly took his first star turn as a featured performer with Ringling.

By the summer of 1944, the Ringling Bros. and Barnum & Bailey Circus was reported to be the largest and most successful traveling show in the world, often attracting audiences of more than 10,000 people to each performance. With a regular corps of 1600 workers and performers, the circus was a self-contained city on rails, a primarily nocturnal community of gypsies who considered themselves members of the same entertainment family.

Although the circus business had always been consistently lucrative, the continuation of World War II had steadily eroded attendance, placing a strain on Ringling's recent earnings. In an effort to decrease their operating expenses before the 1944 summer tour began, Ringling reduced the size of their traveling crews. They also reduced their insurance coverage to a mere $500,000 liability policy underwritten by Lloyds of London.

After a successful indoor run in New York and Boston, Ringling's outdoor season got under way on June 6—the same day that Allied forces stormed the beach at Normandy in an effort to turn the tide of the war. In Philadelphia, the first city on the tour, a small fire broke out on a canvas flap during the afternoon show. Although fire was an ever-present risk to the circus each year, a risk to which the Ringling troupe had grown accustomed, the early Philadelphia fire would cast a cloud of concern over the performance family that would never truly disappear.

On June 30, after a week of shows in mid-sized Connecticut communities, Ringling rolled into Portland, Maine, the northernmost city on the New England tour. As usual, there was intense pressure to set up in time for the afternoon show. The layout and elevation of the main tent was the first and most important task of the day. Spanning the length of two football fields, the Big Top was a square mile of canvas that soared more than five stories and required hours of pre-performance rigging. With the drastic reduction in crews, the stake teams were nearly twenty men short for the job, so Edward "Whitey" Versteeg, Ringling's feisty, short-tempered roustabout boss, was forced to select a gang of powerful local boys to help fly the Big Top.

One of the boys hired to raise the main tent that day was a slow-witted, strong-armed eighteen-year-old with close-cropped hair and chiseled-granite features. A drawling downeaster accent revealed that he had been born and raised in northern New England. The kid was shy and quiet, but he could swing a sledge hammer with vengeance. Strength would be his ticket of admission. None of the circus managers could have guessed that he was actually a fourteen-year-old runaway who had lied about his age in order to join the Ringling team—or that he was a deeply troubled spirit who had been setting fires since he was seven years old.

In the fall of 1930, Robert Dale Segee was born into a nomadic family headed by an unpredictable man with a volatile temper. The Segee clan drifted back and forth between Portland, Maine and Portsmouth, New Hampshire, renting twelve different apartments in the first ten years of Robert's life. The youngest of seven children, he seemed strange from the start. He exhibited what his family would later call a nervous condition: biting his nails, eating very little, crying easily. As he got older, he rarely spoke to his parents, and he seemed especially afraid of his father, who was quick to anger.

By the time Robert started school, he had become a loner. He found it difficult to get along with other kids, who taunted him because of his moods and his silence, so he often preferred to stay alone in his room. He would watch from a window on the third floor while the kids in the neighborhood played outside. During those rare moments when he overcame his reclusion and ventured into the world, he would spend all his time with his brother, Eugene, the only child who showed a willingness to tolerate him.

Over the years, Robert's eccentric psychological traits grew worse, leading to even greater isolation and a simmering anger. When he was seven, he started a small fire in the family's South Portland home by tossing newspaper onto an oil stove. He was amazed by the flames, which sent him into a trance-like state. When Eugene rushed into the room, Robert quickly threw his jacket onto the stove, quenching the fire. As a result of the blaze, the Segee family was forced to move. Within a year, Robert set a closet on fire, driving his family out of their home once again. Over the next six years, 68 suspicious fires would be reported within a ten-block radius of the Segee family's Portland apartment.

The family's suspicions about Robert increased with the frequency of local fires, and relations with his father grew increasingly strained as time went on. Robert soon became afraid to go to sleep at night because of the nightmares that had begun to haunt him. By the age of nine, he would routinely sneak out of his house and roam the streets until dawn. His strange, vampire lifestyle was preferable to the dangers he would be forced to confront in his dreams. Prolonged exhaustion, coupled with an IQ of 78, soon made it virtually impossible for Robert to succeed in school. All the other kids—including his own brothers and sisters—teased him for his dullness, and his teachers became indifferent toward him.

As the years went by, Robert was forced to repeat several grades—an effort by his teachers to help him acquire the rudiments of an education. He was fourteen by the time he reached the sixth grade. Ironically, he had grown larger and stronger than most boys his own age, as if some undefined act of genetics had stimulated the strength of his body in order to compensate for the weakness of his mind. But his unusual physical size—even more exaggerated when compared to the younger boys in his class—made scholastic life more difficult. After failing every subject that year, he decided to leave school forever.

A few months later, Robert Dale Segee ran away to join the circus.

Three

Before every summer tour, Ringling always waterproofed the nineteen-ton Big Top at the circus sail loft in Sarasota, Florida. Since 1942, however, the best materials for that purpose had been restricted for wartime use by the government. Prior to the start of the 1944 season, Ringling management resorted to an alternate method developed and used by circuses around the world since the nineteenth century: they sealed the Big Top with a pasty mixture of 1800 pounds of paraffin wax and 6000 gallons of gasoline.

Circus tent ropes, like braided nautical lines, were woven from highly flammable jute and sisal. Minutes before the Portland matinee began on June 30, a small fire was discovered on one of the ropes high above the main entrance. Neil Todd, a member of the Ringling seat crew, caught the attention of an usher, who quickly extinguished the flames without damage to the Big Top—and without injury to anyone in the audience. Todd reported the incident to Leonard Aylesworth, boss canvasman, but the fire was considered a one-time accident that represented no threat to the Ringling circus, so it was soon forgotten.

After two successful performance days in Portland, Ringling struck its tent and prepared to travel to Providence, Rhode Island. Just before dawn, Bob Segee appeared at the rail siding and approached Whitey Versteeg. He asked if he could travel with the show for the rest of the New England tour. The rookie roustabout was strong, and he was needed, so Versteeg agreed.

Several hours later, Ringling arrived in Providence. With Segee's strength added to the 200-man tent crew, the towering Big Top was set and the lighting rigged well before the two o'clock deadline. That afternoon, a hole burned through a tent flap just prior to the matinee. Once again, the flame was extinguished without loss or injury. But this time, something had changed.

Circus folk have always been very superstitious people. They have never liked performing under a full moon—especially on Tuesdays—and they have never liked fire. Recognizing fire as a force capable of destruction and death, a potentially devastating force beyond human control, the Ringling Brothers circus trained its crews and performers in the prevention of disaster. In the summer of 1944, there had been a fire in Philadelphia, and fire had twice threatened performances in Portland and Providence. Multiple bursts of flame in such a short time were more than unusual, so rumors of a jinx began to spread. As fear entered their hearts and minds, the Ringling performance family went silent, concerned that even a whisper of fire would bring their superstitions to life, turning entertainment to tragedy.

July 3, 1944   10:13 PM

Mildred stood in the doorway of her bedroom, studying her three children as they slept soundly on jury-rigged beds made of pillows and blankets. Their cramped quarters were very different than the accommodations the kids had grown used to while living in Southampton, but they were the best that Mildred could provide. She had been anticipating their holiday visit for weeks. Now that Don, Honey and Edward were finally with her, she did not want them to leave.

Uncle Ted had brought the children to Hartford hours earlier, leaving more than enough time to prepare for their holiday adventure. There had been some awkward moments at first, as with all their recent visits, but Mildred had been surprised and relieved by their loving attitude toward her. If she had her way, she would have spent days just holding them close, asking thousands of questions about the lives they were leading without her. But she knew they needed time to adjust, so she had restrained herself.

Mildred had planned to take the kids to Bushnell Park for the Fourth of July fireworks display that would explode over the Connecticut River once the sun went down. The celebration would have provided neutral ground, a zone of emotional safety in which they could all grow comfortable with each other again. Mildred harbored a fantasy that the kids would be awed by the explosions that would rip the skies above the golden dome of the capitol building. Honey would seek shelter in her mother's arms during the loudest bomb blasts. Her brilliant blue eyes and blonde hair would grow brighter in the fiery light. And by the time the show was over, all three children would be openly vying for their mother's attention. Then they would all make their way back to the apartment together, and there would be moments when Mildred could allow herself to believe that they were a family again, and that they had never been apart. However, fate would intervene, forcing her to abandon her fantasy.

July 4, 1944   8:25 AM

On the morning of the Fourth, Mildred packed a lunch for the children and hustled them off to Pope Park for a few hours of swinging, sliding and talking. Being the oldest, Don did his best to impress his mother by showing how strong he had gotten since she had last seen him. The joy of wrestling his lithe and jovial six-year-old brother, Edward, to the grassy grounds of the park frequently offset his interest in the snacks that Mildred brought along.

Running the risk of spoiling the children she rarely saw, Mildred gathered the kids and announced that she had one more tantalizing adventure planned for them. After their picnic lunch, they would spend the rest of the afternoon at Churchill Park in Newington, riding on the swings and playing in the pool. Coupled with the promise of a trip to the circus the next day, the news of a journey to a park in another city for an afternoon in the water made the children cheer.

Time was not an issue, so Mildred focused her attention on the kids during the bus ride to Newington, a southeastern suburb of Hartford. It was a beautiful summer day, and Mildred knew the kids loved being outdoors in the company of other families and children. When they arrived, Don and Edward raced away to play together, leaving Mildred and Honey to spread the blanket and set out the lunch that had been hurriedly prepared before their surprise trip to the park.

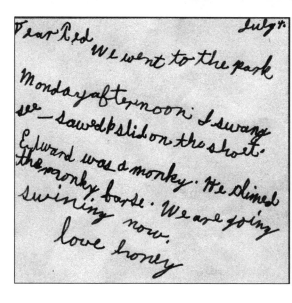

Honey's note to Uncle Ted, written on Tuesday, July 4.

NOTE COURTESY OF DON COOK

Searching in the shade of a towering elm tree, Honey picked some wildflowers and placed the prettiest ones on her mother's lap. Mildred was suddenly aware of how mature and self-confident her daughter was. Ted and Marion were obviously taking wonderful care of her, and their loving attention showed in Honey's personality. That thought made Mildred both proud and sad.

"Do you like the flowers?"

"Very much. Thank you."

"They're just like the ones in my garden at home."

Honey immediately recognized that the last word spoken could have hurt her mother, since the only home the children knew was one that she did not share with them. Mildred did her best to contain her emotions, focusing on Honey in an effort to distract herself from her own disappointments. In the moments that followed, it was Honey who found her way to the questions that Mildred had hoped to avoid.

"I like it when we're with you," Honey said decisively. Mildred smiled, pleased by the underlying sentiment of her daughter's simple declaration. "Edward cries for you at night sometimes, but Don and I don't." Mildred found herself uncertain about how to react to this news, so she remained silent. Honey studied her mother carefully before continuing. "Will we ever live with you again?"

Mildred's hands had grown busier, as if working to cast off the troubling emotion that this question had stirred. Then, as if through divine intervention, the need to respond was suspended, their conversation interrupted by shouts and cries from the area surrounding the pool. They turned toward the commotion and saw dozens of people rushing toward the water—with Don and Edward following them. Instantly terrified, Mildred and Honey chased after the boys in an effort to protect them from whatever danger might have presented itself.

A large group had gathered near the pool, and they had encircled Don and Edward in the process. Mildred and Honey broke through to the front of the crowd, where her sons were standing in shock. On the ground before them lay an eight-year-old girl who had just been pulled from the water. Her lifeless body made it appear that she was simply sleeping. Except for a few whispers, the crowd remained silent. Even Mildred found herself staring in disbelief, unable to tear her eyes away from such a dreadful image.

Moments later, the little girl's mother appeared and began to wail in anguish, shocking Mildred back to reality. As she struggled to compose herself, Mildred reached for her sons, covering Edward's eyes as she ushered the children away from the tragic scene. The suddenness of the child's death had revived Mildred's sense of impending danger.

Over her children's objections, she moved deliberately to the blanket and gathered the rest of the food in a bundle. There would be no further celebration. Their afternoon in the park had ended in sorrow. Although all three children were curious about the child who had drowned, it was Edward who needed the most reassurance. Mildred did not offer much of an explanation except to say that the little girl had gotten hurt and that they would have to hurry to catch the bus back to Hartford, a trip that was sure to be taken in silence.

The tragedy at the park and the sad ride home left Mildred and the kids emotionally exhausted. As they walked back to the apartment from the bus stop, Mildred reluctantly decided not to take them to the capitol lawn for the fireworks display. Instinct told her that she had made the right decision, but Mildred was still badly disappointed. The fiery light show had been the cornerstone of her plans for the holiday.

The kids nibbled on some dinner, then they dashed off some postcards and a letter to Uncle Ted and Aunt Marion. Shortly after eight, Mildred tucked them into their beds, aware that memories of the afternoon might haunt their dreams. After kissing the kids goodnight, she began to hum *Jesus Loves Me*, Honey's favorite hymn.

"Is she in heaven, mommy?"

Momentarily stunned by the question, Mildred stopped humming. As usual, her insightful daughter had found her way to the heart of the issue. "I'm sure she is, Honey."

"Do all children go to heaven?"

Mildred realized that her daughter was coming to grips with the tragedy she had witnessed that day, and that her bedtime thoughts had turned to issues of mortality. "When Jesus calls them, all sweet children go to heaven, my baby." Reassured by her mother's answer, Honey nestled deeper into her bed and closed her eyes. Mildred brushed the hair away from her daughter's face and kissed her cheek. "Go to sleep now. We have a big day at the circus tomorrow."

After one last glance at the sleeping children she loved with all her heart, Mildred turned out the light and closed the bedroom door. All at once, a wave of concern washed over her mind as she reviewed the circumstances of the day. She was reminded of an old superstition that she had heard when she was a girl. Her father had once told her that pennies placed on railroad tracks would bring disaster to the train that passed over them. Mildred could not keep herself from wondering if someone had placed pennies in the path of the circus train, crushing the coins into shining copper wafers, tokens of admission to a nightmare from which there would be no escape.

Seconds later, in the quiet calm of night, Mildred berated herself for having given so much credence to an ancient tale. She had always placed the lives of her children in the hands of God, and He would never abandon them. Don, Honey and Edward had put aside their fears—despite having witnessed the death of a little girl hours earlier—so Mildred called upon herself to follow their example. After all, if there had been any danger, it surely must have passed over them by now.

Four

Whenever the children were with her, Mildred tried to maintain her maternal authority. She told herself that her parental responsibility could not end, even though the continuity of their lives had been suspended. But try as she might to be consistent, guilt would often intervene, leading her to relax the rules she would have otherwise imposed when the kids became too demanding. On this holiday, Mildred expected that Don and Honey would awaken her shortly after sunrise, jumping on the bed and pleading to be allowed to run down to the railway by themselves. She knew they would want to meet the Ringling circus train as it sped across the bridge into town, and they would beg for their mother's permission.

Mildred had always loved trains. When she was a girl, her father would occasionally surprise her by asking if she would walk to the East Street station with him. He would glance at his silver pocket watch and urge her to hurry so they could be there before the 7:03 freighter slid along the rails toward Boston. Those moments were wondrous, making Mildred feel special in the eyes of the man she adored. Her father would always avoid the city streets and follow the path through the woods along the river, knowing the trip would take longer that way. Although he never acknowledged it, their walk to the station was an excuse to spend time with his daughter, precious time for just the two of them. He would take

Mildred's hand without saying a word, glancing down at her with the affectionate smile she loved so much, his quiet strength filling her with confidence and pride.

Mildred remembered how much she cherished having her father all to herself. And she remembered how he listened so carefully to the things she said, even the little things, as if they were the most important words she had ever spoken. He would answer her questions and offer advice, guiding her by his example. The arrival of the train always made her sad because it signaled the end of her special time alone with her father. As her children slept, Mildred inwardly acknowledged that she wanted them to experience the unique magic of trains—even though their father would never share the magic with them.

July 5, 1944

The first section of the eighty-car Ringling rail caravan, called the Flying Squadron, raced into Hartford minutes after nine in the morning, and the atmosphere seemed wrong from the moment they arrived. The train was several hours late because of a government-ordered routing delay, and Whitey Versteeg knew the razorbacks and rigging crews would need more time to set the tents, so the decision was made to scratch the matinee that was scheduled to begin at two o'clock. When news of the cancellation made its way to the performers, a black mood descended upon them. Circus tradition had always demanded that the show go on, regardless of any impediments. The superstitious troupe of performers believed that a missed or canceled show was a sign of bad luck, even a warning of impending disaster.

Circus road managers—including James Haley, a director of the company since his marriage to a member of the Ringling family—were troubled by the cancellation, aware of the financial loss it would impose. Haley knew that newly-elected president Robert Ringling and the board of directors would hold him accountable, and he was uncertain of the corporate consequences.

Because the United States government considered the circus to be an important entertainment institution, Ringling had been able to sustain its usual performance schedule, even after the attack on Pearl Harbor. The traveling show had received extra allotments of precious rationed goods such as gasoline, tires, rope and canvas in order to ensure that the company's performance tradition would continue, if only to promote national morale. But their late arrival in Hartford could not be avoided, and the delay gave Ringling very little time to prepare. In addition to the strenuous manual task of setting the tents and prepping the show, a flurry of legal obligations had to be satisfied before the Ringling circus would be allowed to perform on municipal property.

Given the pressure of limited time, the permit to conduct the three remaining shows had to be obtained quickly. Herbert DuVal, Ringling's legal adjuster and advance man, paid a $300 fee to the Building Department for a two-day rental of the circus grounds. Then DuVal hustled to police headquarters and provided fifty free tickets to Chief of Police Thomas Hallisey, who ensured that the necessary paperwork was completed in a matter of hours—even though Ringling had not provided the city with the certificate of insurance required by municipal statutes. Although Hallisey signed the license, which called for compliance with the laws of Connecticut and the City of Hartford, the document was never signed by any circus official.

When told of Ringling's arrival, officers of the Hartford Fire Department recognized immediately that they would not have time to inspect the circus tents and grounds prior to the evening performance. Nonetheless, senior fire officials—including Chief John King—expressed no concern. After all, the circus had been coming to Hartford since the nineteenth century and there had never been an accident or an injury. This would be the tenth year in a row that Ringling performed on the Barbour Street grounds, and King was certain that he had no reason to suspect that something would go wrong in the summer of 1944. Comfortable in that belief, he saw no need to order men or equipment to the circus grounds as a precaution against fire.

Three rambunctious children were racing through her tiny apartment, and Mildred was running late. The lunch she had prepared lay untouched on the kitchen table because Don, Honey and Edward were too excited to eat. The anticipation of an afternoon at the circus had stolen their appetite. Having taken some extra time to fix the bows in Honey's hair, Mildred knew they would all have to hurry if they wanted to be in their seats when the two o'clock show began.

As they headed toward the door, Honey placed a postcard on the table. "I wrote Aunt Marion a note, and I told her about the little girl."

Mildred was not surprised by the straightforward innocence revealed in the brief note. *"Dear Mom. We're getting ready to go to the circus now. When we were at Newington a girl got drowned. We just got to the bus on time. xxx Honey "*

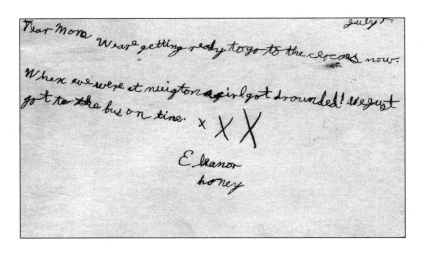

Honey's note to Aunt Marion written on July 5

POSTCARD COURTESY OF DON COOK

Mildred understood and accepted Honey's use of the word "Mom," especially since Mildred had forfeited the opportunity to be with her children in their daily lives. She felt a pang of guilt and regret as she read, no matter how hard she tried to deny it, but it was important not to reveal her feelings to Honey.

"Would you like me to mail it for you?"

"Yes, please."

Mildred dropped the postcard into the pocket of her dress, along with her own letter to Marion and postcards to Ted from Don and Edward. Moments later, she and the children were racing to the bus stop, hoping against hope that the circus would not begin until they had found their way to their seats. The ride across town seemed interminable—especially with three eager kids in a crowded vehicle on a blazingly hot day. Aware of the time, Mildred hurried the kids off the bus and scurried them along Barbour Street toward the main entrance marquee.

Circus management had been given approval to stake their tents on a large open lot on Barbour Street, between Kensington Street and Cleveland Avenue, near Keney Park. Given Ringling's late arrival that morning, the mandatory parade through the streets of the city had put the show even farther behind schedule. The tent was about 425 long and 180 feet wide, covering an area of 75,000 square feet, with a seating capacity of more than 9000. The top itself was supported by heavy poles and guy ropes secured to a double row of stakes about fifteen feet beyond the tent. The largest poles had a maximum diameter of twelve inches, equal in size to most telephone poles. These six center poles, each nearly sixty feet tall, flew American flags that could be seen waving above the canvas.

Ringling was traveling with a staff of about 1200, smaller than the usual peacetime complement of 1600 performers and crew. A gang of roughnecks laced the canvas sections of the Big Top together on the ground and guyed the canvas to the stakes that had been driven a day earlier. Once the canvas sections were bound together and the side poles were in place, the Big Top was hoisted with the powerful assistance of elephants prodded by hook men. Quarter poles could then be inserted as under girders for the immense canvas roof. The process of flying the top was long and arduous, and it could not be rushed.

As the two o'clock deadline approached, crowds clutching tickets for the matinee—the first of four shows over a two-day stand—began to arrive. Fans expected to see a fully functional circus, with a bustling midway, a menagerie stocked with exotic creatures, and sideshow barkers calling out above the cries of the calliope—a vision that constituted their shared fantasy. Instead, they were told that the first show had been canceled and that refunds, or exchanges for tickets to other performances, were available at the gate.

When Mildred and the children discovered that the performance would not take place, they were crestfallen. She had planned this holiday meticulously, and she had not expected that it would begin with disappointment. A glance at the shocked and saddened faces of Don, Honey and Edward gave Mildred new resolve. They had four days together, and she would make sure they enjoyed every minute. After exchanging her July 5 tickets for the next day's matinee, Mildred turned to the children and announced that she would take them to the movies for the afternoon screening of *See Here, Private Hargrove*, a new comedy starring Donna Reed. The film depicted the humorous misadventures of a family living on an Army base, and Mildred was certain the kids would enjoy it.

That night, once the kids were tucked in, Mildred sat by the kitchen window to write a letter to Marion. Brilliant light from a blood-red moon made it possible to see clearly, without using the table lamp. The Parsons family was accustomed to writing to each other frequently, and the tone of Mildred's letter was warm and conversational, reporting the adventures that she and the children had experienced in their first two days together, as if Marion were sitting at the kitchen table with her. As Mildred wrote, some neighborhood kids set off small rockets in honor of the holiday. The missiles flew right past her window, and she was certain that the noise would wake at least one of her children. When she checked on them, they were all sleeping soundly.

The same blood-red full moon that cast its light on Mildred also cast a threatening pall over the performers in the Ringling Brothers circus on the night of July 5. In the wake of fires in Philadelphia, Portland and Providence, and following the superstition-triggering cancellation of the first show in Hartford, the moon offered no relief from their shared sense of impending disaster. Like the Native Americans who had given birth to the legend, circus entertainers believed that blood on the moon warned that many would die.

Five

What is devastating about the unexpected is that it comes upon us with full force, no portion of its power or effect diluted in advance. On the morning of July 6, the people of Hartford could not have known that the fragile physics of the moment would soon be shattered. They had no inkling that Fate would allow a dangerous stranger into their lives, or that his explosive secrets would ignite a catastrophic chain reaction, leading their sleepy city to the brink of destruction.

As the morning progressed, Mildred and the kids could feel the excitement crackling in the air, excitement that was generated from within their own supercharged spirits. They were certain that circus day would be the very best day of their vacation together. From the kitchen, Mildred heard Honey practicing the piano, something she could be counted on to do—even without a direct order. The ancient, out-of-tune upright had been left behind by the previous tenant, probably by choice. As she listened to the music, Mildred reminded herself to mail the postcard that Honey had written to Ted and Marion. It was simple and beautiful, especially with its childish misspellings, and she knew it would make them happy.

"Dear Mom & Ted. I like you. I have a nice home. I'm thinking you are really nice. I hope you are good."

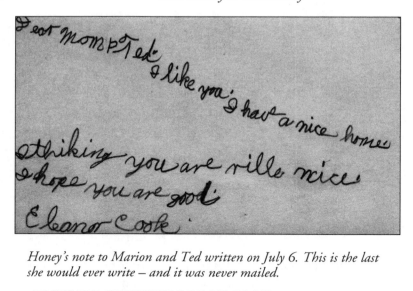

Honey's note to Marion and Ted written on July 6. This is the last she would ever write – and it was never mailed.

POSTCARD COURTESY OF DON COOK

Don and Edward raced in and out of the tiny kitchen, releasing some of the energy they always found so hard to control. Minutes later, they landed safely at the table as Mildred dished out homemade oatmeal. Aware of how easily the boys got dirty, she issued her standard mealtime warning.

"Remember. These are the best clothes you have, so be careful." The admonition carried extra weight today, since the kids were wearing new outfits bought especially for the holiday. Moments later, the piano music ended and Honey entered the kitchen, following the aroma of warm maple syrup.

"I hate the piano," Don declared.

"That's because you don't like to practice," Mildred answered. "If you did, you'd find out how much fun it can be."

Even with his mouth full, Edward had questions about the circus. "Will they have lions and tigers, mommy?"

"Of course they will," Mildred said.

"And clowns, too?"

"Sure," Mildred answered. "It wouldn't be a circus without clowns."

Don seized the moment. "When I get big, I want to join the circus. I'll be the lion tamer." As if to underscore his point, he growled in his brother's face, making Edward cringe.

"You'll never grow up unless you eat your breakfast," Mildred warned. "Besides, the circus isn't all fun and games. It's a lot of hard work."

Honey agreed. "Yeah, like feeding the animals."

"Even worse," Mildred added. "Cleaning up after them." As if on cue, Edward spilled his oatmeal into his lap. Wide-eyed and messy, he looked at his brother and sister, and then at his mother. Seeing no other choice, they all burst out laughing.

The circus was a meta-community of masks and manipulations. It had always been a simple task to conceal one's identity upon entering the circus world, submerging as the person you once were, and emerging as someone—or something—else. Criminals could elude capture by working on a circus crew, sheltered by the anonymity that a nomadic community could provide. On July 6, Robert Segee had been with the Ringling Brothers circus for exactly one week. And in that time, he had successfully kept his true age a secret. He had also proven himself to be stronger than most of the other men with whom he worked, so Whitey Versteeg—the roustabout boss who had hired him in Portland—had given him additional responsibility.

Robert became a member of the lighting crew, and he was trained to set the interior lights for every show. As he and the other young riggers prepared for the two o'clock matinee, Robert mishandled one of the spot units and it fell from his hands, shattering when it hit the ground. The commotion attracted Whitey's attention. He was half Robert's size, but twice as ornery. When he saw the damage, he railed against the kid and slapped him across the face in front of the other boys. Then he threatened to throw the rookie off the Ringling crew if he were ever careless again. Robert was visibly angry because Versteeg had humiliated him in public, but he controlled himself and returned to work. Once the rigging was complete, he and his fellow workers were free until the end of the show. Robert and the other boys planned to travel into town to have some fun and meet some local girls. They had three hours to themselves, more than enough time to make the trip and be back at the Big Top by four o'clock.

> We went to the circus grounds yesterday & no circus - too late in arriving. Some saw "See It's Pri. Hargroves". Come home & all went to bed. Busses were crowded during the rush hour. Donald was really sick - cold sweat etc. He slept for an hour & then as good as new. He is again preparing for the circus this P.M. Emily just called. Her class was discontinued

Page One of Mildred's July 6 note to Marion. Sadly, it was never mailed.

NOTE COURTESY OF DON COOK

Mildred and the children got to the circus just in the nick of time, racing through the Barbour Street entrance at 2:03 p.m. When she learned that the show was behind schedule, Mildred breathed a sigh of relief. There would now be a few minutes to spend the last of the money she had set aside for this occasion. The children were exploding with excitement as they reached the main entrance. Mildred handed four tickets to the gate man, who smiled at the kids, then she guided her young family past the brightly-painted Ringling banners and through the marquee.

Page Two of Mildred's unmailed note.
NOTE COURTESY OF DON COOK

    Candy apples, ice cream—even live chameleons—were being hawked along the midway. Mildred bought cotton candy for Edward and some popcorn for Don. Honey was content with a balloon that trailed in the air behind her as the family rushed back to the main entrance, past the sideshow barker who did his best to attract their attention with his spiel. The geek shows promised "continuous performances," although the human oddities gathered there could hardly be called performers. They simply stood on projected platforms, various degrees of deformity on display for those who had paid for the privilege of gawking and gasping. By the summer of 1944, attractions such as the Tattooed Strong Man, the Fat Girl, the Rubber Man, and an assortment of midgets failed to amaze modern crowds. They were much more intrigued by Gargantua the Gorilla, whose size and personality had become legendary—especially after his widely-promoted "marriage" to a female gorilla nicknamed Mrs. Gargantua by the press. Don showed some interest in the grotesquely-exaggerated banners depicting the Snake Man, but Mildred would not allow herself to be distracted. Having been denied the chance to see the show the day before, she was determined not to be late for the July 6 matinee.

Gargoyles, myths, satyrs, cherubs and other exotic images carved in high relief had always adorned the gold-hued Ringling circus wagons. These were symbols of another world—a world within the mind—and another time in history, when the Catholic Church threatened excommunication for circus attendance. Despite the religious obstacles and the risk of recurring nightmares, the circus had become a long-standing American tradition, a ritual that provided reliable family entertainment every summer, a spectacle that often surpassed any other holiday event in the pre-television era. Hartford was known by circuses around the world as an especially inviting town for traveling shows. The city had held its first Circus Day in 1795, hosting a riverfront performance by Rickett's Equestrian Circus, and it had continued its tradition of support ever since. Even at the peak of World War II, enormous audiences could be expected.

Ringling management knew that, whenever and wherever large numbers of people gathered together, there would always be a risk of injury. Acknowledging that risk, the circus trained its workers in the necessary safety precautions for every show. The troupe had its own police chief, a Ringling veteran named John Brice, who enjoyed friendly relations with police officials in cities on the Ringling circuit. Water wagons were placed strategically around the lot for use in the event of an emergency, and buckets of water were positioned beneath the oval of bleacher seats and grandstands. Ushers and seat men, such as William Caley and Neil Todd, stationed themselves beneath the bleachers once a performance started, ready to snuff out a flaming match or a smoldering cigarette carelessly discarded into the sawdust from above. Since the first show in Philadelphia that season, Todd and his co-workers had been kept busy. Between May and July, there had been twelve minor canvas fires that had damaged the sidewalls of the Big Top. After each incident, sailmaker George Kelly had made the necessary repairs.

On July 6, however, Ringling workers neglected to place charged fire extinguishers at their respective positions beneath the bleachers, leaving most of the units on the trucks, instead. They also neglected to check the distance from the Big Top to the nearest municipal fire hydrants, and they did nothing to ensure that the circus hose couplings would match the hydrant fittings.

Emmett Kelly heard the bugler sound "First Call" at 1:45. The musical signal meant he had 45 minutes to finish his makeup, which was smearing because of the humidity. Kelly was concerned that his big round clown nose, a mainstay of his stage persona, would melt in the blistering heat. Kelly provided necessary "comic relief" for the audience whenever they became frightened by the maneuvers of the Flying Wallendas, who risked death during every performance. But the putty for Kelly's nose had gotten too soft, prolonging his preparations. The audience was arriving, and the famous clown was running late.

It was an oppressively hot and humid afternoon. By two o'clock, the temperature had soared to 88 degrees, and waves of radiant heat were flowing over the audience. An unmerciful sun beat down on the square mile of canvas that flew over the heads of the audience, most of them women and children. According to Everett Dow, a reporter for the *Hartford Courant*, "the flag hung limp in the still summer air, and the intensity of the sunlight was excruciating" in the moments before the show began.

True to Hartford's reputation as a circus town, nearly 8000 people turned out for the afternoon show. Some of the fans presented free passes for admission, their reward for having purchased war bonds. Members of the armed services were always allowed into a Ringling show without charge, and several groups of soldiers recovering from wartime injuries were ushered to their seats in the southeast bleachers with the assistance of Red Cross nurses. The atmosphere inside the tent was stifling, many degrees hotter than the temperature outside. Nearly everyone seated under the Big Top folded their paper programs and used them as makeshift fans, but there was no relief. Light summer dresses and shirts clung like a second skin. There would never be enough lemonade to quench the thirst that arose inside the tent that day.

The bandstand was positioned at the far end of the tent, between the northeast and southeast bleacher sections, directly opposite the main entrance. That section served as the performer's entrance, called "back door" by the Ringling troupe. In the summer of 1944, Merle Evans was celebrating a quarter century as conductor of Ringling's 29-piece all-brass band. Evans was a circus veteran, and he had loved every moment of his gypsy career. He and his men wore sparkling white uniforms trimmed in gold, making them look as sharp as they sounded. Evans was known as a master of timing, serving up nearly 200 musical cues during every show.

At 2:18, Evans ordered the band to begin the National Anthem, signaling the opening of the show. The near-capacity crowd strained to keep their balance as they rose from wooden folding chairs that were not tethered to the bleachers. Even as the matinee began, hundreds of people were still threading their way to bleacher seats high above the center ring. Dozens of mothers did their best to help young children negotiate the narrow wooden stairways placed over iron cage chutes strung across the east and west exits on the north side of the tent. The chutes would allow the wild cats to enter the ring for their performance early in the program. Mildred and her three kids were among the late arrivals who considered themselves fortunate that the performance was behind schedule. They climbed to their seats near the very top of the blue bleachers, to the right of the main entrance.

The oval track that enclosed the ring was approximately thirty feet wide, and it was used by most of the attractions as the show progressed. Through most of the program, circus fans were kept away from the track by metal railings that circled the arena. The railings prevented easy access, just as the cage chutes did. The July 6 show began with a brief parade of animals around the track, with brassy march music to liven the spirits of the audience. Clowns ran back and forth across the tanbark, pitching buckets of sawdust into the air, triggering squeals of mock-terror from surprised kids who were amazed that they had not gotten drenched by the contents of the buckets.

A Matter Of Degree

Karl Wallenda, patriarch of the famous Wallenda family of flying daredevils, stood at the base of the ladder with his wife, Helen, and two of Karl's cousins, waiting for their cue to climb to the high wire. They would soon deliver three tiers of true terror, with Helen standing alone at the top of the pyramid, supported by her husband, who balanced himself in a chair on a crossbar as the family rolled across the suspension cable on specially-built bicycles that gripped the wire. The mere thought of the daring act made most people cringe, but Helen described her work as an exhilarating necessity driven in the early years of her career by actual hunger.

When she was thirteen, Helen had answered an employment ad that called for a young girl with courage. She quickly became a member of the Wallenda troupe and later married Karl, on whose shoulders she first climbed to the peak position of "the human pyramid" at the age of seventeen. She had been raised in a European circus family, and she shared a strain of daring with her new husband, whose grandfather had once trained wolves for a living. Helen claimed to be perfectly comfortable at the top of the pyramid, a position she called "upstairs" that took her to the top of the circus tent, rising nearly fifty feet above the gathered crowd—with no net below to cushion a fall.

Minutes into the program, the lights grew dim and the music became more sinister as May Kovar ordered her eighteen leopards and panthers through their snarling paces in the cage ring on the west side, while Joe Walsh presented his lions and bears in the cage ring on the east side. Mildred and the children were immediately captivated by the wild cats. Don and Edward loved the growling animals, and they shouted their approval. But when one cat lashed out with its claws, as if to tear flesh, Honey hugged her mother tight, seeking assurance that she would not be harmed.

The cats that Mildred Cook and her children enjoyed so much had been brought into the ring through the iron cage chutes strung across the northern exits of the Big Top. The chutes were four feet high, with open bars approximately fourteen inches apart, and they allowed direct access to the performance area from animal wagons placed outside the main tent. Once the cat act ended, the lions and panthers were to be driven out through the chutes, which would then be disassembled, allowing the exit path to be reopened. Although no one knew it when the show began, the cage chutes would soon become a deathtrap.

Six

The searing heat of the day drilled its way through the Ringling canvas as the matinee continued. Hartford Police Chief Thomas Hallisey was standing just inside the main entrance, passing time with his old friend, John Brice, as Kovar worked her leopards and panthers. Neither man noticed anything unusual in the first few minutes of the program.

By 2:35, many of the people in the audience—all of them seated on the bleachers along the southwest border of the Big Top—began to feel intense heat at their backs, as if the sun had defied the laws of physics, sinking lower in the midday sky, all the while maintaining its radiant force. Unsure of the reason for such heat, they tried to ignore it.

Kovar's cat act ended at 2:38, and she commanded four of her panthers off their perch with a crack of the whip, running behind them toward the chutes that would lead the cats out of the ring. At that moment, Emmett Kelly applied the last of his layered makeup and left his cubicle, shuffling along in his floppy shoes toward "back door," the performer's entrance behind the Big Top. He was four minutes behind schedule—all because of the humidity and its effect on his makeup. Now he was racing toward his position beneath the high wire.

Almost unnoticed by the crowd, the Wallendas climbed into the darkness, taking their places on the lip of the platform, fifty feet above the audience. Karl was poised to begin the daredevil high wire act for which he and his family had become famous when Merle Evans and the Ringling band played the first notes of *Waltzing Matilda*, the Wallenda performance cue. Emmett Kelly heard the music and glanced at his watch, which read 2:40.

Seconds later, a flame was born. Witnesses said it appeared to be the size of a man's fist, a horseshoe, a softball, a grapefruit, a basketball—and they would all be right. It would depend on where they sat, and when they first observed the birth of the beast. Chief Hallisey looked to his right and saw "flame about halfway up the side curtain, crawling toward the top." At that point, the fire was still small, no more than eighteen inches in diameter, so Hallisey believed there was a chance to control the beast.

Helen Wallenda noticed a "tiny tongue of flame" on the sidewall canvas, and she alerted Karl. Although the flames were creeping steadily up the sidewall of the tent, the audience remained calm, seemingly oblivious to the fiery threat. Karl believed there would be time to make a "calm descent down the rope." He glanced around the arena, and came to the conclusion that the audience was "momentarily stupefied and incredulous," and that only those seated directly opposite the flames understood the "full danger of the situation." Somewhere in the stands, a woman yelled "Fire!" but the audience was too stunned to move. Many of the women and children simply stared, transfixed by the flames as they climbed higher and spread wider, rising steadily toward the Big Top. Karl signaled his family, and the Wallendas instantly abandoned the platform, sliding down the ropes to the ring.

Sensing the growing threat, band leader Merle Evans immediately captured the attention of his musicians and changed the tune to *The Stars and Stripes Forever*, the traditional circus danger call. Evans conducted musical cues with impeccable timing during each performance, but the Sousa march was never played unless a disaster was imminent. Ringling performers recognized the warning signal right away, and they raced to predetermined positions in an effort to put out the fire. Roustabouts and attendants heard the Disaster March in every corner of the lot. Elephant handlers instantly shouted "Tails!" and their lumbering charges responded to the command. Using their metal hooks, the bull men herded the elephants off the lot to the edge of Barbour Street, preventing a stampede of terrified giants that might crush and kill innocent people.

Hoping to find a telephone, Hallisey raced to the circus office wagon in "front yard," just beyond the main entrance, but there was no phone on the lot. Then Hartford Police Sergeant Spellman ran to a house on Barbour Street and notified the Hartford Fire Department. An officer from the HPD Vice Unit called the fire in from a nearby police cruiser.

Precious seconds flew by, and the beast grew larger. When shock gave way to recognition, a collective roar of terror burst from the crowd, and panic set in. Emmett Kelly heard the voices from the grounds outside the performer's entrance. The aroma of smoke told him that something had gone terribly wrong, so he rushed along the sawdust even faster. Following his instincts, he picked up a water bucket at the elephant tethering area and filled it from a nearby trough, then he lugged the bucket with him as he approached the southwest quadrant of the tent. A frightened Kelly—aided by seat men and canvas crews—tossed buckets of water against the flames, but the blaze had already become an angry engine of death, and it raged on.

The prize-winning photograph of Emmett Kelly, captured as he and other troupers struggled to defeat the blaze.

The picture was taken by Ralph Emerson, Sr.

In their mass hysteria, the crowd raced toward the main entrance. Perilous instinct deceived them into believing that the canvas door through which they had entered the tent offered the only avenue of escape. Those seated in front found it easiest to flee for the exits without impediment. Those in the middle tiers were the most likely to be trapped by loose bleacher seats that promoted the trampling of those who had already fallen. Mildred and the kids were on their feet when the mad scramble began, but Mildred scanned the tent before moving, unsure of which direction to take.

Mommy, we have to get out!
Stay close to me and we'll be all right!

Edward was terrified, so Mildred picked him up in her arms. His weight at six years old made passage difficult, but she would not put him down. She grasped Honey's hand tightly as crazed people streamed by them, knocking bleacher seats to the grass below. All the while, the flames climbed closer to the tent top.

Free to move on his own, Don did not follow his family. Instead, he climbed to the top of the bleachers with other fleeing fans. When Honey and Mildred turned around to check on him, they were stunned to see Don standing several rows above them.

Don! Where are you going?
This is the way to get out, mommy!
No, we have to stay together!

Despite his mother's admonitions, Don climbed higher. When he reached the top, he simply ran across the bleachers and jumped fifteen feet to the sawdust below, groping his way to safety beyond the tent. His family, however, chose to stay inside. They could not have known that Don was right about the route of escape, and they could not have known that, by climbing down the bleachers, they would run the risk of being devoured by flames.

As she gripped Honey's warm, wet hand, Mildred tried to negotiate the steps while carrying Edward. The heat had become intense, and people were desperate to escape, screaming in terror as they ran in all directions. One panicked man, chopping his way through the crowd by swinging a bleacher seat as if it were a machete, nearly knocked Mildred to the ground. Honey and Edward sobbed, beseeching their mother for comfort. They had never shared a nightmare with her before, and they did not know how to wake up without her help.

It's all right. It's all right, my babies. We have to keep going!

As the air temperature rose to more than 500 degrees, it became nearly impossible to breathe. Many people died in their seats after inhaling a single blast of heated gases. Hundreds of others passed out as they ran, making escape even more difficult for those behind them. Many of the fallen would be trampled where they lay. The roar of the flames soon combined with the collective screams of human beings and frightened animals, creating a semi-human sound of madness.

A group of young servicemen—some of them recovering from wounds, others simply home on leave—had come to the circus for an afternoon of entertainment. The courtesy tickets provided by Ringling placed them in the ground-level bleacher seats opposite the fire's point of origin. Seconds after the flames became visible, the unnamed servicemen grasped the implications of the blaze and took immediate action to bring others to safety. First, they gathered up their wounded buddies, lifting those with leg injuries into their arms and carrying them outside. Then they returned to the burning tent, offering assistance and guidance to children and adults alike, then finally confronting the stampeding crowd in an effort to calm them down and prevent serious injuries.

But the crazed mob paid no heed, and the flames continued to climb higher, reaching the canvas roof in less than three minutes. The voracious fire followed the seams of the canvas, burning a gaping hole in the Big Top, through which the American flag could be seen waving in the smoke. The drafting effect that followed created a roaring wind as the blaze sucked oxygen through the hole in an effort to feed itself. Flames flew across the canvas, and the temperature inside the tent soared to nearly 1600 degrees. People continued to die from the inhalation of superheated air, suffocating instantly, and those still standing screamed in terror, desperate to escape the flames that were searing human flesh.

As the inferno enveloped the Big Top, gobs of napalm flame—the product of Ringling's volatile waterproofing mixture—dripped from above, sticking to the skin of the unlucky victims onto whom it fell. Any effort to scrape away the molten substance simply spread waxy flames to other parts of the body. At that moment, it was as if the heavens had opened, raining fire on innocent beings below. In their desperation, those who believed in God cried out to Him, seeking intercession. Those without a god simply cursed their fate and struggled forward, anger and fear woven into the remnants of soul that had not been burned away.

Within minutes, the blaze began to consume the Big Top.
PHOTO COURTESY OF THE CONNECTICUT STATE LIBRARY

The fire swept from the main marquee to the performer's entrance, and the bleachers were soon set on fire by canvas sections that fell like blazing rain. The painted wooden structures served as catalytic fuel for the fire, which chased the fleeing crowd. As if they were waves in a human ocean of panic, people raced in a single, undulating mass toward the northeast corner of the tent. They hoped to escape through the exits opposite the primary blaze, but the iron animal chutes blocked their escape route.

May Kovar forced her cats through the cages, fearful that they might turn in terror and run back into the burning tent. If they did, they would be destroyed by flames—or by gunfire. Terrified leopards and panthers were still inside the chutes as hundreds of people rushed the cages. The chutes were too high to be climbed, and the wooden stairways that were placed over them were useless in a stampede of thousands. As burning canvas fell from above, Kovar turned to assist those who were struggling to climb over the chutes, the only barrier to survival.

Like steerage passengers on the *Titanic*, the mob continued to push against the cages that denied their freedom. Positioned on the opposite side of the chutes, Ringling attendants drove the crowd back with cattle prods, an action that contributed to the madness—and the death count. Children were paralyzed with fear when they came face-to-face with the leopards and lions, who were snarling up at the crowd passing over them. Frantic parents wanted to send their children over the cage chutes, but the width of the open bars made it likely that little arms and legs would fall through, leaving them vulnerable to the growling, clawing animals. Panic and indecision stoked the chaos. Some managed to overcome the opposition of Ringling workers, saving themselves and their children in the process. Many others were not as fortunate. As the inferno roared above them, hundreds of people were crushed against the cages, and dozens of lifeless bodies began to stack up like cordwood.

Bill Curlee was a 29-year-old Hartford native whose job as an aircraft inspector had recently required that he move to Euclid, Ohio. Back in Connecticut on a visit over the summer holiday, he had decided to take his young son, David, to the circus. He also invited his brother-in-law, his niece, and some neighborhood kids to the July 6 matinee. He never dreamed that a day at the circus would ultimately threaten their lives. With their escape route blocked by frightened people, Curlee decided to take action. First, he gathered young David into his arms, lifting him high onto his shoulders. Then he kissed his son and tossed him over the cage chutes, into a pile of canvas on the other side. Seconds later, a red banner fell from the top of the tent and covered the boy where he lay. When David stood up, he ran from the tent—just as his father had instructed him to do.

Assured that his son was safe, Curlee turned his attention to others, especially those who were reluctant to climb over the bodies in order to navigate the cage chutes. At six feet two and 210 pounds, he was an imposing presence that inspired confidence. Poised above the pile of bodies, Curlee reached back to women and children and lifted them over the chutes, offering his assistance in an encouraging manner. Soon, the situation grew more desperate. When he glanced over his shoulder, Curlee could see that the blaze had reached the tent pole lashings, which had begun to burn away. He instantly recognized that those who had delayed their escape, even for a few seconds, were at greatest risk of death from crush injuries.

As the fire devoured the lashings, the poles began to twist and sway, so Curlee stepped up his efforts to save hysterical people, picking them up by their clothes and tossing them over the cages. He held his position until the last moment—even after his own escape had become virtually impossible. One by one, the baling rings crashed to the sawdust and several poles fell across the tanbark and into the grandstands. Moments later, one of the last poles broke loose and crashed to the cages, crushing Curlee to death. His body would be found with those who had died within a few feet of safety.

Others were more fortunate—if only because of their ingenuity. Young Don Anderson, a spunky kid from a tiny farming town in the northeast quadrant of the state, had come to the circus with his uncle. As the fire raged, Don found it difficult to escape from his bleacher seat because of the leg brace he always wore. He could see hundreds of frantic people clawing and shoving in an effort to make headway, unable to move against the surge. So Don took out the jackknife he always carried and stabbed the sidewall canvas, slicing a gash that would set him free. Minutes later, hundreds of women and children poured through the jagged opening that Don had carved, and he hobbled along behind them, unaware that he would be seen as a hero for saving hundreds who might otherwise have died.

Following Anderson's lead, roustabouts and escaping fans slashed the canvas with knives, opening the way for hundreds to flee without burning. Circus personnel rolled the sliced strips of canvas into funnels in an effort to save those who had climbed to the top of the bleachers as the fire raged on. Children sailed along the canvas funnels into Clown Alley, where clowns in makeup caught them and ushered them away from a fiery death. One Ringling veteran, Cliff Chapman, stood his ground against the flames, returning to the tent repeatedly in an effort to save young fans from the blaze. His brightly-painted smile became an ironic symbol, melting in the heat to reveal the sorrow of the man behind the makeup, the man who cried for those who were doomed.

The flames were higher than the main poles by the time the fire headed for Merle Evans and his 29 musicians. The heat of the blaze became so intense that the organ-calliope caught fire. The kettle drum heads exploded from the heat, creating bowls of fire at the rear of the bandstand. Nearly 75 miles of hawser ropes and cables guyed the poles that supported the Big Top. Now, the ropes were on fire and the cables were melting. Burning canvas and flaming cables fell toward the band, but Evans and his men dodged the flames and played on.

The Big Top was being devoured by thunderous flame, generating a searing heat capable of setting human bodies on fire. Gasping for breath and unsure of what to do, Mildred and the children were caught up in a last stampede to safety. No matter where she looked, escape seemed impossible. Moving with a surging mass of people, Mildred found it increasingly difficult to carry Edward and maintain her grip on Honey. Desperation had given the mob superhuman strength, and they were pressing against her, forcing her to move at their will, and at their pace. She could not possibly carry Honey and Edward at the same time, so she gripped Honey's tiny wrist as tightly as she could.

Mommy, I can't see you!

The crush of people began to surround them, paying no heed to the fact that Mildred was a mother with a young child in tow, a child who needed her. Beyond exhaustion, she tried to force her way through the mass of humanity so she could protect her little girl, but the mob would not give ground.

Where are you, mommy?

They crushed against her, forcing her to move with them, in whatever mad direction they chose to take. With her arm stretched to its limits, it wasn't long before her grip began to weaken. Seconds later, after one final push by the mob, Honey's hand was torn from Mildred's grasp, and the angelic child with blonde hair and blue eyes, the child with a loving heart who had brought so much joy to her mother, drifted into a cruel sea of humanity, her voice lost in the screams and sobs of those who drifted toward destruction with her.

Honey!

Mildred cried out in pain, a pain she had never known. Her hand was now empty, but her heart was overflowing with anguish and sorrow, a sorrow that could never be contained.

Where are you, my baby?

The fleeing mass of humanity had taken the child, and there was no way to demand that they return her to Mildred. The urge to search for her lost daughter was overwhelming, but the fury of the blaze and the crush of fleeing people finally overcame her. Edward complained of exhaustion. For some reason, he pleaded to be allowed to lie down for a rest, a few moments of calm after what had seemed like hours of chaos. Mildred battled the voice that cried inside her, the voice that ordered her to keep going.

With her oldest children gone, she could not deny Edward the rest he needed, so Mildred disobeyed her inner voice and gently placed her six-year-old son in the sawdust. Then she lay down beside him, holding him close, offering an island of protective peace in a roiling sea of molten misery. As sorrow overwhelmed her, the only thing left for her to do was pray. *Dear God, please don't abandon us now. I beg you.*

As Mildred prayed, the beast roared, a beast only six minutes old, a flaming beast that rose from the pit of hell, devouring everything in its path.

SEVEN

The first alarm rang in at 2:44 PM, four minutes after the dagger of flame burst through the canvas. Almost simultaneously, the second and third alarms rang in. The calls triggered an immediate response from seven engine and three ladder companies, the nearest of which came from a station only a half-mile from the circus tent. Fire Marshal Henry Thomas was the first fire officer to arrive at the scene. He and his men turned their attention to drenching the flames in the northeast quadrant of the tent, hoping to save those who were trapped inside. Sadly, the fire units that followed Thomas to the circus grounds were of no benefit because the nearest hydrants were too far away—a fact that the fire department had not previously determined. Even if hydrants had been accessible, the main circus entrance on Barbour Street was blocked by Ringling elephants that were pushing water wagons into place in one final attempt to battle the blaze.

According to Emmett Kelly, "the canvas was nearly all burned away and the center poles were crashing one by one" in less than five minutes. There was nothing Ringling troupers could do but watch as their livelihood was destroyed before their eyes. Even Hartford Police Chief Hallisey believed that "no fire department would have done any good because [the blaze] was done before any line was put in."

Deputy Chief Michael Godfrey and his driver were cruising in the north end of the city when they noticed a cloud of black smoke rising from the vicinity of the Ringling performance area on Barbour Street. Instantly concerned, Godfrey sped to the circus grounds. When he approached the tent, he was struck with a ball of superheated air that felt "like a blast furnace." Godfrey later stated that his police uniform began to smoke, forcing him to extinguish tiny flames that broke out along the sleeve of his coat.

Ringling had positioned its own water wagons around the Big Top, but they were quickly proven useless in fighting the blaze because the hose couplings were the wrong size, and they would not have joined with the fittings on the municipal hydrants. Many of the hoses on the partially-charred wagons were still coiled and unused even as the monstrous blaze became more aggressive. Ringling was left with no effective means of attacking the fire that was destroying an American entertainment institution.

Despite the imminent annihilation of the circus tent and the likely incineration of those left inside, clusters of despairing survivors charged back into the flaming tent in an effort to find their loved ones. In many cases, they lost their lives as a result of that decision. Other local residents whose families had gone to the circus that day hovered outside the exits in search of missing relatives. Although their concerns were well-founded, they often blocked the path of imperiled people who were fleeing for their lives.

Once it became evident that it was possible to escape the inferno by jumping from the bleachers, a surge of people climbed and gathered along the top rows. After leaping—or being pushed from behind—they made their way to safety by scrabbling under the sidewalls. Army servicemen from Bradley Field held portions of the canvas up above their heads, enduring horrific heat in order to allow people of all ages to race through the tent walls to the smoke-filled grounds. As they ran, they were often confronted with obstacles in their path, such as Ringling tractors and water trucks being driven closer to the flames in an effort to stem the tide of destruction.

Experienced firefighters recognized immediately that they had arrived too late, because the tent was almost entirely consumed by flames. As a last resort, Thomas ordered a Hartford Fire Department pumper truck to be brought dangerously close to the blaze in order to provide water. The wheels of the pumper could have exploded into flame from the intense heat of the blaze, but the firefighters held their ground. Suddenly, the cotton-faced hoses themselves caught fire. Every attempt to deal with the most destructive force in nature was being thwarted.

The band continued to play, even through the worst of the blaze. Many believed they would never get out alive, but Merle Evans signaled his men to flee at the last possible moment. Seconds after their escape, a quarter pole crashed across the bandstand, crushing the forward section of the eight-foot structure. After being driven from the Big Top by waves of flame that threatened their lives, the Ringling band regrouped on the midway grounds and continued to play, despite the scorching heat that spread like a thick blanket over the circus grounds. The circumstances seemed to call for mournful blues, as if the occasion were a funeral procession in New Orleans. Inside the tent, the organ-calliope burned steadily, its melody silenced by the flames. The Ringling circus disaster might be seen as an ironic echo of the *Titanic* tragedy. While one group of victims died in freezing water and the other group died in raging flames, all the victims died to the accompaniment of music played by men who refused to abandon their responsibilities—even in the face of extreme danger.

Fire Chief John King raced to the scene as soon as he heard about the blaze. When he and his driver reached the grounds, the tent was fully engulfed and nearly in ruins. They threaded their way through the panicked crowd that was fleeing toward scores of victory gardens that had been carefully planted and tended by Barbour Street families. People were already on fire, running from the flaming beast that had begun to devour them. King ordered his men to rescue as many of the women and children as possible before the still-angry flames could overtake them. King actively assisted his men, pulling a number of people from the rim of the burning tent. Other hysterical victims, their clothing and bodies on fire, ran past the firefighters toward an uncertain fate.

Hugh Alcorn, Sr., former State Prosecutor, had taken three of his grandchildren to the July 6 matinee. Seconds after the first eruption of flame, he and the children escaped without injury by climbing to the top bleachers and jumping to safety, as dozens of other fans had done. After placing his grandchildren into the protective custody of a police officer, Alcorn approached Chief Godfrey and used the police phone to call his son, Meade, the Hartford County prosecutor, to inform him that the Ringling circus was on fire, and to assure him that his children were safe.

As fate would have it, State Police Commissioner Edward Hickey was also attending the matinee on July 6. He had taken a gaggle of nieces and nephews to the circus, and was surprised to see his friend Hugh Alcorn seated in the adjacent bleacher section with his own family. When the flames rose aggressively, taking Hickey by surprise, he gathered his kin and ushered them along the top row of bleachers, then dropped each one to the ground below—just as Alcorn had done. Before jumping to safety, Hickey glanced around the arena, witnessing images of destruction that would stay with him forever. Human beings who had been set on fire as if they were living torches rolled on the ground in an attempt to extinguish the flames that were inflicting deadly misery. Other patrons raced toward the exits, only to find the route to safety blocked by masses of desperate people. Those trapped below were screeching in unearthly tones, as if banshees had been sent to warn of impending doom. Hickey knew that the toll caused by the circus fire would be devastating for both the city and the state. The loss of humanity he envisioned was certain to make this fire the worst tragedy in Connecticut history.

On the grounds outside the flaming tent, a howling from within the human spirit replaced the cries of fear. Some of those who heard the chorus of pain would suggest that it was as if a horrible force from the nether world had entered those who were dying, demanding their submission, the last of their humanity screaming as it left them.

Once Hickey and the children were safely beyond the blaze, he made contact with Chief Hallisey and placed notification calls to Hartford Mayor William Mortensen and Governor Raymond Baldwin. Hickey realized immediately that the cooperation of city, state and civilian services would be required in order to deal with the catastrophe. By the time Meade Alcorn and fellow prosecutor Burr Leikind raced onto the circus grounds, Governor Baldwin had authorized Hickey to take charge of the scene.

Alcorn would later become the lead prosecutor in the case against the Ringling Brothers circus.

At the peak of the blaze, the temperature had risen to nearly 1600 degrees, far too explosive for any form of effective firefighting. Ringling crewmen recognized that nothing could be done to save the Big Top, so truck chief David Blanchfield—a Hartford native—and his men risked their lives by driving the diesel-powered generators out of the fire path, preventing a lethal secondary explosion. Then they turned their water hoses on the victims who were trapped inside the flaming tent. Within seconds, even those who had been brave enough to endure horrific heat in an effort to save lives knew that the time had come to save themselves. Police officers and Ringling troupers alike ran toward the eastern exits. If they came upon someone who could be saved along the way, they swept them up and carried them to safety. The others were placed into the hands of God.

The inevitable occurred moments later, when the last tent poles crashed to the earth, creating a forest of destruction. The still-flaming Big Top fell with a deafening roar, dooming most of those still alive inside. Superheated air was driven out of the tent by the pressure of the descending canvas. The blast of fiery air punched its way through the atmosphere, burning human flesh as well as trees and equipment arrayed along the northern rim of the circus grounds. Those who watched the Big Top die were impressed by the image of American flags flying above the canvas roof. It seemed as if they were stubbornly defying the fiery threat, the banners becoming the last vestige of resistance against the tyrannical and malevolent flames that would ultimately consume the Ringling circus and the national symbol of independence.

By the time the fire department hoses were fully charged, the Big Top had been destroyed, so Thomas ordered his men to spray the bodies that had accumulated on the circus grounds. The fire would continue to feast on canvas remnants for the next thirty minutes before burning itself out. Despite frustration and regret over having been unable to fight the circus blaze, Fire Marshal Thomas and his men remained hopeful that they might be able to save some of the victims by cooling the stacks of charred bodies with water from the fire hoses. Their hope was well-founded, since several survivors were able to escape with minimal injury after being rescued from the bottom of a group of victims. Those who had already perished offered refuge from incendiary heat.

The last of the the Big Top is consumed, claiming the lives of those still trapped inside.
PHOTO COURTESY OF THE CONNECTICUT STATE LIBRARY

Other victims were less fortunate. Many of those who had not even been touched by flame were severely burned nonetheless, intense radiant heat searing their skin, penetrating to the core of their being. Firemen found one mother whose arms were wrapped around her young child, their bodies fused together in death by the hellish heat. Even coins in the pockets of some survivors had been welded together, proving beyond question that the blaze had generated otherworldly temperatures. Most of the victims who had been trapped inside, especially the 65 women and children crushed at the cage chutes, were burned beyond recognition, often to charred remains. To them, it must have seemed as if the jaws of hell had opened, announcing the arrival of the devil himself.

Many Hartford residents heard about the catastrophe from radio bulletins that broke into regular programming. As word of the fire spread, normal city life ground to a halt. All interest and attention turned to the circus and the fire that was laying waste to innocent victims of all ages, unsuspecting human beings whose only thoughts and expectations minutes before the fire broke out were of joy and laughter at the circus on a summer afternoon.

Along with a shroud of absolute silence, a cloud of ashes—and the unmistakable odor of roasting human flesh—descended upon the Barbour Street neighborhood. Linda Donahue, a teenager at the time of the fire, would later scoff at statements made by Germans and Poles who denied any knowledge of Nazi crematoria operating in the vicinity of their homes at the height of the war. Given what Donahue had experienced in Hartford, she knew it would have been impossible for European villagers to deny that human beings were incinerated in concentration camp ovens.

The circus fire was a devastating event, so monstrous in scope that it made worldwide headlines in the wake of a Flash message sent across the news wires by the *Hartford Times,* the first such bulletin in the paper's history. The reality of battlefield sacrifice had come home to Hartford in a way that could never have been predicted. According to Mayor Mortensen, the city had experienced its own wartime holocaust, an explosion of flame from which there was little chance to escape. From beginning to end, the fire required only ten minutes to reduce the Ringling Brothers circus to smoldering rubble, changing the red, white and blue colors of holiday joy to the blackness of death.

EIGHT

Only minutes after the first flames had appeared, the circus lay in ruins. Some witnesses found similarities between the Ringling fire and the explosion of the *Hindenburg* seven years earlier. In both cases, the remains offered little evidence of the grand structure that existed prior to the disaster. In a surreal testament to the institution that once was, Ringling's main entrance marquee and the sideshow billboards remained standing, despite the fact that the Big Top had been consumed. The circus grounds themselves were strewn with twisted metal, charred bodies, and tent poles that had fallen like giant matchsticks across the grandstands, crushing anything—and anyone—in their path.

Shell shocked survivors shuffled through the simmering rubble, as if in a waking nightmare, calling for their lost loved ones, hoping against hope that they had escaped unharmed. Many of those who had suffered severe burns were unaware of the extent of their injuries. Unless emergency medical treatment was forced upon them, they simply drifted through the smoke that rose like steamy spirits from the killing ground. To the accompaniment of a soft, almost inaudible murmur of mournful crying, a glassy-eyed woman stumbled aimlessly without shoes, her dress torn, reciting the names of her dead children.

Nearby, families that had escaped the blaze knelt down after being reunited, offering prayers of thanks for the intervention of God. Behind them, a semicircle of bright red Ringling wagons, untouched by the blaze, stood in sharp contrast to the blackened remains of the circus grounds. Just beyond the perimeter of the lot, the neighborhood victory gardens formed green links in a chain that bordered the site of the blaze—a chain that Ringling would later claim had dangerously restricted the movement of circus wagons and safety equipment.

An aerial view of the charred Barbour Street circus grounds after the blaze. The victory gardens can be seen above the blackened remains of the Big Top.

PHOTO COURTESY OF THE CONNECTICUT STATE LIBRARY

In the wake of the fire, the circus suddenly came to represent a world at war, a world gone mad, a world that could no longer be trusted. Some residents of the city reacted angrily, directing their bitter fury at Ringling employees. But circus workers, performers and their children were also deeply affected by the tragedy. Like the fleeing fans, circus troupers found the event incomprehensible, and they stood in shock during the aftermath, struggling to come to grips with the implications of what had occurred minutes earlier. Miraculously, every circus worker and performer had escaped death. All of them expressed gratitude that the blaze had not been born minutes later, with the show fully engaged and the performance oval filled with camels, horses, wagons, elephants and an enormous assortment of Ringling troupers entertaining the audience. Had the fire occurred at that moment, the extent of the catastrophe would have been incalculable.

The Ringling circus physician, Dr. Robert Harris, treated dozens of injured spectators who collapsed in "back yard" after escaping from the flaming Big Top. A crush of victims filled his small hospital tent, but Harris remained calm, offering medical care under circumstances similar to those seen in a battlefield surgical unit. Minutes after the fire began, additional doctors and nurses were called to the disaster scene in an effort to wage war against imminent death, and the carnage they encountered would never leave their memory.

Once the bodies of the dead were gathered onto the circus grounds, initial assessments were undertaken by Dr. Walter Weissenborn, the Hartford County Medical Examiner. A preliminary cause of death was determined at the scene, and the evaluation process continued throughout the afternoon. Priests were called to administer the last rites to the dead and dying, regardless of the faith they had embraced in life. Because the bodies of many victims had been fused together by extreme heat, they had to be carried away in pairs on jury-rigged gurneys made of double wagon ladders that were hoisted by eight or more men. Merle Evans and his musicians set their instruments aside to serve as stretcher bearers in the emotional aftermath.

Although no Ringling lives were lost, the American tradition of which they were a part had been destroyed, and the traveling meta-community was forced to face its own forms of fear and suffering. The devastation left an indelible impression on circus performers, whose grief revolved around the death of their fans, especially the children. Risk had always been a fact of circus life, but the effect of the Hartford fire upon the Ringling troupers themselves was beyond comprehension. Theirs was a life led on the road, a transient life with little permanence. On July 6, fire and death would settle into their memory and reside there forever.

Emmett Kelly and several other clowns—all of them wet and exhausted from their efforts to contain the blaze and assist the desperate audience as they fled—stood at the edge of the rubble, watching masked soldiers from nearby Bradley Field remove the last bodies, many of them children. Kelly moved deeper into the ruins of the Big Top to retrieve an abandoned clown doll that was lying face down in the charred sawdust. As the smoke drifted slowly around him, he hugged the doll—symbol of the lost children—and wept in silence. News accounts would soon report that, from that day on, Kelly would paint a tear beneath his right eye before every Ringling performance, in honor of the innocent victims who had lost their lives. Whether true or not, the union of the man and the image seemed wholly appropriate in the aftermath of the tragedy.

Emily Gill shared a Southampton duplex with Mr. & Mrs. Clarence Tolson, whose son, Ron, was a friend of Emily's young nephew, Don Cook. After learning about the tragic circus fire from a radio broadcast, Mrs. Tolson hurried to inform Emily, who knew that Mildred had taken the children to the July 6 matinee. Throbbing with fear, Emily immediately called her brother, Ted, and told him that the circus had burned to the ground. Ted and his wife, Marion, had been raising the Cook children since the dissolution of Mildred's marriage. The kids had only been gone for a few days, and Ted had assumed that they were having a wonderful vacation with their mother, so news of the Ringling disaster sent a shudder of fear along his spine. All at once, Emily's announcement that the entire family could be in mortal danger shattered the calm of the summer holiday.

Even though Ted was barely able to formulate logical thoughts in the moments after he learned about the fire, he found his way to a plan. Since phone calls to Mildred's apartment had not been answered, there was no way to be certain that she and the kids were safe unless someone made a journey to the city. He urged Emily to drive to Hartford right away, hoping that she would be able to locate Mildred and the children.

Ted was reluctant to alarm Marion without reason, since she was visiting her sister in Randolph, a farming town near the eastern end of the state. Nonetheless, he felt obligated to warn his wife that the children could be at risk. Marion cried when she heard the news, and she made Ted promise to call her the moment he had any additional information.

Minutes later, Ted jumped into his car and drove to Hartford. Alone with his thoughts, he prayed that his entire family was safe, and that they would soon be reunited.

When World War II began, Hartford prepared for civil disaster by establishing a War Council comprised of well-respected municipal leaders. The Council was granted extraordinary emergency powers, all of which were intended to ensure survival should the Nazi enemy ever mount a bombing raid on the city and its war-related industries. The Ringling circus fire provided the first opportunity to mobilize the relief services envisioned by the Council members. More than 1000 volunteers reported for duty in the wake of the disaster, most of them arriving less than thirty minutes after the blaze was discovered. Despite such an extensive increase in support staff, the unprecedented demand imposed upon the city would continue to expand in the hours after the blaze.

Police and fire services were soon stretched to the breaking point, so civil defense machinery operated in high gear in an effort to support the city's hospitals, all of which were being overrun with patients. In order to facilitate the transport of the dead and dying, buses and conveyance vehicles were halted and more than fifty ambulances were directed to the circus grounds immediately after the blaze was discovered. Most of the emergency vehicles were delivery trucks that had been specially outfitted under an order from the War Council. The recently-converted ambulances were sent by Hartford retail businesses such as Brown Thomson, G. Fox & Company and Sage-Allen.

The greatest number of dying and seriously injured patients were taken to Municipal Hospital, a treatment facility that had never cultivated financial resources equivalent to those acquired by Hartford Hospital, the city's namesake medical institution. Proximity to the circus grounds, however, made Municipal the facility of choice for those who had been burned or injured in the fire. The physicians and administrators of Municipal were unprepared for the extent of the tragedy that confronted them on July 6, and the enormous influx of trauma patients pushed the hospital and its medical staff to the brink of their professional capacities.

Those who witnessed the arrival of the dead and dying called the scene heartbreaking, and the circumstances were repeating themselves at every other city hospital at the same moment.

Once word of the fire made its way across the city, emotional chaos spread to hospital corridors, where frenzied relatives searched desperately for any word of their missing loved ones. Moving with the tide that had swept into the Municipal Hospital lobby, one worried man cradled a young boy who had been burned brown—especially around the eyes. Stanley Kurneta had taken his mother and son, as well as his niece and nephew, to the Ringling matinee. When the fire broke out, he saved the members of his family by pushing them up and over the iron cage chutes near the northeast exit. But in the dash to escape, Stanley lost sight of his six-year-old nephew. Unable to locate the boy on the circus grounds, he returned to the flaming Big Top, risking his own life in the process.

After fleeing from the tent a second time, Stanley found his semiconscious nephew lying near a Ringling circus wagon. Ignoring his own injuries, he scooped the boy into his arms and carried him onto an Army truck, comforting his badly burned nephew during the torturous ride to the hospital. Weaving his way into the Municipal emergency room, Stanley noticed a priest standing in the hall. After announcing that he was the boy's uncle, he offered his nephew to the priest, who took him into his arms. The grieving man told the priest that his nephew's name was Raymond Erickson, and he asked that the boy be given the last rites of the Catholic Church. The priest agreed, and Stanley left the building without speaking another word. Shocked from his own injuries and stunned by the threat to his young nephew's life, he returned to the circus grounds, where he informed his family of Raymond's condition. Hours later, the family would begin a desperate search for the little boy they loved, a search that would lead to a cluster of questions that would never be answered.

In addition to the more than 100 victims who had died in the first minutes of the blaze, there were hundreds of secondary injuries that required treatment, a situation made worse by the psychological trauma evidenced by the survivors. Most of the casualties died a horrible death, either from flames or from having been trampled during the frenzy. Those who were still alive were badly burned and, in most cases, the cause was intensely superheated air. The extreme temperatures generated by the fire had blistered the lips, faces and bodies of men, women and children who had escaped from the Big Top, and the human devastation created by the flaming circus tragedy led some witnesses to wonder whether the community would ever recover.

Fortunately, the city's all-encompassing advance planning for a wartime emergency had eliminated any shortage of critical medical materials. A stockpile of 5000 units of plasma in both frozen and liquid form was readily available, and supplies of dressings and treatment gels were enormous. Plasma, morphine and penicillin had been tested successfully under battlefield conditions, and they were considered vital medical interventions of the day, so they were used extensively on July 6.

The seemingly incessant and nearly overwhelming flood of patients soon required that the halls of every hospital become treatment areas. If patients were conscious on arrival, their pain was excruciating, so virtually all burn victims were given necessary doses of morphine. Plasma was often administered with great difficulty because of the badly damaged condition of the victims. In many cases, superficial veins had been destroyed by flame, so physicians were forced to cut to the femoral artery in the thigh in order to infuse required fluids. Once active treatment began, wounds were salved with petroleum jelly and wrapped in sterile gauze. In order to minimize the aroma of burned human flesh, doctors and nurses dabbed camphor cream at their nostrils, or placed drops of scented oil on their face masks.

In the middle of the afternoon, one young victim was brought to Municipal Hospital, and the uniqueness of her appearance and condition would leave a lasting impression upon those who struggled to save her life. She was approximately eight years old, with blonde hair and blue eyes, and the nurses who received her were immediately taken by her tragic beauty. Although the girl was still alive, she remained unconscious. Her forehead revealed evidence of crush trauma, and her left wrist was mildly burned.

Other than a minor char mark on her left cheek, her face was untouched by flames. While forcing intravenous fluids in an effort to revive her, nurses wrapped her wrist in a support bandage. Along with many other seriously injured patients, the little girl had been brought to the hospital alone, so she could not be identified. After initial treatment, she was wheeled into the corridor, where efforts to save her life would continue.

At about the same time, a badly burned woman who appeared to be in her late thirties was brought to Municipal with her young son. Both mother and child had been burned over the majority of their bodies, and they needed aggressive treatment if they were to survive. However, the woman refused to release her grip on the boy's hand. Although her burned and trampled son was unconscious and unaware of his mother's concern, she continued to object whenever medical staff tried to remove the child from her arms. While one nurse sifted through the woman's belongings in an effort to identify her, a second nurse worked to pry the boy's hand from his mother's grasp. Then a dose of morphine was injected into the woman, the wounded woman named Mildred Cook, who wailed for her son until she slipped into a drug-induced coma, a state that would shelter her from pain.

Across town, Hartford Hospital accepted its first batch of patients from the circus fire at three o'clock. Seconds after receiving notification of the disaster, Dr. Donald Wells, a noted burn expert, had implemented the emergency medical plan he had drafted in the wake of the horrendous 1942 Cocoanut Grove fire in Boston. Under the direction of Wells and senior attending staff, trained trauma teams were instantly mobilized, treatment rooms were prepped, and the triage process was initiated, as if a battle were being waged at home.

Dr. Wells recognized the benefits of prior disaster training as the culling and sorting of the injured continued. Despite the efficiency of the emergency plan, the overwhelming influx of flame-damaged patients became an unexpected crisis for the city's hospitals, all of which were routinely short-staffed because many young physicians had been called for service in World War II. Doctors and nurses available anywhere in the city were contacted with an urgent request that they return to their medical posts as quickly as possible in order to assist in the aftermath of the Ringling fire.

Burn patients often exhibited an advanced state of shock, so the true extent of their initial injuries was difficult to assess. Wells knew that pneumonia and infection were the greatest risks faced by fire victims, so tetanus shots were given to every patient burned beyond first degree in an attempt to reduce the threat of systemic infection. Those who developed fevers within 48 hours of admission were given "liberal doses" of penicillin, a precious wartime antibiotic. The onset of a secondary infection could become a death sentence for burn victims, so their sterile gauze bandages would not be changed for the first ten to fourteen days of hospitalization. Across the city, a total of 140 seriously burned patients would be required to undergo long periods of recovery and rehabilitation, with painful skin grafts a necessary and recurring component of their treatment. Doctors recognized that, like the city itself, circus fire victims who survived would carry lasting physical reminders of the trauma they had endured.

NINE

Aware that his city was under siege, Hartford Mayor William Mortensen took an early and active role in the aftermath of the blaze. Immediately after receiving notification of the disaster, Mayor Mortensen toured the smoky circus grounds to assess the extent of the devastation and to synchronize the activities of the city's emergency services. As soon as the flames receded, he ordered Fire Marshal Henry Thomas to begin a preliminary investigation into the cause and origin of the Ringling fire.

As the impact of the disaster impressed itself upon him, Mortensen crisscrossed the city to offer assistance and compassion to victims, survivors and families, a process that quickly became personal rather than political. Mortensen was deeply wounded by the tragedy that had befallen his city, and he moved through its homes and institutions in an effort to offer condolences that rose from the depths of his heart. At the same time, he knew that a controlling municipal authority would have to be established in order to quell the chaos and address the interests of press and public alike. Since Governor Baldwin had told Mortensen that State Police Commissioner Edward Hickey was the right man for the job, the mayor took comfort in allowing Hickey the necessary freedom to coordinate rescue and recovery services, and to undertake an official inquiry.

Edward J. Hickey was not a lawyer, nor was he a fire investigator. First and foremost, he was a politician. In the early years of his career, he had been a Pinkerton detective, then a state police trooper. Along the way, he had acquired the nickname "Bull" because of a thick build and a tenacious—even pugnacious—personality. Through a combination of high-profile cases and political connections, Bull Hickey was appointed Connecticut State Police Commissioner in 1939, the same year his good friend "Cappy" Baldwin moved into the governor's mansion. Given the way the laws were written at the time, the State Police Commissioner also served as the State Fire Marshal. Although the titles differed, two enforcement agencies had been consolidated into one office, granting dual investigative authority to a single state official. No one had ever expressed any concern about the lack of professional objectivity that might result from such a legal framework, so the enabling statute was still in force in 1944.

Commissioner Hickey and Governor Baldwin confer at the State Armory shortly after the blaze.
PHOTO COURTESY OF THE CONNECTICUT STATE LIBRARY

At three o'clock on July 6, just minutes after the appointment of Commissioner Hickey as the state's senior investigative official in the aftermath of the Ringling fire, Governor Baldwin addressed the people of Connecticut by radio. Like so many other people who were just learning about the blaze and the scope of its devastation, Baldwin was overcome with human emotions, and he had all he could do to control himself before the broadcast. His compassion and sorrow triggered tears that had to be held back in order for him to speak at all. In his address, he urged the people of Hartford to be calm, and he warned against a hysterical overreaction to the tragedy.

However, the people of Hartford were anything but calm in the hours after the fire descended upon them. As expected in times of tragedy, they were desperate for news of loved ones who had attended the circus that afternoon. Frances Madden was on duty as an operator for the Southern New England Telephone Company when the fire occurred. Phone calls in and out of the city were completed by hand jacks at the time, and Frances worked furiously with other young operators to service worried callers, but she could not fulfill the multitude of requests that flew across the lines once news of the fire began to break. After the Big Top collapsed, neighbors in the Barbour Street area offered the use of their telephones so that survivors could contact their anxious relatives. A rumor quickly began to spread about one woman who placed a sign in her window announcing access to a telephone—and who then allegedly stood like a ghoul at the first-floor entrance to her home and collected a dollar from each of the traumatized survivors who asked to make a call.

The most frantic inquiries centered on the safety of children who had attended the July 6 matinee with friends or relatives. Lost children, some of them newly orphaned by the blaze, were clustered into the care of Hartford police officers. One by one, they were taken to the Brown School on Market Street, the designated gathering place for kids who had escaped the flames. As soon as they arrived, efforts were made to identify each child so they could later be reunited with their loved ones. As the hours went by, anxious families streamed into the school, often after having searched the city's hospitals for word of their children's safety. Parents who recovered their children would cry tears of joy. In a cruelly ironic twist of fate, children who had not been claimed by nightfall would cry tears of sorrow as they faced the possibility that they might never see their parents again.

The casualty list grew rapidly in the minutes after the blaze, sealing the tragic fate of the circus fire's initial victims. By mid-afternoon, a number of bodies were still being assessed on the lot adjacent to the circus grounds, and funeral homes all across the city were reaching capacity, so Commissioner Hickey recognized that a large public building would be needed in order to facilitate the identification of the dead. Working in concert with Governor Baldwin and Mayor Mortensen, he arranged for the use of the State Armory on Broad Street as a temporary morgue.

An imposing gray granite structure with long, dark hallways surrounding a cavernous rectangular space called the drill floor, the armory prompted subliminal comparisons to a tomb, making it an appropriate repository for bodies. The fragility of life was made evident there, the sacred character of every human being was recognized there, and the solemnity of death was respected there. Fragile, sacred, solemn—and absolutely silent. Those who had expected, or feared, mournful wails heard none. Hartford had been visited by death before. When it arrived this time, sorrow had no sound. Death simply placed a blanket of silence over the grieving community, as if to offer comfort and condolences for having come at all.

Hundreds of off-duty nurses had been summoned by radio appeals broadcast in the wake of the blaze. Mrs. Thomas Tyszka, a senior Red Cross volunteer, was one of those who answered the urgent call for emergency medical support. As she dashed out the door, she warned her ten-year-old son not to come anywhere near the armory while she was gone. Like so many inquisitive boys, young Billy found it difficult to resist temptation. His mother's admonition had stimulated an interest in the Ringling circus fire—and the mysterious rituals that were taking place at the armory. Billy and three of his friends made a secret journey to the state capitol that afternoon. From a knoll overlooking the armory, they witnessed the arrival of trucks bearing what seemed to be hundreds of coffins, all of which were ferried into the stone structure in preparation for the removal of the men, women and children who had died at the circus. Standing together in silence, imagining the cold dark isolation that would surround the human beings enclosed within those coffins, Billy and his friends came to understand the reality and permanence of death.

A Matter Of Degree

As soon as worried families learned where their lost loved ones were likely to be found, long lines formed at the entrance to the armory, lines that soon streamed around the northwest corner of the building. Ironically, worried relatives could view the activity inside the lobby, but they were prevented from entering the armory en masse by an iron lattice barrier that rose to the capstone of the gateway. Even though the sun had lowered in the sky, the temperature remained high, so the Red Cross served cold drinks to those in line. The refreshments provided comfort from the heat—and preparation for the grim search that family members would soon be forced to endure.

Anguished relatives and friends waiting to enter the State Armory.
PHOTO COURTESY OF THE CONNECTICUT STATE LIBRARY

Many of the souls gathered within the armory offered precious little evidence of their former humanity, having been charred to cinders. The medical examiner, Walter Weissenborn, moved among the rows of bodies that had been placed on army cots and arranged by age and gender along the north end of the drill floor. Accompanied by Dr. Edgar Butler, a local dentist, Dr. Weissenborn assessed the bodies before him, noting any remaining clothing, identifying marks, the number of teeth, and a description of any dental work. He also listed the probable age of the victims, although his estimates were wrong by a factor of ten or more years, in some cases. Once the medical examiner completed an assessment, the body was covered with a blanket, pending formal identification.

After being admitted to the lobby of the armory, relatives of the missing were asked to supply information about their loved ones. A dozen female clerks served as the official registry, collecting the names of anxious searchers and maintaining multiple lists of the missing and the dead. Once the paper work was processed, relatives were brought to the drill floor in small groups. In every case, those searching for a missing loved one were escorted by a nurse or a Red Cross volunteer and a Connecticut State Trooper, ensuring that those who found a family member at the armory would have physical and emotional support at the moment of discovery. Jennie Heiser, a seasoned nurse who had witnessed more than her share of misery over the course of her career, was struck by the steely reserve exhibited by those who undertook the morbid quest to identify the dead.

Either because of emotional denial or an inability to distinguish the features of their badly disfigured loved ones, some relatives were unable to identify those who had died. Formal identifications were often made by the recognition of a ring, or a necklace, or a fragment of clothing—items that provided only the most meager proof that the individual who had once occupied that body was in fact the person they were asserted to be. But human beings who have been wounded by the loss of someone they love seek a catalyst for closure, an opportunity for healing, and the first component on July 6 was identification. In the days following the Ringling blaze, many Hartford residents rushed to purchase silver plated bracelets, then they engraved their names on them, because a symbol of their identity—the means of assuring themselves and the world that they existed—had suddenly become more important than ever.

The fire had been over for more than two hours by the time Emily Gill got to the city. With no real plan other than to find Mildred and the children, she drove directly to the apartment on Marshall Street. Racing up the stairs, Emily prayed aloud that her sister and the kids would answer the knock at the door, but there were no sounds of life inside the apartment. A tide of panic washed over Emily as she considered her options. Although she did her best to resist dire thoughts, intermittent images of fire and suffering and death and sorrow and loneliness forced their way into her consciousness like pulses of lightning against a storm-blackened sky.

Moments later, Emily blinked away her tears as she drove toward Barbour Street and the circus grounds. The scent of smoke grew stronger as she got closer to the core of the disaster, and a razor thin layer of ashes covered some of the lawns like early-winter snow. Curious residents and stunned survivors stared as Emily rolled past them, the pace of her progress reduced to a crawl because of lingering crowds and emergency vehicles parked pell-mell around the fire zone. Throngs of residents gathered along the perimeter of the disaster site, their collective weight pressing against the cordon of snow fence and police lines that restricted access to the killing ground.

Unable to travel any further, Emily told a policeman that her family had come to the circus, and she asked if he knew where she might locate them. His response was simple and straightforward: they would probably be found at one of the city's hospitals, and Municipal was the most logical choice. He added that many children had been separated from their families during the fire, and that those who had not been reunited with their parents had been taken to the Brown School, which was just a few blocks away.

As the battle between hope and despair raged within her, Emily willed herself to continue her quest for Mildred and the kids. Her heart began to pound with anxiety and anticipation when she reached the Brown School. Standing in surreal contrast to the smoldering devastation Emily had just observed, dozens of children were laughing and squealing with delight as they played together on the swings and chutes in the backyard of the school. For a fleeting moment, Emily could almost forget that the circus fire had ever occurred, but reality intruded once again when she asked about her niece and nephews. The news that none of the Cook children had been brought to the school that day sent a dagger of dread through Emily's heart. In a fragile voice that threatened to shatter at any moment, she asked that Don, Honey and Edward be added to the list of missing children. Then she walked away from the squeals and laughter that drifted in the wind, and she drove in silence toward Municipal Hospital.

Operating under an order from Governor Baldwin, State Police Commissioner Hickey began his initial investigation while the ashes from the circus fire were still warm. Given the crushing losses suffered by the city, Hickey ordered the Ringling circus to remain in Hartford until the official investigation was completed, and he impounded their train and equipment to underscore his intention to attach the remaining assets of the circus in the interests of the city and its people.

Before leaving the circus grounds, Mayor Mortensen had asked Hickey to obtain as much fresh evidence as possible in the hours following the fire, so Hickey had called for and received assistance from the Connecticut State Police. Troopers from headquarters barracks in Hartford were assigned to search the circus grounds—despite the fact that much of their work would be done in darkness.

As a political appointee with no legal or fire investigation credentials, Hickey had no experience in the cause and origin of fires—especially those that had resulted in death as well as destruction. Had he investigated fire scenes at any time over the course of his career, he would have known that trampling through charred grounds, especially at night, was an excellent way to destroy evidence. Nonetheless, he ordered his men to seek and retrieve any items that might suggest the origin of the blaze.

Complicating matters even further, Hickey did not order his troopers to seal or secure the fire scene, an oversight that allowed virtually anyone to wander through the grounds of what amounted to the worst public catastrophe of the twentieth century. Although Hickey did not recognize it at the time, his investigative decisions would impede the discovery of the true cause of the Ringling circus fire.

Given the immense human interest that arose in the aftermath of the blaze, the news media—which meant press and radio, in 1944—were ravenous for information from the moment they first acquired the story. For years, they had heard of fires during the circus season, but none had been as destructive or deadly as the one Hartford had just experienced. As soon as wire service reporters and journalists from national newspapers and magazines received word of the Ringling fire, they assumed that a blaze of that scope had to have been set. With that assumption in mind, they were quick to probe Commissioner Hickey, clamoring for a cause—and a suspect. Ironically, Hickey had an opposing assumption, placing him at odds with some members of the press from the beginning of the investigation.

While questioning Hartford policemen who had been assigned to the circus grounds that day, Hickey was told by one officer that an angry spectator had claimed that "some sonofabitch" had thrown away a burning cigarette just before flames broke through the sidewall canvas. Even though the statement was reported by a sworn officer, it amounted to little more than hearsay, and secondary hearsay at that. Nonetheless, the assertion left an impression on Hickey, who soon began to speculate to the press that the fire could well have been caused by a carelessly discarded cigarette.

TEN

As the complexity of the investigation began to reveal itself, it became apparent that Hickey and Assistant State Prosecutor Burr Leikind would need a central location in which to conduct interrogations and consider evidence. The McGovern Granite Company—ironically, a grave monument provider—was located on Barbour Street, adjacent to the circus grounds. After an informal request from Leikind, the McGovern site was made available as an interim office during the initial phase of the state inquiry. In the early hours of the investigation, more than a dozen key Ringling managers and employees were sought for questioning. Under orders from Leikind, Hartford police officers and Connecticut State Police troopers fanned out across the lot in search of the men who were believed to possess information valuable enough to advance the state investigation.

Among the first Ringling workers to be interviewed by Leikind were the seatmen charged with ensuring the safety of spectators in the bleachers and grandstands. Questioning began in the early evening, and would continue throughout the night. Neil Todd reported that he was on duty at the north end of the Big Top when he saw the fire "in the top of the tent over the men's toilet" area. Todd asserted that, by the time the seatmen realized that fire had broken out, panic had already set in and spectators were screaming and running toward the exits. He noticed that the cage chutes blocked the northeast exit, and that the chutes prevented many people from escaping with their lives.

In his own statement, seatman Charley Ryan reported that he first saw the fire "at the top of the tent, to the right of the main entrance," where a "large area was burning at the time." Like Todd, he had seen no evidence of flames prior to their appearance on the sidewall canvas. His testimony was supported by Charley Mitchell, another Ringling seatman, who claimed to have seen flames "on the top of the tent at the west end" of the Big Top. Mitchell added that, by the time he noticed the fire, "it was not a very large area burning at that time" but, from his position, there was nothing he could do to smother the flames. When the time came for Lymoine Reiff to offer his statement, he reported that the fire was "burning very badly at the top of the tent over the southwest corner."

All of the Ringling seatmen had indicated that the fire was first seen high on the sidewall, very near the top of the tent. Their uniform testimony served as an important indicator of the nature and position of the fire. Most troubling to Leikind, though, were their comments about the cage chutes that obstructed the exits, leading to the deaths of about 65 people who were found clustered together in the remains of the Big Top. When briefed about the testimony later, Commissioner Hickey ordered Hartford police officers to return to the circus grounds and retrieve evidence of the cage chutes for examination. The officers recovered several cage segments in the remnants of the tent near the northeast and northwest exits, performance areas where the largest number of victims had been found.

For several hours after the fire, two parallel investigations were under way. Fire Marshal Henry Thomas had been directed by Mayor Mortensen to begin his own inquiry, and the evidence was rapidly accumulating. Mortensen was especially interested in determining what actions the city itself had taken prior to the blaze, but the information that had been obtained was not encouraging. Mortensen was told that the fire department had not stationed men or equipment on the circus grounds, and that they had not done a safety inspection of the circus prior to the first performance. Most troubling of all, however, was the fact that municipal and police officials had not obtained a certificate of insurance from the Ringling circus—despite the fact that proof of insurance was required under city regulations. News of these municipal failures infuriated Mortensen, who developed an immediate and lasting antipathy for Police Chief Thomas Hallisey, whose office issued the final permit that granted Ringling the right to perform in Hartford.

Unaware of the city's official pre-circus conduct, Commissioner Hickey vigorously continued his own investigation. Hickey's men rounded up the Ringling workers one by one, compelling their testimony under threat of legal action. By early evening, Prosecutor Meade Alcorn had joined the investigation, and he was avidly interested in Leikind's questioning of Edward "Whitey" Versteeg, Ringling's chief electrician. Versteeg indicated that he had been short-staffed all season and that his men were working long hours to compensate for the lack of manpower. As soon as the fire was discovered, his electricians cut the power running into the main tent, then they ran to help quench the flames.

When asked about the possibility that Ringling equipment might have triggered the blaze, Versteeg stated with confidence that there was never any risk that the diesel engines providing power for the troupe were malfunctioning, and there were no sparks that could have ignited the fire. Versteeg seemed to engage in some protective evasion, however, when he claimed to be unaware of any regular placement of fire extinguishers at selected areas within the main tent. Sensing an opening, state investigators continued to probe, asking Versteeg about the condition of the Big Top itself. The Ringling veteran took Leikind and Alcorn by surprise when he reported that the top had been waterproofed with a flammable mixture of paraffin and gasoline prior to the summer season. Versteeg's unexpected revelation lent new significance to the investigation. With questions of criminal liability in mind, subpoenas were issued for the appearance of James Haley, George Smith, Leonard Aylesworth, David Blanchfield, John Brice, and John Carson.

James Haley, vice-president of the Ringling corporation, was the most important of those circus officials Leikind intended to question, but Haley could not be found in the first hours after the blaze. As the evening wore on, an increasingly perturbed Leikind directed Herbert DuVal, Ringling's legal adjuster, to assist police officers in their search for Haley. Minutes after becoming involved, DuVal led the investigators to Haley, who was in his private rail car on the Ringling train. Served with a subpoena to compel his testimony, Haley had no choice but to prepare for his first appearance before Commissioner Hickey.

By nightfall on July 6, the death toll from the fire had risen to 120—and it was still climbing. As the hours went by, more and more grieving relatives scoured the armory in search of their lost loved ones. Once an identification was made, registry clerks typed the name of the deceased on partially prepared death certificates. With the assistance of Dr. Henry Onderdonk, Medical Examiner Walter Weissenborn obtained and reviewed the identification information for every claimed body. On each certificate, Dr. Weissenborn declared that the victim had died either from third and fourth degree burns in the "conflagration" on the Barbour Street grounds, or from severe trauma. However, the actual cause of death would never be certifiably known because no autopsies were performed on the deceased, and because even the most severely burned victims could have died from the inhalation of superheated air before flames ever touched them. Weissenborn's decision to list fire as the cause of death was a simple clerical necessity.

As bodies were removed, more bodies were brought in to replace them, and it seemed as if they would be replenished until the community's storehouse of endurance had been exhausted. In an effort to keep anxious family members informed while their gloomy quest continued, the names of survivors who had been found at other locations were intoned over the loudspeaker of a state police radio car that was stationed on the drill floor. Announcements were made many times over the course of the evening, granting a reprieve from misery to a fortunate few whose loved ones had escaped death. For others, however, hours of anguished waiting would result in abject sorrow.

Like so many European immigrants, Anna DiMartino had come to America with the hope of achieving the dream of freedom and opportunity. Her husband, Sal, worked as a laborer in an effort to scratch out a decent living for his family of eight young children. On July 6, he and Anna had gone to the circus in high spirits, eager for a holiday afternoon of laughter and joy. Hours later, their shared dream became a singular nightmare. After overcoming his initial reluctance to search the armory for his missing wife, Sal found Anna there. She had died of severe burns, and the truth of her death pierced her husband's heart. With his strength stolen by shock and sorrow, Sal fell into the arms of the nurse and trooper who had accompanied him on his search. He had always counted on Anna's emotional support throughout their years together. Now that the love of his life had been taken from him, he would rely on the strength of strangers to help him find his way home.

After learning that his wife had died, Sal DiMartino is assisted by Armory volunteers.

PHOTO COURTESY OF THE CONNECTICUT STATE LIBRARY

Most of the searching relatives were forced to accept the death of one, perhaps two, of their family members. Although every death was devastating in its own right, none could compare to those cases in which entire families had been annihilated in the circus fire. For some surviving families, a declaration of death would have been acceptable in its closure and certainty—and far more preferable in its finality than the mystery that surrounded the loss of their loved ones.

Six-year-old Raymond Erickson had been brought to Municipal Hospital by his uncle, Stanley Kurneta, in the first minutes after the Ringling blaze. Raymond's father was on duty with the Navy, stationed in the southern tier of the United States, so Raymond's mother was required to face the situation on her own until her husband could be brought home on compassionate leave. When the terrified Sophie Erickson rushed into the hospital to inquire about her son, she was told that there was no record of Raymond—or of the priest who was alleged to have received him.

Unwilling to believe that her little boy had not been treated for his injuries, or that he had somehow been lost in a medical morass, Mrs. Erickson pressed hospital officials for more details. In a meeting with Mary Sullivan, the superintendent of Municipal, Mrs. Erickson asserted that it would have been impossible for a nurse or doctor to forget her young son. In addition to being much taller and stronger than the average six-year-old boy, Raymond would have been easy to recognize because of the unique identifying marks on his body, including "stains of gentian violet on his left hand and lower arm, for blisters from a cast" he had worn after breaking his wrist one month before the fire. Still, no record of his treatment or disposition could be found.

The fact that no one could remember anything about the priest who was said to have attended dying victims in the corridor of the hospital that afternoon made the disappearance of young Raymond even more mysterious—and disturbing—for the Erickson family. In one final attempt to assist the grief-stricken mother of a lost child whose disappearance could neither be explained nor accepted, Mrs. Erickson was taken to the Social Welfare Department of the hospital. While there, she was allowed to search through a collection of clothing that belonged to the victims who had been treated that day. In a crowning moment of parental sorrow, Mrs. Erickson found her little boy's socks and shoes. A knot that she had tied in the laces and tucked inside one shoe so as not to be seen served as a poignant reminder of the care Mrs. Erickson had taken before Raymond left for the circus that day. Sadly, the little boy in the navy blue sailor suit would never return to his mother—and no trace of him would ever be found.

As with Sophie Erickson, it was the fear of permanent loss that compelled Emily Gill to visit Municipal Hospital on the night of July 6. An information area had been set up in the lobby, so it was there that Emily's search for Mildred and the children began in earnest. A clerk leafed through the records and determined that Mildred had arrived at the hospital hours earlier with severe burns. Visions of her sister's suffering instantly raced through Emily's mind, but she could not allow herself to dwell on them. As devastating as Mildred's medical status was, the news quickly got worse. The clerk stated that a little boy who was presumed to be Mildred's son was brought in with her, and he was taken to Room 505 for ongoing care. When Emily asked about Edward's condition, the clerk answered in one word: grave. Because medical treatment was still being administered, Emily was not allowed to visit her sister and her nephew. Adding to her concerns, the hospital had no information about Mildred's other children, Don and Honey. Recognizing Emily's state of distress, the clerk tried to offer a ray of hope by suggesting that the children might be found at the Brown School. She could not have known that Emily had already reported the children missing after searching for them there.

Bearing only fear and sorrow in her heart, and with a growing sense of doom throbbing within her body, Emily returned to Marshall Street, where Ted was waiting for her. Within seconds, she offered the details of her search, denying herself the freedom to cry as she shared the sad facts with her brother. Given that Mildred and Edward had been found, Ted instinctively turned his attention to the search for Don and Honey. Aware that the accumulation of information increased and evolved over the course of time—especially during an immense disaster such as the circus fire—Ted contacted the Hartford Police Department in the hope that they would know something more about Mildred's missing children. He and Emily were rewarded with the first joyous news of the day.

Don Cook had been found wandering the circus grounds minutes after he jumped from the bleachers and scrambled out of the tent. The nine-year-old knew there was no way to go back inside to help his family escape, so he waited anxiously near the eastern border of the tent, hoping they would come out, but they never did. Discovered by a Hartford couple who did not want to see any children left alone after such a horrible event, Don was taken to the safety of their home. He was given time to rest and to have something to eat, then the family contacted the police to report that they were caring for the boy. When Ted called the department to inquire about Don, they gave him the address of the family that had sheltered him.

Ted and Emily were jubilant over the discovery that Don was safe, but they were still haunted by the question of what had happened to Honey. Emily had searched for her at the Brown School and was told that they knew nothing about her, and the clerk at Municipal Hospital had no record of Honey having been treated there. Although Ted was reluctant to entertain the idea that Honey might have died in the blaze, he forced himself to consider that possibility. Having heard radio reports that the state armory was being used as a temporary morgue, he finally decided that he and Emily should review the bodies that had been gathered there, even if Honey were found among them. Ted broached the subject as gently as he could, encouraging Emily to steel herself for a passage through the armory, a familial necessity that promised to be one of the most difficult they would ever have to endure.

By the time James Haley entered the makeshift hearing room in the McGovern Granite office on the evening of July 6, Commissioner Hickey had returned from his initial duties at the state armory. During a preliminary interview that was anything but cordial, Hickey asked about the composition of the circus and its corporate officers, about the roster of its employees, and about the seating arrangements at each performance. Haley answered to the best of his ability, sometimes deferring to other Ringling managers who possessed more information specific to Hickey's line of questioning. When asked about the fire itself, Haley stated that about one fourth of the Big Top had already been consumed by the time his attention was attracted by the sound of human screams. He added that, like many other Ringling employees, he was unable to alter the course of the blaze, but he later assisted in the removal of bodies. At that point in Haley's initial testimony, Commissioner Hickey brought the interrogation to an end. Then he suspended the hearing and declared that all further questioning would be done at State Police headquarters on Washington Street. At his urging, however, the search for evidence would continue long into the night.

Ted and Emily sat in stony silence during the drive to the armory. If any hazy fantasies of their gruesome task arose in their minds, they did not reveal them. Just as other anxious searchers had done, they disclosed personal details to the registry clerks, who wanted as much information as Ted and Emily could provide. Other than a description of Honey, their details were few—especially since the children had spent all their time with Mildred in the days prior to the circus fire. During the identification process, searchers scrutinized remnants of clothing worn by fire victims, but Emily had no idea what the children were wearing on the day of the circus, so she offered few suggestions. Once the registration was complete, a state trooper and a Red Cross volunteer were assigned to escort Ted and Emily into the armory, then up to the drill floor.

No matter how well they had prepared themselves, they could not have imagined the sights, or the smells, that would await them there. Emily was offered a surgical mask, which she readily accepted, and she instantly placed the soft cotton cloth over her nose and mouth. In a matter of seconds, she and Ted were brought to the front section of cots where the youngest victims had been gathered. An attendant gently uncovered the face of a child whose morgue tag number was 1565. The sight of the child—who seemed to be sleeping, a perception that made the reality of her death even harder to accept—sent Emily into the arms of her brother. The little girl had blonde hair of medium length, and she seemed to be the same age as Honey. But this child appeared to have been trampled, and the contour of her forehead had been changed. Still, there was something about her that seemed strikingly familiar, especially since her face had been untouched by flames. Nonetheless, Ted and Emily came to the conclusion that the child who lay before them was not Honey, and they reported their opinion to the clerks. Moments later, brother and sister left the armory together, hand in hand, unsure of what had happened to the little niece they loved so deeply.

Eleven

As the lethal consequences of the circus fire expanded and the death count rose, Commissioner Hickey and Mayor Mortensen realized that an inquest into the cause of the Ringling blaze would have to be conducted. The need for such a judicial inquiry became more urgent after Hickey discovered that the Big Top had been waterproofed with a flammable mixture that had accelerated the blaze and enhanced its killing power. Mayor Mortensen knew that the people of Hartford would plead for answers, and, with more than 100 known fatalities, they would certainly demand justice. Hickey and Mortensen held a phone conference with Coroner Frank E. Healy, who was vacationing at his summer home. The mayor made it clear that preparations for an inquest would have to begin immediately. Hickey indicated that a state police investigation was already under way, and that sufficient forensic evidence would be gathered over the next several days. He estimated that the interrogation of witnesses would be concluded in time for an inquest as early as Monday, July 10. However, prudence suggested that Coroner Healy open his judicial inquiry on Tuesday, July 11, allowing an extra day for any administrative exigencies that might demand attention. Within an hour of their conversation, Healy was on his way back to Hartford, and subpoenas were issued by the prosecutor's office on behalf of the Coroner. By early evening, police officers William Mackenzie and James Finnegan served William Dunn, secretary of the circus, along with James Haley,

George Smith, Leonard Aylesworth, Whitey Versteeg, John Brice, Herbert DuVal, and more than a dozen circus seatmen and ushers, all of them placed under court order to appear at the inquest. The State of Connecticut had made it clear that Ringling would atone for the deaths caused by the circus fire.

Shortly after eight o'clock that night, Ted and Emily were reunited with Don, who appeared to be physically unscathed by his ordeal. An openly loving child, he had never been reluctant to show his affection, so he warmly hugged his aunt and uncle when they arrived to take him home. Emily's tears flowed freely while Don was in her arms, empathy allowing her to imagine the emotional turmoil that her nine-year-old nephew was experiencing as he wondered where his mother, sister and brother were, never daring to ask if they were still alive. After expressing their appreciation for the rescuing family's kindness and concern, Ted and Emily took Don back into their care. Even before they came for him, they had decided that he would accompany them to Municipal Hospital, where they knew at least two of his closest family members could be found.

Ted and Emily had agreed that Don would be given the chance to be with his mother and brother, regardless of the outcome of their treatment. Whatever emotional repercussions Don might suffer in the days or weeks following his hospital visit would be dealt with as they arose. In the meantime, Ted and Emily believed it was preferable to grant the boy his familial right to reunite with his mother and brother, spending whatever precious private time the Lord allowed. Although they had no inkling about the medical condition of either Mildred or Edward at that moment, they drove to Municipal Hospital together, three frightened beings drifting in a rising sea of sorrow.

On her first trip to the hospital, Emily's request to visit Mildred and Edward had been denied because they were undergoing emergency treatment. This time, she and her family were allowed to see their injured loved ones—after being forewarned that their condition had not improved. Ted and Emily reeled when they were told that Mildred had been burned over 85 percent of her body, and that she remained in a coma due to her injuries and the morphine being administered for extreme pain. The nurse added that Mildred had been bandaged like a mummy, so she would not be able to communicate with them. Even more troubling, Edward's medical status was extremely grave, and he lay near death. Given the dire circumstances, the nurse agreed that the family should spend some time with Edward, although their privacy would be minimal because there were other children in the same fifth-floor ward with him.

Armed with sufficient information to prepare themselves for their hospital visit, the Parsons family moved through the corridors in silence. An unmeasured depth of concern led Emily to disconnect from the reality of the moment. Time seemed to pass more slowly, expanding or contracting, although she did not know which of those forces took precedence. Visual impressions occurred in pulses, sequences and waves, as if Emily were selectively editing her conscious life, admitting through the gateway of her mind only that which was absolutely vital. Then, with no memory of how long the physical journey had taken, Emily found herself inside Mildred's room, staring at her sister from an uncertain distance, unsure of how far they were from one another in that shared space, or how they had made their way to that moment. Sight and sound soon settled in again, waking Emily to the risk that Mildred faced, a risk underscored by the quiet tears being shed by the frightened little boy cuddled against Emily's hip, the little boy whose mother's face lay hidden from him, swaddled within a veil of protective gauze. In that moment, Emily stepped beyond herself to fold Don into her arms, and she assured him that his mother would awaken and return to this life—and to him.

Minutes later, Ted and Emily led Don to Room 505 so he could be with his younger brother, but there was no way to determine if the gravity of the situation impressed itself upon him. Ted and Emily had all they could do to get through the moment themselves, knowing that the sweet nephew they loved so much was likely to die. Ted gently ushered Don a bit closer to Edward's bedside. Although the circumstances were extreme, the boys shared a tender moment. In a weak and weary voice, his breathing labored, Edward expressed concern about Mildred and Honey. His injuries and his age made it impossible to tell him the truth, so Emily promised that his mother and sister were fine—a benign deception intended to ease the mind of a dying child. God would surely forgive her. Moments later, Ted brought the visit to an end so his six-year-old nephew could get some rest—if rest were possible. Don placed a tender hand on Edward's arm and said goodbye, unaware that he would never see his brother again.

To the amazement of armory attendants, only two dozen victims of the blaze had been identified by ten o'clock on the night of July 6. At 10:15, Mayor Mortensen was given airtime by WTIC and other Hartford radio stations to broadcast an update on the disaster. Mortensen expressed his gratitude to the Red Cross, the Salvation Army, and to the members of the War Council. He also mentioned the exceptional effort and professional commitment of State Police Commissioner Hickey and Deputy Police Chief Godfrey. Ironically, there was no mention of Thomas Hallisey, the city's senior police official. Although the listening audience was unaware of it, Hallisey had been removed in principal from the active investigation because Mortensen believed the portly career cop had been derelict in his duties. In return for his negligence, Hallisey would soon be forced to retire. Given that the mayor's late-night broadcast was solely intended to be informative, he never discussed the corrective action he planned to take in the future. Instead, he read the names of those children who were still being cared for at the Brown School, and he concluded by somberly announcing the names of the known dead, as compiled and reported by all of the area hospitals.

Fire Marshal Henry Thomas surrendered all of his collected evidence and transferred his investigative authority to Commissioner Hickey at eleven o'clock. As of that moment, Hickey became the state's sole investigative authority, charged by the governor to continue his inquiry into the horrific Ringling blaze. Just after midnight, the investigation was reconvened in the hearing room at Connecticut State Police headquarters on Washington Street. The initial phase of Hickey's interrogations would last well into the early morning hours of July 7. During that same period, state troopers and Hartford police officers stomped through the charred remains of the circus, seeking evidence and snapping pictures in an effort to discover the origin of the blaze. In accordance with Hickey's orders, any evidence deemed valuable was removed from the fire ground and brought back to the state police offices for inspection, rather than being evaluated on-site.

Pursuant to Commissioner Hickey's order, James Haley and other key circus employees appeared at state police headquarters as the hearing resumed. The witnesses were kept isolated from each other, interrogated independently in order to guard against preconceived testimony. Meade Alcorn and Burr Leikind were present when Hickey began his questioning, and James Haley was the first circus official to testify. Haley reported that Robert Ringling, president of the corporation, had been traveling in Illinois, but Haley had called him from the Bond Hotel in Hartford to inform him that the circus had been destroyed by fire. Curiously, Commissioner Hickey never asked Haley about the substance of that conversation.

As the interrogation continued, Haley was able to estimate the seating capacity of the Big Top, although he deferred to George Smith on the actual layout of the tent and the firefighting equipment deployed by the circus. Haley's most important contribution to Hickey's investigation was his confirmation that canvas manager Leonard Aylesworth was responsible for the waterproofing treatment applied to the Big Top. Satisfied that he had obtained what he needed from Haley, Hickey indicated that he would refer all testimony to the Prosecutor of Hartford Police Court for the purpose of filing formal charges. Hickey added that he would recommend that bond be set for Haley's release, and he asked that Haley remain in the city so that he could be interrogated again. Before daybreak, four more key Ringling men would endure the same intense questioning—and suffer the same judicial result.

George Smith, the circus veteran who served as general manager for Ringling, was the next official to appear before Commissioner Hickey. In response to direct questioning, Smith indicated that John Carson managed the ushers, and that Aylesworth and his seatmen were responsible for the fire buckets. Smith confirmed that the fire extinguishers were under the control of Whitey Versteeg, the chief electrician. After eliciting Smith's description of the waterproofing application process, Hickey turned to the issue of fireproofing the Big Top.

Hickey: Is there any process at all applied to the canvas for fireproofing?
Smith: No.
Hickey: None whatever?
Smith: No. As far as we could determine, there's nothing that would fireproof it and waterproof it at the same time, and this year it was impossible to buy what you'd call fireproof equipment.

Hickey listened as Smith explained the method of application in more detail, describing how the wax-and-gasoline compound was heated to boiling and brushed on with brooms, "sealing all the pores in the canvas." Then Hickey returned to the issue of fireproofing.

Hickey: Did I understand you to say that this year you were not able to get the materials for fireproof purposes?
Smith: That's right.
Hickey: Was the canvas top for the previous years fireproof?
Smith: No, sir.
Hickey: How long since you have been fireproofing?
Smith: We never fireproofed.

Going further, Smith indicated that Ringling had communicated with a Baltimore company, Hooper Manufacturing, in an effort to obtain a fireproofing compound. Smith asserted that Ringling had obtained some samples of the Hooper material, but it could not be used because the canvas still burned during pre-season testing. The circus had only become involved in the search for fireproofing material because Robert Ringling, the corporation's new president, had insisted on it "by all possible means."

With thoughts of financial consequences in mind during his interrogation of Smith, Commissioner Hickey asked a series of questions intended to elicit the extent of Ringling's liability coverage. Hickey was stunned to learn that the circus was vastly underinsured, carrying a single liability policy from Lloyds of London in the amount of $500,000. Coupled with the recently-revealed fact that city officials neither inspected the circus nor obtained the mandatory certificate of insurance from Ringling prior to the first performance, the discovery of the corporation's lack of insurance sent a shock wave through Hickey's body.

The Ringling Bros. and Barnum & Bailey Circus had come to Hartford and burned to the ground, leaving the entertainment institution on the verge of bankruptcy. With the death toll already in excess of 100 victims, Hickey envisioned millions of dollars in claims, even lawsuits, in the wake of the disaster. He instantly realized that, once the attorneys for the plaintiffs learned that the circus would not be able to compensate their clients in full, those lawyers could be counted on to include the name of a second defendant in each lawsuit—and the second defendant was certain to be the City of Hartford.

At the conclusion of Smith's interrogation, Hickey referred the testimony to Prosecutor Leikind so that formal charges could be filed. Hickey then called Leonard Aylesworth, the man responsible for waterproofing the Big Top. When asked who had determined what mixture should be applied to the canvas, Aylesworth indicated that he had learned the technique from his predecessors on the circus. Although he usually inspected the seating areas prior to each performance, he was in Springfield on the morning of July 6, preparing for the next day's engagement. He did not leave anyone else in charge during his absence. When Hickey asked Aylesworth about other firefighting equipment used by the circus, the thirty-year veteran stated that the boss electrician had responsibility for the deployment of fire extinguishers. During Aylesworth's inspection on the night of July 5, he noticed that the fire extinguishers had not been placed under the bleacher seats, but he did not mention that fact to anyone. Commissioner Hickey was immensely disturbed by Aylesworth's apparent negligence, but the canvas manager had provided some details that heightened Hickey's desire to obtain the sworn testimony of Whitey Versteeg, Ringling's chief electrician. After dismissing Aylesworth, Hickey declared that Versteeg would be the very next man to testify—a requirement that was certain to extend the first phase of the hearing.

The task of identifying the dead continued as the hearing progressed. By one o'clock in the morning, the volunteers who had assisted at the state armory since mid-afternoon carried the scent of smoke, just as the victims did. Although hundreds of relatives had streamed through the building over the course of nine hours, only fifty bodies had been identified and released for burial. Many family members had walked to the armory when news of the disaster first broke, then they had waited in line for extended periods before being given the opportunity to view the victims. In some cases, they walked among the gathered bodies more than once, taking in the details of death while searching for a symbol of the human life that existed before that moment. If such a symbol could be found, their loved ones could be identified and taken into the memory of their families. Given the grief that permeated the hearts of those who had found their missing loved ones in the armory, relatives with no other means of transport were driven home by Hartford policemen. In order to give the volunteers and the mourners some badly needed rest, the War Council closed the armory and locked the lattice gate shortly after one o'clock. The building would reopen at eight, and the quest for identifications—and solace—would begin again.

Twelve

As the night wore on, Commissioner Hickey opened his interrogation of Whitey Versteeg by establishing the professional background and credentials of the 44-year-old electrician. Versteeg testified that he had apprenticed as a gaffer at the MGM and Hal Roach film studios in Los Angeles, and had spent more than twenty years in show business before joining the Ringling troupe in 1942. During questioning, Hickey learned that Versteeg had first observed the fire when the flames were as high as forty feet above the circus grounds, a position just beneath the Big Top itself. Hickey led Versteeg through a description of the fire, then on to the issue of greatest importance during the initial investigation.

> Hickey: You have charge of the fire extinguishers, haven't you?
> Versteeg: I have charge of the ones in my department.
> Hickey: Only one?
> Versteeg: The ones in my department.
> Hickey: Are you charged with the duty of looking out for all the fire extinguishers that are on the lot?
> Versteeg: The ones in my department.

There was a disturbing repetition in Versteeg's responses, indicative of either fear or evasion. Because Hickey believed that the deployment of fire prevention equipment was central to the question of criminal negligence, he pursued Versteeg again.

> Hickey: What I want to find out is, how many fire extinguishers have you control of?
> Versteeg: Well, I would say about eighteen altogether. Eighteen to twenty.
> Hickey: How many has the circus?
> Versteeg: Well, that I couldn't say exactly.
> Hickey: They're all—You are the man that has charge of all the fire extinguishers, aren't you?
> Versteeg: Not outside my department, like the trucks and things like that.

Versteeg went on to state that he and his men only distributed the extinguishers at points within the main tent when they were ordered to do so by senior circus management. The issue was important enough for Hickey to continue the line of questioning, despite the intrinsic reluctance of the witness.

> Hickey: Since you arrived in Hartford, did you unpack or unload any of these fire extinguishers for distribution about the tents?
> Versteeg: We unloaded them, but they weren't distributed around.
> Hickey: You unloaded them, but they weren't distributed around?
> Versteeg: They were taken out of the containers, of course.
> Hickey: None of them were distributed about the main tent?
> Versteeg: No, they weren't distributed about the main tent.
> Hickey: And you don't do that unless you get orders?
> Versteeg: When we get orders, we distribute them around.
> Hickey: But that wasn't in Hartford?
> Versteeg: No, it wasn't here, no.
> Hickey: Neither yesterday or today?

Versteeg: No.

Hickey's persistence paid off in the end, when Versteeg was forced to acknowledge that his own common sense should have suggested that the fire extinguishers be deployed at every performance. Having elicited that response, Hickey realized that Versteeg's value as a witness had been exhausted, so the interrogation came to an end. The last key circus worker to appear before Hickey that night would be David Blanchfield, a 57-year-old Hartford native who served as the lead truckman for Ringling.

Early in the questioning, Blanchfield's testimony inadvertently lightened the mood of the investigation when it was revealed that he and Hickey had known some of the same local families during their youth in Hartford. Blanchfield had been a part of the circus world for 25 years by 1944, and he had been employed by Ringling in the summer of 1942, when a deadly fire tore through the menagerie during a four-day stand in Cleveland. Blanchfield's experience with circus fires made him a valuable witness to the events of July 6.

Blanchfield: I started the trucks over to protect the wild animal cages, and someone told me there were people in there burning, and I countermanded the order and put the trucks to work.

Hickey: Someone told you there were people burning?

Blanchfield: They told me there was a little boy burning in the exit, and when the trucks came to the exit, I stopped them and had them play water onto those people.

Hickey: What became of the truck that was over at the light section?

Blanchfield: When he finished with the light plant, he came back to the back door. The fire was still going. They moved the wagons away from the fire. The wheels were on fire, and as they pulled them away, we put the wheels out.

Blanchfield made it clear that the circus lighting trucks carried flammable materials, increasing the risk of injury or death once they caught fire. His understated description of the bravery shown by his men—and of his own courage during the blaze—was unexpected, and it generated a modicum of respect within the hearing room. As the questioning continued, Blanchfield confirmed that the circus water wagons carried only two-inch hose, too small to be mounted on municipal hydrants. The truckman was honest enough to acknowledge that it was his responsibility to instruct Ringling drivers in firefighting procedures, but he had never given them any formal guidance. Blanchfield knew how deadly a circus fire could be, and he willingly offered his opinion to Hickey and the prosecutors. "It's impossible to save a circus tent," he exclaimed. "There's no way to do it, unless you was right there and put it out with your foot." The circus veteran continued, his English becoming more tortured as his emotion increased. "As I say, gentlemen, no one that's never seen a big top burn don't know how quick it burns. You ain't got the least conception of how quick a big top goes."

Blanchfield's testimony had offered Hickey, Alcorn, and Leikind a vivid depiction of the intensity of the Ringling fire, underscoring their impression that those who had been trapped inside the Big Top would have had little chance of escape, once angry flames reached the canvas roof. With that testimony, the fate of the circus men was sealed. In the dark hour before dawn on the morning of July 7, Prosecutor Leikind ordered the arrest of Haley, Smith, Aylesworth, Versteeg, and Blanchfield on ten counts each of involuntary manslaughter. Escorted by Detective Paul Beckwith, the accused men were taken to Hartford Police headquarters for booking and printing. Reporters flocked around the defendants when they arrived, shouting questions about the cause of the fire and the nature of the testimony offered by the Ringling men, testimony that had led to formal charges that could send each of them to prison upon conviction.

James Haley—by all accounts, a man of impeccable reputation until that moment—spoke with reporters about the court proceeding and the impact of his arrest. The language he used when addressing their questions suggested that the reality of his circumstances had just begun to impress itself upon him. "I don't know what caused the fire," he said. "All of us were overwhelmed by the catastrophe, and I know I can't seem to think that anything, any of the court arraignment this morning, or being released on $15,000 bond, is real. The only real thing is death, and the grief the circus feels for the families of those who died. I never thought this could happen." The reporters could sense that Haley was deeply troubled by the tragedy, and that he was speaking from his heart, especially when he described how he had participated in the removal of the dead from the circus tent. "I wish this were a dream," he added. "We all know the circus is hazardous, but none of us thought this tragedy possible. I would have given my life to prevent the fire."

There was strength in Haley's words, and in his demeanor. A natural leader, he had maintained a military officer's bearing throughout the proceeding. Haley and his fellow circus defendants were represented by Dan Gordon Judge, a New York attorney retained by the Ringling corporation in the hours after the fire. All five defendants, looking drawn and disheartened, stood silent during their arraignment, after which Haley posted his bond—the highest amount imposed. The other defendants each posted a $10,000 bond, then all five men were released on their promise to appear at a hearing scheduled for July 18.

Five Ringling Brothers employees during their arraignment on charges of involuntary manslaughter.

PHOTO COURTESY OF THE CONNECTICUT STATE LIBRARY

On the performance days immediately prior to their arrival in Hartford, the Ringling Bros. and Barnum & Bailey Circus had experienced fires in Portland, Maine and Providence, Rhode Island. Given the extraordinarily long odds against three fires occurring within the same week, law enforcement professionals could have focused their investigative attention on the circus workers themselves. Furthermore, they could have suggested the possibility that an arsonist had infiltrated the Ringling troupe. Had any such suggestion been made, the more seasoned—and superstitious—circus workers would have agreed. After their late arrival in Hartford and the cancellation of their first show, and after the appearance of the blood red moon on July 5, followed one day later by the deadly conflagration, the Ringling gypsies had grown fearful. A focused search for an arsonist within the troupe would have been an intrusion on their privacy—and a source of resentment, especially since it would have derived from suspicion directed at the performers themselves—but the capture of an incendiary threat to the circus would have outweighed the inconvenience, easing the Ringling troupe's fears in the process. Curiously, no such suspicions were ever raised by Commissioner Hickey during his investigation, so a young man who had been harboring explosive secrets was allowed to remain hidden within the Ringling circus community.

The prospect of loss hovered over Ted and Emily like an ominous thundercloud. Since they shared the same fears, no words needed to be spoken in the hours after they stepped beyond the darkness of Municipal Hospital. If their thoughts were made visible, they would have appeared in the same form, in the same moment, and in the same sequence within their minds. Like planets orbiting the sun upon whose power their survival would depend, their thoughts revolved around family. Don was huddled between Ted and Emily, wrapped warmly within the silence that had enveloped each of them in their moment of uncertainty. In the interest of his emotional welfare, they had taken him home to Marshall Street, where he would be reminded of those he loved most. Placed into bed, sung to sleep as if he were still an infant, Don was offered rest—and peace. Ted and Emily, on the other hand, were denied the rest they so badly needed. As night slipped toward dawn, thoughts of Honey seeped into their minds, followed by questions of where she might be found, followed by a premonition that she might have been taken from them forever. Ted marveled at the logic with which his thoughts arose, arriving in a sequence that was at once inexorable and inevitable, leading him to accept the reality of Honey's absence. His soul could feel her leaving, as surely as if she were in the room, stroking his hand as she said goodbye, allowing Ted to absorb the truth of Honey's death, a cold hard truth that froze within him like New England winter.

Thirteen

The people of Hartford had taken their grief and suffering to bed on the night of July 6. It was to be expected that their sleep would be disturbed by fiery nightmares and dreams of danger, real or imagined, in the aftermath of tragic experience. When they woke on the morning of July 7, they learned from their newspapers and radios that the death toll from the circus fire had risen to 127, and that 176 additional patients had been admitted to city hospitals. The painful statistics proved that the fire and its deadly effects had not been the products of dream or imagination.

The *Hartford Courant* reported in its July 7 editions that previous fire department administrations had ordered at least one apparatus to the site of circus performances over the course of the city's history, ensuring public safety in case of an emergency of any kind. The newspaper questioned the judgment of Chief John King, who had not ordered fire equipment to the Barbour Street circus grounds while Ringling was in the city. The implications of the *Courant* article were clear: questions had begun to arise about the city's conduct prior to the deadly blaze.

Ringling public relations chief Roland Butler skillfully guided press reaction to the disaster, all the while assuring the community that the corporation would not evade its responsibilities. In one release, he indicated that the circus "must keep moving to new audiences to make the money necessary to pay our obligations" to the victims of the blaze. Butler reported that Ringling had decided to open an office in the city to ensure that "justice is done everyone, because the circus is now a part of Hartford." As if in response, both the *Courant* and the *Times* wrote favorable articles asserting that the circus was "an American institution that should not die" because of the tragedy of July 6, 1944.

With the death toll rising and the story of the fiery disaster published for all to consider, communal grief and anger began to peak and the ravaged city began to express its bitterness toward the circus. Ringling workers and performers, still struggling with their own sense of personal loss, had taken their jitney bus from the rail yard to the circus grounds early that morning. Along the way, groups of furious residents threw stones at the troupers who were seen as having caused the deadly conflagration. Ringling employees—all of whom had been ordered to remain in the city while the state investigation continued—began to fear that they might be harmed by a cadre of irate citizens bent on retaliation.

The city could not have been expected to understand that the troupers had woken to their first day without a show to mount—and without a certain future for themselves and their children. An inspection of the Barbour Street grounds early that morning revealed total destruction of the circus, with only a small section of bleachers standing after the blaze. Ringling troupers roamed the grounds, contemplating the implications of the tragedy that had befallen them. During an interview, Merle Evans stated that he had been through "blowdowns" and previous fires, but the Hartford blaze was the worst experience of his career.

Roland Butler estimated Ringling equipment losses at approximately $250,000—a staggering sum in 1944. Dozens of wagons had been charred, two lighting plants had been completely destroyed, and trapeze rigging and ring gear had been consumed by flames. The gypsy community considered itself fortunate that no trouper had been killed. May Kovar and the Wallendas were the only performers under the Big Top when the fire broke out. However, sixty crew members suffered burns and injuries in the blaze, many of them the result of efforts to rescue terrified people in the audience. According to F. Beverly Kelley of the Circus Fans of America organization, "burned roustabouts and ring stars didn't have their wounds treated" until hours after the blaze was over.

For the people of Hartford, there was no escape from the pain and suffering inflicted upon them by the circus fire. Many of those who had attended the July 6 matinee made their way back to Barbour Street the next morning to search for possessions that had been lost in the mad scramble to safety. Those who were rescued from the flames knew that their loss of property was meager when compared to the loss of life suffered by their fellow residents. Grieving families returned to the state armory at eight o'clock to search for missing relatives who, by that time, were considered among the dead. Using treatment lists compiled at city hospitals, Dr. Milton Fleisch assembled a roster of the dead and injured. In the aftermath of the blaze, the flood of incoming patients had made it almost impossible to obtain the medical records of the wounded who were treated and released, but Dr. Fleisch was meticulous in his details. When analyzed, the roster revealed that the city had been fortunate that so many spectators had survived. Although the facts offered no comfort to those whose loved ones had perished, the Fleisch records made it clear that the deadly fire could have claimed far more lives. Instead, the vast majority of hospital visits were for minor injuries, such as sprains and abrasions.

As the day wore on, the careless smoker theory, first touted to the press on July 6 by Commissioner Hickey, began to take hold, but Ringling representatives vehemently denied that it would have been possible to ignite the tent—especially the sidewalls—with a cigarette. When reached in Evanston, Illinois, Robert Ringling denied that the waterproofing mixture could have endangered human lives. Like those circus officials who had been charged with manslaughter, Ringling continued to claim that fireproofing compounds had not been available during wartime. He vowed to make full restitution to the victims of the blaze.

Published accounts of the circus tragedy offered conflicting reasons for the deadly fire, so the people of Hartford were led to speculate about the true cause of their misfortune. Given the strong cultural commitment to the American war effort, rumors of sabotage soon began to drift through the community. There was no doubt that the destruction of the Ringling circus by Nazi sympathizers would have eroded national morale, but Ringling's press representative, Hal Olver, dismissed suggestions that a bomb or arson device could have triggered the blaze. Nonetheless, Commissioner Hickey requested the assistance of the FBI. Federal agents were quickly assigned to examine the evidence, but no signs of sabotage were ever found.

In the quiet of Room 505 at Municipal Hospital, young Edward Cook succumbed to his injuries on the afternoon of July 7. As Edward's soul departed forever, his mother lay in a drug-induced coma, unaware that her son had died, another precious child lost to the circus fire. Before signing the documents that would release her gentle nephew's body, Emily Gill maintained a loving vigil at Edward's bedside, tears spilling from her eyes as she mourned the loss of the shy little boy whose mother often called him "the cat who walks alone." Minutes later, Emily drove to Mildred's apartment on Marshall Street, where she informed her anxious brother that their nephew had died.

Through their sorrow, Emily and Ted decided that Don—Mildred's only surviving child—should be taken back to the Parsons home, where he would be surrounded by family members who would console him as he recovered from the loss of his brother and sister. Of course, their joint decision meant that Emily would be faced with the ongoing responsibility of searching for Honey, a task Emily willingly accepted. That evening, Ted drove Don back to Southampton, a journey marked by silence. After putting his worried nephew to bed and assuring himself that the boy would rest easily through the long dark night, Ted made an entry in his personal journal:

"At Hartford all day. Edward died from burns. Honey not to be found."

Emily knew that Mildred was dedicated to her job at Liberty Mutual, so she felt an obligation to report her sister's medical condition—and the likelihood of an extended hospital stay and a long period of recovery. When William Tally, an executive with the insurance company, discovered that Mildred had been seriously injured and that two of her children had died, he surprised Emily by offering his personal assistance as she continued her search for Honey. An hour later, Tally escorted Emily during her second passage through the state armory.

Emily accepted her grisly responsibility as well as any grieving family member could. Shortly after seven o'clock, she was shown the body of 1565—the same child she and Ted had seen the night before. Once again, Emily was conflicted with emotion about the little girl who seemed so familiar: her blonde hair, blue eyes, and the features of her face led Emily to believe that the child was Honey, but her teeth appeared to be different somehow. Emily could have sworn that Honey had eight permanent upper teeth, but 1565 was said to have only two permanent lower incisors—contradictory estimates that ranged too high and too low to be anatomically appropriate for a child judged to be between six and eight years old. Except for the number of teeth, Emily would have been able to identify the dead child as her missing niece. Instead, she stated for the second time that she did not know who the little girl was. The only thing Emily claimed to know for certain was that 1565 was not a member of her family.

There were no other children who matched Honey's description in the armory that night, a fact that frustrated and saddened Emily and those who had assisted her. Since there seemed to be nothing more that William Tally could do for Emily, he could have wished her well and returned to his family. Instead, he remained by her side. Recognizing Emily's distress, Commissioner Hickey ordered State Police Trooper Sam Freeman to assist in the quest for Honey. Hickey suggested that Freeman, Tally and Emily undertake a search of all the funeral homes to which circus fire victims had been taken. Over the course of several hours, they viewed the children at Dillon's, Farley's, Newkirk's, Pratt's, and Talarski's—but they did not find Honey.

Only fifteen victims remained unidentified at the state armory after Emily's visit on the night of July 7, and the medical examiners were becoming concerned about the condition of those bodies. After a brief consultation with Commissioner Hickey at 7:30, Dr. Weissenborn ordered that the last fire victims—including 1565—should be transferred to the refrigerated morgue at Hartford Hospital, where they could be viewed by those who sought to identify them. With the assistance of military and police personnel, the transfers would continue until nearly midnight.

As the night wore on, Freeman, Tally and Emily continued their mission. Their search of city funeral homes lasted more than three hours. Just after eleven o'clock, Freeman suggested that they return to Mildred's apartment so Emily could obtain a photograph of Honey. With a picture in hand, they would visit Municipal Hospital for another round of inquiries about the missing child. It seemed logical to Freeman that Mildred and the kids would have been taken to Municipal at the same time. The investigator was convinced that someone on the nursing staff would remember Honey—especially since a social worker had told Emily that a child answering Honey's description had died at the hospital around six o'clock on the night of the fire. However, the first phase of the search had left Emily emotionally exhausted. Having pushed herself beyond her limits, she told Freeman that she would provide the photograph he needed, but she did not have the strength to continue the quest that night. Recognizing the extent of Emily's loss, Freeman accepted her decision.

When Emily arrived at the Marshall Street apartment, her sister-in-law Marion and Rev. James Yee—a Southampton minister and family friend—were waiting for her. They had come to the city together hours earlier and had gone directly to the state armory, but they had found no trace of Honey there. The emotions that had accumulated over the last two days overflowed when Emily greeted Marion. They cried for their lost loved ones, and welcomed the solace they could offer each other as women sharing sorrow. Then, the need to find a photograph of Honey interrupted their commiseration. As Emily sifted through Mildred's memorabilia, she explained to Marion that Trooper Freeman intended to use a photograph of Honey—a smiling Honey with white ribbons in her hair—as the map that would guide him in his ongoing quest for Mildred's missing daughter. Minutes later, Emily offered the picture to Freeman, who was instantly spellbound by the beauty and innocence captured in the portrait. Emily thanked Freeman for his support and dedication, then she walked into the darkened courtyard leading back to Mildred's apartment. Alone with the photograph, Freeman studied the beautiful face of a lost child, a face that would inspire him to continue his mission long into the night.

The picture that motivated Trooper Sam Freeman's July 7 search.

PHOTO COURTESY OF DON COOK

On July 8, the *Hartford Courant* reported that Fire Chief John King denied the newspaper's earlier assertions that the Hartford Fire Department had stationed equipment at circus performances in previous years. King's denial suggested that he recognized the need to defend his decision not to order men and equipment to the Ringling circus grounds on July 5 and July 6.

In its own July 8 editions, the *Hartford Times* reported that the Ringling officials had been arraigned in Hartford Police Court in the early morning hours of July 7, and that city officials had promised "more arrests" in the circus fire inquiry. The paper also reported Mayor Mortensen's public announcement that Fire Marshal Henry Thomas had not inspected the circus prior to the first performance. To some readers and residents—including Police Commissioner Edward Hickey—that published fact left the City of Hartford vulnerable to claims of negligence.

Hours earlier, Commissioner Hickey ordered state police officers back to the circus grounds on Barbour Street to sift through the rubble in search of additional evidence. Troopers and police officers recovered "two small pieces of burnt canvas, assumed to be part of the sidewalls," along with "three jacks and small boards from the west bleacher section," the area that was thought to have been the point of origin. Troopers also recovered a section of the iron cage chutes and a portion of the wooden steps that had been placed over the chutes prior to the performance. The collected evidence was delivered to Hickey's offices on Washington Street, where investigators would determine that the cage chutes constituted a death trap for spectators who had tried to escape from the north side of the flaming tent.

Conditions at Municipal Hospital had become dangerously overcrowded in the aftermath of the fire, posing a risk of infection that could prove lethal to burn patients. On the morning of July 8, City Health Officer Dr. Alfred Burgdorf decided to reallocate some stable patients to other area hospitals in an effort to ameliorate the demand on Municipal facilities and to maintain proper levels of care for Municipal's remaining patients. One of the burn victims scheduled for transfer to Hartford Hospital that day was 38-year-old Mildred Cook. While her youngest son, Edward, was alive and undergoing active treatment, doctors had prevented Mildred's reassignment. After Edward's death, there was no longer any reason to postpone his mother's medical transfer.

That same morning, Hartford police detectives Tom Barber and Ed Lowe returned to duty. They had worked steadily since the first moments of the fire, continuing their official responsibilities long into the night of July 7 at the state armory, where they served as witnesses for families in search of missing loved ones. The assignment had been emotionally draining for the two veterans, who quickly concluded that the Ringling tragedy had imposed too much sadness for their community to endure. Given the importance of identification, however, Barber and Lowe devoted themselves to their assignment, doing whatever they could to ensure that a name was supplied for every victim. A morgue photo of a little girl—one of seven souls who remained unidentified as of July 8—began to circulate among state and city personnel, and the photo intrigued the two detectives. The child was beautiful, even in death, and her face had barely been touched by fire. Barber and Lowe were certain that someone in the city had to know who she was, so they began to display the photo of the innocent victim they soon came to call "Little Miss Fifteen Sixty Five."

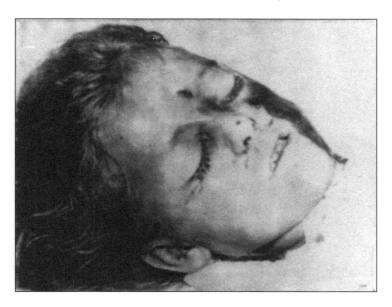

The widely published photograph of Little Miss 1565, sent around the world in an attempt to identify her.

PHOTO COURTESY OF THE CONNECTICUT STATE LIBRARY

A missing person report had been filed at Hartford Police headquarters on the morning of July 8. Judy Norris, a little girl from Middletown, had gone to the circus with her family, but there had been no trace of Judy or her family since the fire first occurred. As the day progressed, Barber and Lowe heard about the report, which led them to believe that they might have found a clue to the identity of Little Miss 1565. Hoping to solve the mystery, they traveled to Middletown and began a search for someone who could identify the child in the photograph. Barber and Lowe questioned families who lived in the Norris neighborhood, and they questioned a number of children who had known Judy at school—and they even questioned the postman who delivered mail to the Norris home—but absolutely no one could identify Little Miss 1565. All they knew for certain was that the child in the photo was not Judy Norris. Deterred but not defeated, Barber and Lowe vowed to keep searching.

That same afternoon, Ted Parsons traveled to Northampton to select a proper coffin for his nephew. In the hour before dawn, Ted had completed plans for a ceremony that would honor the memory of Mildred's youngest children—even though the family had received no official confirmation of Honey's death. Having come to the conclusion that his niece would never come home again, Ted undertook a meticulous plan for a dual funeral that would be held in Mildred's absence.

The memorial service was held in Southampton at three o'clock on Sunday afternoon, July 9. Within three days of the circus tragedy, the Parsons family and the community in which they lived had come to accept the loss of Honey, as well as Edward. Although Honey's body had not been found, family and friends mourned for her with the same finality as if her death were certain. The joint service was led by Rev. James Yee, pastor of the Congregational church. In a special tribute, Edward and Honey were remembered by fifty of their classmates from the Sheldon Academy and friends from Sunday School. The sad-faced children paraded single file to the Parsons home on East Street to take part in the service honoring two young friends who had lost their lives in the circus fire three days earlier. As a final expression of devotion, four of Edward's young cousins bore his coffin to the hearse that would ferry him to Center Cemetery.

Of the 168 victims who died in the Ringling circus blaze, all but seven had been identified by Monday morning, July 10. Over the weekend, a few searchers had visited the Hartford Hospital morgue in an effort to identify missing loved ones, but the last victims—most of whom bore little resemblance to the human beings they once were—remained unknown and unclaimed on Monday. One of the last seven, an infant listed as Victim 001, had died of crush injuries on the circus grounds, and the dismembered body had been cremated at Hartford Hospital on July 7. Although some would later claim that the child was simply a collection of body parts, Dr. Walter Weissenborn wrote a narrative description in the child's death certificate that established Victim 001 as a single human being at the time of death. "It is my impression," he wrote, "that this body was crushed by a falling pole, and the rest of the body was burned and trampled beyond recognition." Weissenborn's declaration of death brought the official number of unidentified fire victims to seven.

By mid-morning, no one had called to inquire about the identity of the remaining victims, so Dr. Weissenborn was left with no other choice but to release their bodies for burial. When he signed the official documents, the medical examiner gave each unknown victim the identical cause of death: "Burns by fire, 3rd and 4th degree." On that same day, funerals for a total of sixteen victims of the circus fire were held at various places of worship in Hartford. Mourners would always remember the pungent aroma of smoke that emanated from the closed coffins of their loved ones, despite the fact that four days had passed since the fire claimed their lives.

The last six unknowns were mourned together in a specially-conceived municipal ceremony designed to serve as a means of closure for the city. At three o'clock, six black hearses drove to the entrance of Hartford Hospital, where six caskets were waiting for them. Squads of six pallbearers, each squad comprised of policemen and firemen, placed the caskets into the hearses, then the sad parade drove to Hartford City Hall, where a group of officials that included Mayor Mortensen joined the cortege. Led by three motorcycle officers, the procession drove north on Main Street. All along the funeral route, people lined the sidewalks in an effort to pay their respects to the six unknowns. Men held their hats over their hearts, women cried, and young children—unaware of the true meaning of the event that was unfolding before them—hid behind their mothers, who clutched their children close, as if to protect them from unseen dangers.

Northwood Cemetery in Wilson, which lies at the northern border of Hartford, had prepared for the ceremony by opening three graves for the youngest unknowns, and three larger graves for the adult victims. Although three of the victims were children, only Little Miss 1565 was placed into a coffin appropriate for her size. More than 200 mourners, including Mayor Mortensen and his wife, various city officials, members of the Common Council, police and fire officials, and a large gathering of city residents, attended the group funeral. The 36 policemen and firemen who had served as pallbearers stood in a semicircle around the graves, as if standing guard in honor of those being buried. Because no one knew what religion the unknowns might have practiced during their lives, three ordained representatives were asked to perform the sad duty of the day.

Rev. Warren Archibald of South Congregational Church, Rev. Thomas Looney of St. Michael's Church, and Rabbi Morris Silverman of Emanuel Synagogue offered the burial prayers and rituals of three faiths. Rev. Archibald read the Twenty Third Psalm, then Father Looney read from the Eighteenth Chapter of the Gospel of St. Matthew, then Rabbi Silverman recited Kaddish and the El Mole Rahmim. Those who had gathered there found the ceremony touchingly sad, and a number of people wept openly as the service progressed. Once the six unknowns had been placed into their graves, city officials and the mourners who had witnessed the burials returned to their lives, mindful of the wounds suffered by the city itself, wounds from which they would all need time to recover.

Little Miss 1565 was buried without her name, but she had been adopted by the city as one of its own. Because she belonged to no one, she could belong to everyone. After her death, she became the symbol of shared loss and the focal point of communal grief, offering the means to mourn for the romantic innocence that had been lost forever. Hartford had been shaken to its spiritual foundations, but it would still remain "the city of hope."

Fourteen

The very first lawsuit seeking damages in the wake of the circus fire was filed on July 10 by Sal DiMartino on behalf of his wife, Anna. The suit called for $15,000 in compensation for the young woman's death. Later that same day, the City of Hartford was named as co-defendant in numerous lawsuits filed on behalf of fire victims. Interestingly, those suits were initiated just 48 hours after Mayor Mortensen announced that the city had not inspected the circus prior to its first performance. The suits alleged that "the city acted without first requiring that proper safeguards and inspections be installed and maintained to protect the general public against fire and other hazards." The suits also alleged that the city or its servants "were negligent, reckless and careless in that they leased [the Barbour Street grounds] to the defendant [Ringling Brothers] when they knew or should have known...that it was hazardous and dangerous to permit the defendant to invite the general public to view a performance under such circumstances and in such a setting."

A steady stream of similar suits—most of which named the City of Hartford as co-defendant with Ringling—arrived in the days that followed. In many of those cases, which collectively amounted to millions of dollars, the property of city officials such as Fire Chief John King and Fire Marshal Henry Thomas was attached as collateral. With claims on behalf of the dead and injured accumulating every day, and with the threat of further lawsuits spreading as fast as the fire that had triggered them, Commissioner

Hickey and Mayor Mortensen knew that a plan of containment had to be crafted that would allow the city to cope with the legal fallout of the Ringling circus tragedy. Given that they could not undertake the responsibility for such a plan themselves, they had to find someone with the time and talent for the task. So they contacted a man on whom they could rely, a brilliant young lawyer with the credentials to initiate a legal strategy that would satisfy everyone. Best of all, he was also a friend of "Cappy" Baldwin.

Edward S. Rogin had been a member of the Connecticut bar since 1930, and he was the senior partner in a well-respected and growing law firm that he had established with Louis E. Nassau. A well-spoken gentleman as well as a gifted and incisive lawyer, Rogin differed from Hickey in both manner and style, but he was judged by Baldwin and Mortensen to possess the skills required to navigate the jagged shoals of litigation that the city was certain to face. From the very first meeting on the subject of liability, Rogin proved himself invaluable.

Rogin predicted that claims were likely to rise, and lawsuits were likely to continue—especially since the Ringling Brothers circus had been found to be seriously underinsured. With that in mind, Rogin immediately sought to forestall any possibility that Ringling would be forced into federal bankruptcy because of immense property and casualty losses caused by the fire. From Rogin's point of view, the city's first order of business was to ensure that a receivership could be created in Connecticut that would legally obtain control over the circus and its assets. If accomplished, such an action would provide assurance to the injured survivors and the families of the dead that any claims or suits would be paid from the ongoing business of the Ringling circus. In reality, the first step in Rogin's legal plan had already been taken by Hickey when he impounded all of Ringling's property.

Rogin soon concluded that a special form of arbitration would have to be agreed upon in order for claims to be paid in an equitable manner. He decided to summon a group of prominent lawyers—many of whom had already filed suit against Ringling and the City of Hartford—and engage them in the concept of capping their demands and their fees in order to distribute awards to all victims. Rogin had met with Dan Gordon Judge,

Ringling's attorney, who assured him that the circus accepted responsibility for the fire and would pay all claims, no matter how long the process would take. In each claim, Ringling would pay the amount decided upon by a three-member arbitration team established by Rogin. Under the plan, Ringling would continue to operate its business, accumulating cash for all subsequent claims. Rogin and Judge knew that the plan they had devised was the only effective method by which the victims of the circus blaze would be adequately compensated, especially in light of Ringling's financial losses on July 6. After sealing the agreement with Judge, Rogin was faced with his most formidable task as a mediator: to persuade his fellow members of the Connecticut bar to accept the circus arbitration plan.

In the days following the circus fire, numerous press reports discussed the unknown child who had become the focus of community interest. Known by more and more people as "Little Miss 1565," her image gnawed at the grieving soul of the city—even after the burial ceremony on July 10. Lingering questions about her identity led to the publication of three theories that would become elements of an expanding urban legend about the unknown victim. The first theory suggested that she was a circus waif who had been traveling with the Ringling show; the second theory suggested that she was simply a runaway; and the third theory suggested that her entire family had died in the blaze, a multiple tragedy that would have accounted for the total absence of inquiries about her. While the residents of Hartford pondered these possibilities, municipal officials sent notices of her death, along with a copy of her photograph, to newspapers around the country. Their search even extended to Europe in an effort to find anyone who could identify the child. As always, hope underscored their actions.

On Tuesday morning, July 11, the *Hartford Courant* ran an article about Mildred Cook's missing daughter. Because Mildred was still in a coma at Hartford Hospital, the newspaper was forced to rely on descriptive information provided by Emily Gill, who had not seen either her niece or her nephews for several days prior to the circus fire. The *Courant* described Mildred's daughter as "eight years old and tall for her age, with light brown hair and blue eyes." The article went on to assert that she had been wearing "a red plaid play suit, red socks, and white summer shoes." The story was a poignant reminder of ongoing loss, reviving thoughts of the tragedy that struck the city so unexpectedly.

Later that morning, Coroner Frank E. Healy opened his judicial inquiry into the cause of the Ringling circus fire. The inquest—conducted at the County Courthouse even as Commissioner Hickey's investigation continued—generated reams of incendiary testimony that would be weighed in order to determine whether any criminal culpability existed in the case. For the six Ringling officials who had been arraigned on charges of involuntary manslaughter days earlier, freedom would depend on Healy's findings.

The Ringling defendants were not Connecticut residents, so they had no objective means of determining which member of the state bar would be the most able defender of their legal rights and interests as the circus case proceeded. Ed Rogin, however, was aware of a man who would be willing to serve as defense counsel, working in concert with New York lawyers who had been sent to Hartford by the Ringling corporation to assist in the proceedings. The local attorney's name was William Hadden, and he was one of Rogin's longtime friends and political associates. The Ringling defendants would soon come to rely on Hadden, trusting his advice as the legal risks increased.

Coroner Healy opened his inquest by suggesting that the Ringling circus did not provide proper safety precautions for the public event, a premise that would serve as the throughline for the entire proceeding. Healy began by questioning Police Chief Thomas Hallisey, who asserted that "the fire went just like a breeze" across the tent top, "[dropping] the tent into oblivion" in less than ten minutes. Hallisey claimed that "fire came on those people," forcing them to stampede in an effort to escape death. The career cop claimed that spectators on the northeast end were "in turmoil," and their panic contributed to the loss of life. Some of Hallisey's officers assisted those who were trying to flee, and they held their perilous posts inside the tent until the heat became so intense that their uniform coats began to burn. Crazed parents threw their children from the bleachers into the arms of policemen. In one case, a Hartford officer "had his own child put into his arms," according to Hallisey.

Some of the Ringling employees did their best to counter the effects of the early inquest testimony. David Blanchfield, the Hartford native who had directed Ringling water trucks into position to battle the flames, declared that the circus tent was "just one solid mass of flames," and that even the Hartford Fire Department would not have been able to save the Big Top on July 6. Later, George Smith, circus general manager, stated that fireproofing materials had not been available at the time preparations were being made for the summer tour. Leonard Aylesworth, boss canvasman, attempted to deflect his own legal perils by asserting that the gasoline and wax waterproofing process had been "handed down by [his] predecessors," and that the same formula had been used by circuses around the world for generations. Given the scope and diversity of the testimony, Coroner Healy quickly surmised that it would take several months to determine the guilt or innocence of the Ringling circus employees.

As the inquest continued on July 11, the *Hartford Times* published its own description of Mildred's missing daughter in the evening editions. Like its morning-news rival, the *Times* relied on information provided by Emily Gill. By press time, the little girl's clothing had evolved from a "red plaid play suit" to a "blue and red plaid play suit," and her height was reported to be "four feet four," or 52 inches—extraordinary physical stature, if accurate, for an eight-year-old girl. Although neither the *Times* nor the *Courant* could have predicted it at the time of publication, the descriptive details contained in their July 11 articles would become profoundly relevant to the issue of Little Miss 1565's identity more than forty years after her death.

In the months prior to the Hartford fire, John Ringling North had been jockeying for control of the circus corporation. Standing in opposition to North's controversial schemes were Robert Ringling and his mother, Edith—a family ally of Aubrey Ringling, the young widow who had recently married James Haley. Aware of the overarching desire for domination that permeated John Ringling North's personality, Edith and

Aubrey had entered into a legal arrangement that obligated them to vote their stock shares jointly on every important issue of circus management. This "Ladies Agreement," as it was colloquially known, thwarted John's unbridled ambition. In the wake of the tragic fire, Edward Rogin drafted his temporary receivership plan with the approval of Edith Ringling and Aubrey Ringling Haley. To the astonishment of John Ringling North, the Ladies Agreement soon included a gentleman from Hartford.

As he implemented the first phase of his plan, Rogin faced one legal problem immediately: Connecticut courts were in a summer recess, so the odds of finding a sitting judge were less than excellent. Rogin and his legal team scoured the state and finally located Judge John King, who had been scheduled to conduct hearings in his Willimantic chambers during July 1944 as part of the court's provision of interim judicial services.

During a hearing on July 12, Rogin petitioned the court on behalf of the City of Hartford. His application stated that the primary reason for receivership was the "numerous suits and attachments of [Ringling] property and assets, and the numerous suits pending or threatened." He added that the bankruptcy or liquidation of the circus would restrict or deny appropriate monetary awards to victims and survivors for injuries and damages. As of that date, nearly $5 million in suits and claims had already been filed, and millions more were certain to follow. Given the facts presented, Judge King granted Rogin's petition without impediment. The uniquely conceived plan immediately placed Rogin at odds with John Ringling North. Mutual antipathy and distrust established a battleground on which both men would wage legal warfare over the next ten years. For the time being, however, the city had been given the right to protect its dead and wounded.

In the course of an emergency Common Council meeting held on the evening of July 12, Mayor Mortensen presented a proposal that called for the creation of a municipal board of inquiry. The purpose of the five-man board would be "to investigate the performance and conduct of city officials before, during and after" the horrific circus fire. In his address to the Council, Mortensen said that "the board must keep unswervingly in mind that no just criticism is too harsh, no law too binding, no form of supervision too rigorous when we have at stake the precious gift of human life." The mayor's proposal was well-intentioned, but it triggered a contentious debate.

Alderman Joseph Fauliso, Democratic minority leader, rose in opposition to the mayor's proposal. "The 168 dead call on us to make a complete disclosure of the truth," Fauliso railed. "The city has failed them. The city has participated in a fraud that caused these deaths." Despite the sound of Council President John Hurley's voice calling for order, Fauliso continued his tirade. "The mayor failed to check the several departments entrusted with the safety of [our] citizens. Checks and double-checks should have been made. We all took too much for granted."

Infuriated by the minority leader's allegations, Hurley pounded his gavel repeatedly, but Fauliso continued to express his anger. "I can only conclude that the mayor's committee will be a whitewash committee," he shouted. Fauliso's final comment so outraged Hurley that he broke his gavel in half when it struck for the last time. "As long as I am president of this board," he screamed, "I will not allow politics to enter into this matter." When the heated exchange was over, Mortensen's proposal was approved, and the official Board of Inquiry was born.

Earlier that day, Mortensen and the city's chief health officer, Dr. Alfred Burgdorf, ordered the circus to remove all of its property from the municipal lot on Barbour Street. In response to multiple complaints from increasingly vocal residents, Mortensen also demanded that Ringling move to the North Meadows, an area in the northeast corner of the city, adjacent to the Connecticut River. During the six days following the blaze, the circus and its staff had been restricted to the lot, where their meals were served at the cookhouse tent.

According to the Circus Fans of America, Ringling troupers had endured their grief in isolation, with virtually no one in the city offering compassion. A lucky few had been taken into the homes of local CFA members who provided welcome shelter from the jeers and stones thrown by angry Barbour Street residents. Some of those residents had long opposed the idea of allowing any performances on the city-owned lot in their neighborhood. They considered the circus a public nuisance, primarily because of the noise that had to be endured well into the night whenever a troupe appeared.

In the wake of the blaze, the CFA expressed concern that there would be "attempts to legislate the circus out of business," so they vowed to "go into action against any attempt to ruin" the Ringling corporation. Writing in the CFA's summer edition of *The White Tops* newsletter, F. Beverly Kelley asserted that "there was no spirit of defeat mingled with sorrow in the hearts of Ringling troupers" after the catastrophe. Kelley claimed that, in the time since Robert Ringling took over as president of the family company, the circus had been "trying to secure materials with which to flameproof its canvas." Kelley added that "those materials [had] not been available in wartime to nonessential industries," so the circus was forced to assume the risk of performing under flammable canvas. The company had relied on its sixty-year tradition of safety, a period in which fire had never claimed the life of any Ringling customer.

On July 13, a section of yellow canvas from the south wall of the men's toilet tent was obtained by state investigators, who then delivered the sample to Commissioner Hickey's offices. The fact that such evidence was collected one full week after the circus blaze implied that Hickey had begun to focus on the men's room tent as the likely point of origin for a concealed blaze, as suggested by witness testimony.

Governor Baldwin addressed the state by radio on Saturday, July 15, offering additional details of the aftermath. Baldwin stated that "a thorough investigation [was] being made to determine how and why the tragedy occurred." The governor promised that, "if any criminal negligence [was] involved, everything in the power of the state [would] be done to bring to justice those who may [have been] responsible." Baldwin went on to praise Commissioner Hickey for his decisive action in the moments after the circus blaze. Hickey's most valuable achievement lay in his assessment of emergency need, and in the implementation of the War Council actions in response to the catastrophic fire, a disaster similar to that which the city could have suffered from a wartime bombing raid. Baldwin closed by saying that the circus fire had deeply saddened residents all around the state. "We shall not soon recover from this blow," Baldwin stated, "but we can be intensely proud of the spirit with which the people of Connecticut met the emergency. There are heroes, nameless and innumerable, in this tragedy."

Hours before Baldwin's radio address, Connecticut State Trooper Lester Mercier was dispatched to the Norwich State Hospital in order to deliver hair samples to Dr. Lincoln Opper, director of the NSH laboratory. Dr. Opper was prepared to conduct a comparative analysis of a sample clipped from the body of 1565 and a sample from Honey Cook's hairbrush. In a subsequent report citing State Police Case H-25-Z, Dr. Opper indicated that "the several strands of thin brown hair averaging four inches in length show great similarity microscopically to those hairs submitted [from the Cook child's] brush." Dr. Opper went on to state that "most of the hairs are lacking in the medulla. A scanty fine linear distribution of dark pigment is confined to the central portion of the light cortex." Although Dr. Opper knew that absolute identification based on hair samples alone would have been impossible, his report stated that "it may be concluded from this examination that both specimens may have been derived from the same scalp." The NSH report was added to the compilation of evidence gathered during Hickey's investigation, but no state or municipal official took any action on the basis of Dr. Opper's findings.

On July 20, exactly two weeks after the circus fire, Commissioner Hickey retrieved "a small piece of melted iron" and "a piece of wood approximately four feet long, covered with steel" as additional evidence in the state investigation. As described, the samples from the bleacher jacks would most probably be used to bolster Hickey's belief that the fire was started by the careless disposal of a cigarette. Over the course of the investigation, Hickey and his men had questioned hundreds of witnesses, including workers and performers employed by Ringling. Virtually every witness reported that they had seen the first flames break out high on the sidewall canvas behind the southwest section, near the men's room tent. No one ever asserted that they had seen smoke below the bleachers at ground level, nor had they seen a smoldering fire in the grass. Some witnesses, including experienced observers such as *Courant* reporter Everett Dow, claimed that they had seen circus workers snuff out their cigarettes on the sidewalls in prior years, but the canvas had never caught fire. Yet, some of those same witnesses asserted that a cigarette had to have been the cause of the blaze from which they had escaped on July 6—despite the evidence captured with their own eyes.

Given the string of suspicious fires leading up to the Hartford tragedy, James Haley and his management team, along with seasoned Ringling performers such as Felix Adler, were convinced that a pyromaniac had infiltrated the circus and that the Hartford blaze was a deliberate human act. When the investigation began, however, Commissioner Hickey had mentioned the careless disposal of a cigarette as a possible cause of the July 6 fire, and he held to his original theory. Haley was frustrated by what he perceived to be Hickey's apparent lack of interest in the possibility of arson, and he suggested that Ringling managers could provide valuable information and assistance if Hickey were willing to discuss the case with them. Rather than conducting interviews of circus personnel in response to Haley's suggestion, Hickey offered an acerbic rebuttal: Connecticut officials could be counted on to continue the investigation of the Ringling case, and they would follow every lead—regardless of who was involved.

The mechanics of lawsuits and insurance claims continued to preoccupy Ed Rogin in the weeks and months following the circus fire. Claims of every size and scope came across his desk, and he was required to settle all of them. In the context of arbitration, the value of young lives was minimal. Most families received only a few thousand dollars in the name of their dead children. The most severely burned survivors of the blaze were granted the highest awards. Katherine Martin received $100,000 for her pain and suffering, and six-year-old Patty Murphy's family was awarded $90,000 in compensation for the burns that had scarred Patty so badly. One particular claim, however, would trouble Rogin for the rest of his life. Months after the fire, a middle-aged African-American woman made an appointment to discuss her losses. As soon as the woman entered the office, Rogin could see that she had been severely burned—most visibly on her neck and legs—and that alligator scarring had formed in the months since she suffered her injuries. It was evident to Rogin that the woman's burns had to have been excruciatingly painful, so he was prepared to offer her the assistance she needed. However, the woman's simple plea would leave Rogin stunned. Rather than demanding hundreds of thousands of dollars, as many other claimants had done, the woman had only one request: a refund for the price of her tickets. She had paid $2.20, and that was all she wanted. Rogin was not certain that he had heard her correctly, so he asked if she had seen a doctor, and whether she needed further treatments of any kind. The woman shook her head and repeated her request for $2.20. "The good Lord saw fit to save my life," she stated, "and I am grateful to be alive. All I want is the price of my tickets." Unable to convince the woman that she was entitled to a far larger settlement, Rogin simply refunded her money.

Fifteen

In the wake of the blaze, the unidentified eight-year old girl who had come to be called "Little Miss 1565" became the symbol of the city's grief. Her face captivated Ed Rogin, who sent letters around the world at his own expense in an effort to identify the lost child. He had no interest in self-celebration, so he never revealed his private effort to find a name for the little girl who had captured his heart.

Meanwhile, the inquest was progressing well, and Commissioner Hickey came to the conclusion that he and his investigative team had acquired all the information they needed from the performers and crews of the Ringling circus. Many of them had been held in Hartford since the afternoon of July 6, spending six days in subsidized housing provided by the city. By July 12, the time had come to either charge them or set them free. Satisfied that there was no evidence of criminal intent in relation to the circus fire, Hickey issued an order for their release. By nightfall, the Barbour Street lot was stripped to the bone, a charred oval of earth serving as the only remnant of the fiery tragedy.

After Ringling posted a $380,000 court-ordered cash bond to reassure city officials that the corporation would remain accountable for the impact of the disaster, the circus wagons began to roll toward the Windsor Street rail siding, where they were loaded onto waiting flat cars. In the early morning hours of July 13, the circus was released from Hartford and the damaged entertainment institution limped back to its corporate headquarters in Sarasota, Florida. Most of the workers boarded the Flying Squadron and road the rails back home, but the moody roustabout named Robert Dale Segee—the powerful kid who had lied about his age to gain entrance to the Ringling circus community—boarded a bus to Portland, returning to the city where his fiery dreams were born.

In the midst of the ongoing Coroner's inquest, Commissioner Hickey received numerous letters from witnesses and survivors, many of whom sought to commend him for his management of the support systems employed by state and city officials in the aftermath of the tragedy. In other letters, there appeared to be a desire to recount the circumstances experienced during the blaze, as if the writer felt a compulsion to chronicle that which had befallen him, or to describe what he or she had witnessed. Hickey accepted these letters in the belief that they were an element of his public duty. Although many of his responses were brief, if not terse, he answered every one.

In a letter dated July 7, Attorney Carlos Ellis of Middletown described the difficulty he experienced in attempting to save himself and his family as the blaze advanced. Ellis had attended the circus with his three children and a couple of friends. After noticing "a triangular sheet of flame where the tent top joined the sidewalls," Ellis quickly guided his group toward the northeast exit. Circus attendants were in the process of driving three cats out of the steel cage chutes as Ellis and his family approached the exit. According to Ellis, Ringling attendants used their prods to prevent the children from making their way over the chutes, driving them back toward the fire instead. Ellis refused to be driven back, and he urged his children up onto the chutes. By that time, the cats had become frightened by the commotion and began to snarl at the children climbing above them.

Ellis wrote that the sight of "a lion snarling up at him, only two inches beneath his feet, with his jaws wide open" terrified the lawyer's son, Whitney, who drew back and refused to climb any farther. Ellis knew that the fire posed an imminent danger to their lives, so he forced his son onto the chutes once again, but the boy was pushed back by one of the frantic Ringling attendants. This time, the boy "fell down between the [cage chute] and the bleachers, and someone in the crowd knocked him to his hands and knees." Recognizing that his son could be killed in a matter of seconds, Ellis grabbed him around the waist and hoisted him over the cage chutes, ignoring the objections of the animal attendant. Before leaving the tent, Ellis turned to help others over the chutes and through the exit. By the time he was reunited with his family, "ten minutes had elapsed from the time [he] first observed the flames, and the tent was completely burned down and the bleachers were aflame." Nothing more could be done to save the circus, or the souls trapped within the Big Top.

On July 20, Commissioner Hickey received a most unexpected letter from Emily Gill. She had written to him because of his widely publicized position as senior state official during the investigative phase. In her letter, Emily reported that she had searched for her missing niece at Municipal Hospital and "checked the girl who answered to the description, but found her to be the mystery girl, whom I know is not my niece. Because the figures are six unidentified and six missing, I felt my niece must be misidentified. However, she might never have left the tent. God alone knows." Hickey was moved by the sentiment that managed to reveal itself beneath the straightforward language of the letter. The contents offered him very little information, yet he had the impression that Emily Gill must have found it necessary to express her feelings in order to reassure herself that she had done everything possible to find her missing loved one.

As the city continued its multiple investigations, summer began to fade, even if the memories of July 6 did not. By August 1, the death toll from the Ringling blaze had risen to 166 men, women and children. As of that date, more than thirty victims remained hospitalized because of their injuries. The Fire Victims Relief Fund, established weeks earlier by the Red Cross and the *Hartford Times*, had grown to $40,000. The Red Cross received a $10,000 gift from the Ringling circus, a good-faith contribution intended for families who had suffered the loss of loved ones in the July 6 blaze.

In the fall, Hartford's children—those who had not been taken cruelly and unexpectedly—returned to school, where they would find a way to share their thoughts and fears with friends and teachers alike. The 1944-45 school year would give rise to the legend of the fire, a topic that would be discussed each year thereafter, until the mysteries that swirled like smoke around the Hartford circus fire could be resolved.

In early November, the municipal Board of Inquiry issued its formal findings. The board sought to fix culpability, even though the investigations undertaken by Commissioner Hickey and Coroner Healy had not been completed by the time the board issued its report. The board declared that the Hartford Fire Department "made no inspection of the tents, seating arrangements, exits or firefighting equipment established by Ringling Brothers prior to the fire." Using a tortured metaphor, the board called the city's fire protection "the Achilles heel in our defense armor." The report said that, if firemen and equipment had been stationed at the circus grounds, they might have been able to intervene in the early stages of the blaze. The fact that no such provisions had been made was considered a lapse in administrative judgment.

The board also found that the Hartford Police Department had issued a permit for the circus upon the acceptance of a $300 fee, but without certification of an inspection by the fire department. The board made special note of the fact that Police Chief Thomas Hallisey had received fifty free passes to the circus during the permitting process, and the formal report discouraged public officials from accepting gratuities of that kind in the future. The report went on to state that the Building Commission had not demanded an insurance certificate from the circus, nor did the commission stipulate any specific types of safety or exiting requirements in the property contract with Ringling Brothers.

In essence, the Board of Inquiry had found that inadequate protective measures by the police and fire departments, agencies charged with the safety and welfare of city residents—compounded by communication and control failures within other departments of municipal government—had contributed to the tragedy of July 6, 1944. Shortly after the report was issued, Mayor Mortensen announced the simultaneous resignation of Hartford Police Chief Thomas Hallisey and the appointment of Michael Godfrey as his successor. The public would not be told that the change of command had occurred because Mortensen no longer trusted Hallisey to perform effectively on behalf of the people of Hartford.

On November 18, after a four-month struggle for recovery that included multiple skin grafts that had left her badly scarred, Mildred Cook was released from Hartford Hospital. She had spent a month in a coma, and had not been told about the death of Edward and the presumed death of Honey until she regained consciousness in August. The tragic news had pierced her heart, the cold words finding their way to her soul as if they had been formed with the cutting edge of a steel blade, but Mildred refused to cry. Although she never revealed her sadness to anyone, she had been grieving continuously for months.

The memories of July 6 would not fade because the scars on Mildred's body remained visible in the morning mirror. Late in her recovery, someone had told her that she was one of the lucky ones because the fire had not touched her face. How she longed to tell them that luck had had no place in her life, and probably never would. Instead, she sang within herself, trying not to remember, trying not to cry. After regaining her strength, Mildred visited Edward's grave in Southampton for the first time. In the months that followed, she would spend silent time there among the marigolds, savoring the thoughts of the children whose voices would always be with her, even though they were gone. Next to Edward, an empty grave waited for the precious little girl who had never come home.

Just prior to Thanksgiving, Governor Baldwin awarded young Donald Anderson the Connecticut Medal for Distinguished Civilian War Service in honor of his heroic conduct during the fire. The Governor's citation recognized that the thirteen-year-old's selfless action saved lives that otherwise might have been lost.

When the first holiday season in the wake of the Ringling blaze began, Detectives Tom Barber and Ed Lowe visited the grave site of Little Miss 1565 on December 24, 1944. Although the city had continued to publish news of her death in newspapers around the country, there had been no word from anyone about the identity of the child who had come to symbolize the tragic circus fire.

Barber and Lowe made their way to the grave of the still-unidentified child to whom they had become committed and placed flowers on the inlaid marker. Then they made a promise to her—and to themselves—that they would not allow the beautiful blonde child to be forgotten. They would continue their tradition, making three trips to Northwood together each year, until Ed Lowe died in 1965. Tom Barber chose to carry on the tradition alone, making three commemorative visits every year until his own death in 1977. True to their word, Barber and Lowe never forgot Little Miss 1565.

On January 11, 1945, Commissioner Hickey issued the results of his independent investigation. During the course of his inquiry, Hickey had interviewed a total of 146 witnesses. His report began by asserting that Ringling had made "no arrangements...for firemen or firefighting equipment," and that the Hartford Fire Department had not issued an order for men and equipment to stand by during the circus performances. Hickey relied on Chief John King's assertions that his department had never ordered any "protective measures" in prior years, despite the fact that the *Hartford Courant* had previously disputed King's claims. Hickey then listed a number of Connecticut towns in which fire protection for circus performances was required. Inexplicably, he followed that listing with ironic language that appeared to be a veiled defense of the City of Hartford, claiming that "it has not been the practice in Connecticut to assign firefighting equipment at circus performances."

The report went on to state that the only inspection of the circus grounds was made by Building Inspector Joseph Hayes at eleven o'clock on the morning of July 5. Hickey reported that Hayes found that the tent was not ready for a performance, so he returned for another inspection at 3:45 that afternoon. The tent was still not ready, but Hayes granted Ringling the right to perform nonetheless, basing his decision on the assumption that "construction of seats and exits [would comply] as in previous years."

Hickey also reported that, prior to the start of the 1944 season, boss canvasman Leonard Aylesworth supervised seventy men in waterproofing the Big Top with the gas and paraffin mixture. It was Aylesworth's responsibility to inspect the areas beneath the bleacher seats and grandstands before every performance, but he did not make any inspection on the morning of July 6 because he and circus manager George Smith had gone to Springfield, Massachusetts with the Ringling stake crew, and they had been supervising the preparation of the next performance location. Hickey's investigation revealed that, although Ringling had 35 fire extinguishers stowed and accessible on its trucks on July 6, none of those units were placed beneath the seats in the main tent.

Hickey cited witness testimony that placed the flame "on the sidewall canvas inside the southwest section of the main tent." The witnesses all claimed that the fire was "burning the upper portion of the side wall canvas and the lower section of the big top." Many of those witnesses, according to Hickey's report, "saw only the tent top burning." At no time during Hickey's investigation did any witness ever claim to have seen either smoke or flame near the base of the sidewall. Hickey himself—as a witness to the conflagration that day—asserted that "the side wall canvas burned slowly upward. Suddenly, a burst of flame appeared from underneath the west end of the tent top and shot to the northeast corner. Then the entire top became a mass of flames, with portions of it dropping onto the audience, a liquid [dropping] down and inflicting severe burns on people fleeing from within" the tent.

William Caley, a three-year employee, and John Cook, a rookie with only five weeks on the tour, were the seatmen responsible for placement and use of water buckets beneath the southwest bleachers. Hickey reported that Caley and Cook "were required to perform other duties [for the circus] in addition to fire watch service," and that they were also required to "leave their posts and go to the opposite side of the tent to set up the animal cage chutes" at the northwest exit. Their absence had allowed the fire to advance unimpeded up the sidewall.

An usher, Kenneth Gwinnell, reported that he first saw the fire on the sidewall about "five or six feet from the ground." He added that, rather than smoldering for awhile, as a cigarette fire ordinarily did, "this came all of a sudden and it evidently was a match." Gwinnell was speculating about the match, but his instincts suggested that the fire was already furious and forceful by the time the first destructive flames burst through the canvas on July 6.

Other circus employees had testified that "a fire was discovered on the sidewall canvas in Providence on July 4," but the fledgling flame was extinguished quickly. Aylesworth indicated that there had always been numerous cigarette burns on sidewall canvas, but those burns never became active flame. According to Hickey's report, "there had been a dozen fires of that kind" during the 1944 season, including one in Portland on June 30—the day Robert Segee joined the Ringling crew—but each one had been extinguished easily.

The report implied, perhaps inadvertently, that Hickey had obtained testimony suggesting that there was something radically unique about the Hartford fire. Despite the troubling trend in the accumulated testimony, Hickey's report made no reference to the possibility of arson, nor was there any reference to the question of deliberate ignition, or to the role that such a question might have played in Hickey's investigation.

Although James Haley and experienced Ringling troupers believed from the start that the Hartford fire was an act of arson, they quickly came to the conclusion that Connecticut investigators were not interested in their point of view. Early on, Haley wanted the Connecticut State Police to find a suspect in the case—especially since suspicion of a criminal act would lessen the implications for the circus itself—but his requests were rebuffed by Hickey, who replied that "a thorough investigation was under way...and it [was] immaterial to [him] who did it or who [was] involved."

In the end, Hickey steadfastly asserted that "the carelessness of some unidentified smoker" had caused the deadly conflagration of July 6—the very theory he had first espoused. Hickey went on to declare that "the evidence before me does not disclose this to be the act of an incendiary." James Haley's assertions of arson were never mentioned in the final report, nor was there any reference to whether or not Commissioner Hickey was aware of Robert Segee's incendiary background. The report concluded with a suggestion that, as a result of its own negligence, the Ringling corporation had contributed to the lethal effects of the circus blaze.

Later that same day, Coroner Frank E. Healy issued his inquest findings. Healy determined that there had been criminal negligence on the part of Ringling Brothers management and staff. He declared that the circus had ample reason to believe that dangerous conditions existed beneath the Big Top, conditions that led to the deaths of 168 people. Coroner Healy fixed blame on seven Ringling Bros. and Barnum & Bailey Circus employees, declaring that he had found sufficient evidence to conclude that "James A. Haley, George W. Smith, Leonard S. Aylesworth, Edward R. Versteeg, David W. Blanchfield, William Caley and Samuel Clark [were] guilty of such wanton or reckless conduct which makes them criminally liable for the deaths of [168 victims] who lost their lives in the circus fire of July 6, 1944." Coupled with the results of Hickey's investigation, Healy's finding opened the door for the prosecution of the Ringling circus staff for involuntary manslaughter.

There would be no formal trial for the Ringling employees. After Coroner Healy found the seven men criminally responsible for 168 deaths as a direct result of negligence, the pressure to prevent a protracted prosecution increased. Their attorney, William Hadden, a political ally of Ed Rogin and Judge Bill Shea, encouraged his clients to plead no contest to the charges of involuntary manslaughter, placing themselves at the mercy of the court. Having already placed their trust in their lawyer, a man who was presumed to know the inner workings of the Connecticut legal system and the men who operated within it, the Ringling defendants agreed.

Judge Bill Shea had served in the state senate prior to his appointment to the bench. When the judicial vacancy appeared, Governor Baldwin and Ed Rogin collaborated in the decision to appoint him. Ironically, their choice was between Shea and Hadden. According to Rogin, he and the governor were unable to decide between the two, so they tossed a coin—and Shea won. Hadden had taken the news well, proving to Rogin that he had political fortitude—and a political future. Hadden's role in the prosecution of the Ringling defendants would prove valuable to him at the conclusion of the case.

During the arraignment on February 17, Hadden told the court that a jury trial would require a minimum of eight weeks, taking key circus officials away from their obligations to prepare the show for the 1945 season. With that in mind, Hadden asked Judge Shea for permission to enter nolo contendere pleas for each of his clients, and Shea agreed. The judge then ordered a four-day delay in sentencing to allow time for a review of the legal presentations and formal pleas. The charges against Samuel Clark had been dropped, so the Ringling defendants expected leniency in the wake of a tragedy that their attorney had asserted was an unintended accident. However, on the afternoon of February 21, the six anxious men were stunned when Judge Shea sentenced each of them to felony terms on ten counts of involuntary manslaughter.

James A. Haley, of Sarasota, Florida, vice-president of the Ringling circus and a member of the Ringling family by marriage, was sentenced to Wethersfield State Prison for "not less than one nor more than five years" on the first count, with similar sentences on all other counts to run concurrently. Haley, 47, had only been with the circus for fifteen months at the time of his sentencing. Because of his management role as corporate vice-president, his imprisonment was suspended until April 7.

George W. Smith, general manager, and Leonard S. Aylesworth, chief canvasman, both of Sarasota, Florida, were sentenced to Wethersfield State Prison for "not less than two nor more than seven years" on the first count, with similar sentences on all other counts to run concurrently. Smith, 51, was born in Southboro, Massachusetts, and had been employed by various circuses since the age of seventeen. Aylesworth, also 51, was born in West Salem, Wisconsin and had spent a lifetime in the circus world, beginning at the age of fifteen. Because of their importance to the successful production of the Ringling Brothers show, Smith and Aylesworth were granted a stay by Judge Shea so they could assist in preparations for the 1945 summer tour. They were later ordered to begin serving their sentences on June 7, 1945.

Edward R. "Whitey" Versteeg, chief electrician, of Baldwin Park, California, and William Caley, seatman, of Wanamie, Pennsylvania, were sentenced to county jail for one year on the first count, with similar sentences on all other counts to run concurrently. Versteeg, 44, was an orphan at the age of eleven. Seven years later, he left the orphanage to join the circus. Caley, 35, had been employed by the Ringling circus since 1941. Unlike the others, he was not formally arrested until his appearance in court on February 17, the day of his sentencing. He was vilified for having "left his post" beneath the bleachers, at the point where the fire was then believed to have originated. Caley began his imprisonment on the very day he was sentenced.

David W. Blanchfield—ironically, a native of Hartford—chief truckman, received the lightest sentence, which was suspended because Judge Shea respected his forthright testimony. He was ordered to serve six months in county jail on the first count, with similar sentences on all other counts to run concurrently. Blanchfield, 51, left high school at the age of sixteen. He had joined the Ringling circus in 1936.

In March of 1945, a hearing was held on the motion to withdraw the pleas entered by the Ringling defendants. Both Robert Ringling and John Ringling North were called to the stand to testify on the question of each defendant's role and importance in the ongoing operations of the circus. Robert expressed general support for James Haley as a valuable contributor to circus management. John, on the other hand, asserted that competent and experienced men could easily replace all six employees—even Haley and senior managers—during any period of imprisonment. He went so far as to suggest that he had contemplated filing suit for mismanagement against Robert Ringling and other corporate executives. North's courtroom assertions enraged Rogin, who believed that the statements were calculated to promote the bankruptcy of the circus in order to avoid liability for $4 million in settlement fees. On the afternoon of April 7, the original sentences were upheld.

In addition to the individual sentences, the Ringling Bros. and Barnum & Bailey Circus was fined a total of $10,000. Public atonement for the sin of negligence had begun. Even in the face of the shock expressed by the Ringling employees as Judge Shea read his decision, no one in the press corps ever questioned the sentences—or the decision to abandon a defense.

Despite the tragedy that had befallen the city of hope, the era of innocence and romance was still thriving in 1945. People had faith in the institutions of government, and they trusted their leaders. Cynicism had not yet infected American society like an escalating virus. So, when Connecticut officials announced that the Hartford circus fire was an accident, the people of the city believed them. Many residents, however, were stunned by the severity of the punishment imposed upon the Ringling defendants, and they expressed their amazement by writing letters to the editor asking how the City of Hartford had escaped judicial punishment for its own apparent negligence.

A Matter Of Degree

Perhaps in response to public concern, a *Hartford Times* editorial dated July 17, 1945 claimed that "time will determine where blame lies for the death and suffering" imposed upon the city during the fire. The editorial went on to assert that "not all fault [for the fire] was with the circus management" and that city and state officials should share in the responsibility for the disaster. The paper assured Ringling that the people of Hartford bore them no ill will, and that the city wished the circus well "as it [recovered] from the effects of the disaster." The editors also wrote that "it would be most unfortunate were anything to bring about the end of the circus."

Several months after the Ringling case concluded, William Hadden decided to leave private practice. Shortly after his retirement, he became the Attorney General of Connecticut.

With the Ringling imprisonments in the spring of 1945, thoughts of the catastrophic circus fire were allowed to recede, and the healing of the community spirit finally began. The survivors, whose memories of the tragedy would never disappear, hoped for internal peace, and those who had lost loved ones tried to move on with their lives, uplifted by the compassion offered by the city that had witnessed and participated in their loss and grief.

Coupled with the end of World War II, the conclusion of the Ringling case brought an aura of calm to the city of hope. However, the people of Hartford had no way of knowing that a stunningly cruel twist of fate would soon allow the Ringling circus case to come roaring back to life, forcing the city to confront its memories of the flaming beast that had caused such intense suffering in the summer of 1944.

Part Two

Shadow of Fire, Echo of destiny

SIXTEEN

On August 10, 1948, Madeline Davey gave birth to a baby boy. Drifting in and out of a drug-induced haze, she was not allowed to hold her infant son because of the risk she posed to his health. During the last months of her pregnancy, the tuberculosis had advanced steadily, posing a medical threat that made a successful birth something of a miracle. Moments after their son was born, Madeline and her husband, Steve, decided to name him Richard, in honor of Steve's youngest brother. Madeline was given a few extra seconds to kiss her newborn baby goodbye, then she was rushed out of the room and transferred to a remote sanitarium, where she would recover for the next three and a half years.

When his son was just five weeks old, Steve Davey visited his aging mother, who lived in Hartford. While Mrs. Davey cuddled her new grandson, Steve steered the conversation toward a very sensitive subject. In the process, he revealed the true reason for his visit. Madeline's hospital expenses were rising steadily, and the cost of her medications was more than Steve could bear. He was drowning in debt, and he knew he would never make enough money in Hartford to pay his bills.

As Mrs. Davey listened to her son's story, she became increasingly concerned. Steve went on to explain that the northern logging industry was booming, offering a strong man like him an opportunity to make a decent living for himself and his young family. After a brief pause to collect himself, Steve told his mother that he was moving to Maine, and that he would not be able to take his infant son with him. A logging camp was no place to raise a baby. Obviously, the boy would be much safer with his own family—especially with his grandmother.

Steve was careful not to ask his mother for help directly, but Mrs. Davey knew instinctively what he wanted her to do. She was already caring for Steve's older brother, Bud, who had been severely injured in an auto accident years earlier. Although she recognized that accepting full responsibility for a newborn baby would make life much more difficult for her, Mrs. Davey agreed to take her new grandson under her wing.

With his mother and father gone, Ricky—as he was soon known around the house—became very close to his grandmother and Uncle Buddy. In the first few years of his life, they were the only family he had. Because of a traumatic brain injury suffered in the accident, Buddy was unable to work, so he spent most of his time with his impish nephew. As part of Buddy's usual routine, he paid a daily visit to the firefighters at Station 7 on North Main Street. When Ricky got old enough, Buddy took the boy along.

Ricky reveled in the company of the men in blue uniforms. They seemed to enjoy themselves while doing their jobs. And they always included Ricky in their conversations, as if he were more than just an extra visitor who had not been invited. For any young boy, the thrill of the alarm bell, followed by the sight of men sliding down a silver pole, slipping into heavy boots and turnout coats, then racing away in a fire engine with its siren screaming was incomparable, something he would later find hard to describe. It was a myth made real, and Ricky was a witness to its transformation.

Years later, the men in blue uniforms would recognize their mascot's emerging manhood, so they would eliminate the diminutive "Ricky," and they would call their teenage protege Rick, instead. The honor of being accepted by the men of Station 7 would make a lasting impression on the boy, an impression that would lead him to make an important decision once he became a man.

Madeline Davey returned to her mother-in-law's home in 1952. Although the tuberculosis had been cured, Madeline was left with a malaise from which she never fully recovered. Her body had fought the disease, but the battle had left her inner spirit changed, and her physical strength diminished.

When his mother came home to live, Ricky became confused. He was pleased to have a real mother for the first time in his life, but her arrival had stoked the coals of hostility within the house. Conflict most often resulted from a tug-of-war between Ricky's biological mother and his grandmother, the loving woman who had raised Madeline's son. When Steve returned from Maine, he and Madeline quickly decided to find their own place, leaving the inter-parental strife behind. But Steve had not been as successful in the logging business as he had hoped, so the young Davey family was forced to move into a subsidized housing development called Charter Oak Terrace.

Initially designed to house servicemen returning from World War II, Charter Oak had become a haven for families with low to moderate incomes, and a shelter for those on state or city welfare. The sociological shift that resulted made life in Charter Oak Terrace a tenuous enterprise. The circumstances of their lives made the children who lived there prone to aggression, so a young boy like Ricky had to learn the rules of the street in order to survive.

In those early years, Ricky never had an inkling that he and his family were poor, especially since he seemed to have all the things a young boy needed most. His school was very near the apartment, and there were lots of activities and sports for kids to participate in, and he developed a group of friends who could always be counted on for adventure. Many of his friends were multiracial, and Ricky learned to accept people for who they were, rather than reject them for the color of their skin. Not all the adults who lived in Charter Oak shared Ricky's views, so he also learned about prejudice and hatred, lessons he would never forget.

Ricky first heard about the Hartford circus fire when he was in grade school. Every year, the legend would be described in the classroom in an effort to instill an awareness of community history. A catastrophic fire that claimed more than 100 lives provided more than enough fantasy in the minds of young listeners eager for thrilling tales. But there was a terribly tragic component to the story, and the reality of the events that occurred on July 6, 1944 generated more sadness than excitement in the hearts and minds of impressionable students.

Ricky saw the news photo of an eight-year-old girl who died in the blaze, a child who had never been identified, and the picture had affected him. She looked as if she were sleeping, with no real evidence of anything that had hurt her badly enough to take her life. But he learned that she had died nonetheless, and that no one had ever claimed her as their own. For years, Ricky had heard his parents discuss the fire and the lost child, but the picture of "Little Miss 1565" brought the fire into his consciousness in a way that words never could. She was a kid, just like he was, and she had died during an afternoon at the circus.

Children rarely have a reason to contemplate their own mortality. But life can sometimes intrude in a unique and powerful way, forcing a child to consider what death must be like, and to consider its permanence. Ricky had already seen death many times. Given the severe conditions of life in the Charter Oak neighborhood, some men had been driven to suicide by hanging. Others had been murdered with guns that their enemies should never have possessed. Ricky had seen their bodies, and he had come to understand that death often arrived without warning. But the face of Little Miss 1565 stunned him because the number that had replaced her name suggested that she had never lived at all, and that her real name might never be known by anyone, ever. That was something Ricky did not want to contemplate. He told himself that, if he were to die, he would want people to remember him, and you need a name in order to be remembered by the world.

Ricky had been forced to grow up quickly, as children in harsh places always do. By the time he became a teenager, he had experienced enough trauma and conflict in Charter Oak Terrace to teach him that emotions can leave you wounded. They might even kill you. So he taught himself to turn off his emotions altogether, tricking his conscious mind into believing that his soul could not be penetrated, and that nothing could hurt him. Gangs roamed the complex, and membership meant both pride and protection, but Rick's parents had forbidden him to join a gang. Consequently, he often became a target for their sport.

By the time Rick was fifteen, he had grown tired of being kicked around, tired of having his money stolen, and tired of being a teenage outcast, so he decided the time had come for his initiation. He soon found that belonging to a group was the most important value in his teenage life. When he wore his colors, he was someone to be respected, an accepted member of the Charter Oak world, someone with a name.

Rick became proud and vocal while on the street, but he remained shy and quiet while in school. The emotional range of his personality began to emerge with his growing awareness of the poverty in which he lived. Although many teenagers in his neighborhood experienced similar poverty, it embarrassed Rick nonetheless. To make matters worse, he perceived himself to be a weak student. When taken together, Rick's interior impressions left him with the sense that silence was the best way to protect himself. And silence was a weapon he would continue to use, even as he got older. By working behind the scenes, on his own, he would accomplish a scholastic task without impediment—or observation. When the task was done, he would reveal its result. All the while, he would guide himself to the goal, his isolation reducing the risk of embarrassment and shame. In the years that followed, that method would prove valuable. In 1964, however, he would be forced to endure one last profound embarrassment, and the impact of that event would stay with him forever.

There were few secrets in Charter Oak Terrace. Most families in the complex were struggling to make ends meet, especially in a cooling post-war economy, so no one made any judgments about the living conditions of their neighbors. Steve Davey had never been able to earn enough money to secure his family's future, despite his best intentions. When it all caught up to him, there was nothing to do but accept his fate.

Rick answered the door for the sheriff, but he could not bear to witness the eviction first hand. Without saying a word, he climbed the stairs, entered his bedroom, and locked the door behind him. Until it was over, he would be entirely alone. Rick watched from the window as his family's belongings were carried out of the duplex and dumped onto the street. Images of his life were placed on display for everyone—especially his friends—to see. There was intense humiliation in being deposed from Charter Oak. Rick's mother cried as her family life crumbled all around her, but Rick refused to shed a tear. Instead, he vowed that he would never be humiliated again.

Perhaps in response to the difficulties he had experienced throughout his young life, Rick soon developed an adversarial relationship with authority. Beginning with his parents, then with his teachers, and continuing with his superiors in the Army while serving four years in Germany during the Viet Nam War, he pushed the boundaries of discipline in order to assert his independence. When he returned to the states, he realized that the time had come to channel his rebellious spirit and develop a career. The positive memories of his earliest years in Hartford—the days spent at Station 7 with Uncle Buddy—triggered a desire to become one of the men in blue uniforms, one of the men who raced to the scene of a blaze, one of the men to whom terrified children could turn for comfort when flames threatened their lives. Rick Davey would become a firefighter.

Fire is an expression of force, a force that can never be fully controlled. Once born, it becomes a screaming beast whose only purpose is to sustain itself. Generating heat and light as it grows, the beast is driven by a desire for fuel, a banquet of earthly substances that will provide energy to propel the voracious demon along its parasitic path of consumption, moving relentlessly forward until that which has nourished it has been destroyed.

Human beings have learned that they are vulnerable to the beast. Still, there are some men and women who possess the strength and confidence to confront fire. By doing so, they place themselves at supreme risk, demonstrating their willingness to sacrifice their own lives in an effort to protect others from the harsh reality of flame. As a reward for their courage and commitment, society places a badge over their hearts, a symbol of appreciation and an expression of the desire to shield them from harm. The right to wear the badge must be earned, and those who have earned it consider their membership in the fire community an honor and a privilege.

Rick Davey joined the Hartford Fire Department as a probationary firefighter in February 1971. The "probie" from Charter Oak Terrace had a lot to learn, and he learned it on the line. At all times of the day or night, under every incendiary condition imaginable, Rick watched how the beast behaved, what fuel it preferred to feast on, how it could be counted on to do whatever it chose to do because it had a mind of its own, how it glided along the surfaces that outlined the lives of vulnerable human beings who would be devoured after having crossed its path.

In the hands of an arsonist, fire is a profoundly dangerous weapon. As the occasion requires, it can be used as a straightforward method of destruction, or as an instrument of revenge; it can also be used to conceal even more heinous crimes, such as murder. In the firefighting world, there is a line of demarcation between those who don turnout coats and face masks to enter a flaming building to flood the beast until it drowns, and those who enter the smoking rubble after the beast has departed, their sole purpose being to follow its destructive trail. After several years on the fireline, Rick had become familiar with the methods of fire suppression. In 1979, he volunteered to observe seasoned veterans in the Fire Marshal's office, men who sought the evidence that would reveal causes and origins of fire, and whether the fires to which they were assigned had been deliberately set.

Rick was instantly surprised by their methods. The investigators would enter a building or fire ground immediately after the blaze had been knocked down, and they would scrutinize the site, sometimes for hours, always working in silence, always working independently. Throughout every investigation, they never spoke a word to each other. After the investigators had completed their analysis, they regrouped to discuss their findings. At that time, they would discuss the evidence in detail, each officer providing the rationale for his conclusions. If they were unanimous in their opinion about cause and origin, a report was generated. If any one of them disagreed, they all went back to the scene and began the investigation again—from the beginning.

Rick was compelled to ask the veterans why they behaved as they did during an investigation, but he sensed that he would have violated a professional taboo, so he kept his questions to himself. At the same time, he was intrigued by what he had observed because the methods employed by the investigative team seemed tailor-made for his own professional persona: working without words, and working independently. One year later, he moved off the fireline to become an arson investigator.

Before long, Rick discovered the tricks of the trade, developing an instinct for investigations and an understanding of the arsonist mindset. He was tough, thorough, persistent, and he loved to work alone. The veterans said he was a natural, an investigator blessed with an exceptional ability to "read" a fire for burn patterns, depth of char, progression of flame, the presence of accelerants, always searching for cause and origin. Like all the members of the arson team, Rick took great pride in his work, seeing it as a source of satisfaction and self-esteem. After years of adrenaline-surging call-outs in the middle of the night, Rick never needed to sleep very much, so he was always ready for the demands of an investigation. He endured long hours, often without extra pay, and he was willing to work a stakeout until three or four in the morning, take a nap and a shower, then be back on the job by eight. He learned that the arson squad required dedication or madness, maybe both.

Because the arson squad was essentially a division of law enforcement, team members often carried sidearms in order to protect themselves—even though it was against department regulations to do so. Over time, protection seemed to become even more necessary for Rick, since the resolution of an arson case usually meant prison for the person convicted. People in prison often nursed their anger, anger that could explode in revenge once they were back on the street. In one case after another, Rick sent the firebugs away—most often because he had found his way into their minds, using their own thoughts and intentions against them. Although he did not yet know it, there would soon be a case that would require every ounce of his skill and intuition, a case that would require years of his life, a case that no one else had ever been able to solve.

Seventeen

Every year, the *Hartford Courant* ran a story on the Ringling circus fire of 1944, and Rick read each one. The picture of Little Miss 1565 had haunted him since he was a kid, and he had found himself drawn to the stories about her. After absorbing hundreds, perhaps thousands, of published reports over the years, he believed he had memorized most of the known facts about the circus fire. The issue intrigued Rick as a human being, and it captured his imagination as an investigator. He could never understand how an insensitive person in the stands could have tossed away the cigarette that had started the conflagration, taking so many lives in the process. Rick doubted that there would be a way for someone to live with the knowledge that they were responsible for a tragedy of that scope.

He studied the picture of a beautiful little girl who was torn from those who loved her, then buried without her name. Like many other people who had heard the story of the lost child, he wondered how she could have remained unknown for so long. It had been 38 years since the blaze. He told himself that there would be no way to sift through the ashes of a case that ancient. Then, without warning, his reverie was interrupted by Fire Marshal John Vendetta—a trusted friend, as well as Rick's superior officer. John gave Rick an unusual assignment, ordering him to give a speech before a class of junior high school students. The subject would be the Hartford circus fire of 1944.

Rick was surprised, but he saw no divine intervention in the assignment at the time. It was simply another task to be completed. However, this particular task required that he speak to people in an intimate setting, and that he become the focus of attention. The job would not be done in silence, and it would not be done alone, and that meant only one thing to Rick: extensive preparation, if only to avoid public embarrassment.

During his hunt for information, he was led to the fire department archives. Ironically, there were virtually no files on the circus case. No matter where he looked or who he asked, Rick could find nothing more than a thin sheaf of papers that described the fire in cursory terms, ending with a restatement of the state's original finding that the Ringling blaze had been an accident. Troubled by the lack of material, which left him far less prepared than he had hoped to be, Rick went home to rehearse his speech.

It was a bitterly cold March morning as Rick climbed the stairs to the Burns School. The frost-fanged air took one last bite at his face as he entered the building. Ironically, this was the very school that he had attended when he was a boy. When Rick peered through the window of the door to Mrs. Ashton's classroom, he flashed on Miss Demma, his favorite teacher when he was in school. He smiled while he recalled that he had developed a serious crush on her, then she decided to get married—breaking Rick's heart in the process.

The students were eager to hear about the topic that had captured their imaginations, and Rick wanted to quench their thirst for information. However, he could only offer the most superficial details relating to the fire department's actions in fighting the circus blaze, and very little about the aftermath of the tragedy. Armed with the department's meager file, he told them that witnesses saw the fire break out on the canvas walls, and that the death toll had risen to 125 in the wake of the fire, and that a little girl about seven years old had died that day, and that she was still unidentified because no one ever came forward to claim her. And he told them that, after conducting an investigation, the state had declared the fire an accident caused by a discarded cigarette.

Although the students were polite, Rick could read the disappointment on their faces. It quickly became evident that they had done a sizable amount of research into the case, and that they had compiled quite a roster of information after sifting through old news accounts of the Ringling fire. Rick's presentation did not satisfy their curiosity. They immediately asked about the gas and wax mixture that had been used to waterproof the Big Top, and they asked about the cage chutes that had been strung across the exits, and they asked about how the circus could have done those things and still have been allowed to perform in Hartford. They told Rick that there were 168 deaths, including the child who remained unknown decades later, and there were thousands of physical and emotional injuries. The city had been badly wounded by the blaze, and it was clear to Rick that those wounds were still fresh.

As long seconds ticked by, Rick could barely muster the strength to speak. The questions that the students were asking were questions he now asked himself, details he would have tried to uncover and explain—if he had known as much about the blaze as they did. How could he have been so unprepared for questions on a subject about which he had presumed to know so much, if only from the news articles he had read. Those articles always focused on Little Miss 1565, offering little or nothing about the circumstances leading up to the blaze, facts that Rick had never known. He had come back to school without his homework, and the embarrassment struck like a knife. Mrs. Ashton stepped in to explain that the students had embarked on a quest for information as part of a class project. In response, Rick said that he had searched for information, too, but he had not found what he needed. He apologized to the students, and promised to return some other time—whenever he had something meaningful to offer them.

By the time he returned to the office, Rick was nursing a killer migraine from the stress of the speech. There was no denying that his professional head had been handed to him, and it would take some time for his wounded pride to heal. As the scene repeated itself in his memory, one undeniable irony took precedence over every other thought: the circus fire was a devastating tragedy, but there was virtually no information on file in the fire department archives. Rick found the absence of material hard to believe, and even harder to accept. With that incongruity in mind, he vowed to begin a new quest for information, and he promised himself he would learn everything that could be learned about the historic blaze that claimed 168 lives in the summer of 1944.

That night, Rick dreamed about the fire, and the images that presented themselves tore at his subconscious. He could see the flames, feel the heat, hear the screams, witness the people running to escape the beast that chased them, an angry beast unwilling to depart until destruction was certain. By the time Rick woke the next morning, the seeds of curiosity—and doubt—had been firmly planted. The circus fire had occurred four years before he was born, but it had suddenly come back to haunt him, and Rick's instincts told him it would not go away until he resolved the questions that raced through his mind.

Generations of people had grown up and grown old believing that the Ringling circus fire was an accident. That had been the official state declaration, and the people of Hartford had always accepted it as true. The scope of the tragedy had given rise to a legend that had taken hold of the community. Fact had fused with fiction, as if the intense heat of memory had welded them together. Elderly residents lifted their grandchildren into their laps to recite fragments of the circus fire story, even though the story had long since been embellished to the point of myth. It was the caliber of the story that had mattered most, not the facts underlying the tragedy.

For most people, myth will always suffice because it embodies a certain cultural truth all its own, a truth that reaches to the heart of shared experience. For Rick Davey, myth would never provide a resolution to the Ringling case. He came to believe that the information that had been accepted as true might not be true at all. As surprising as that revelation was, he forced himself to accept it. Experience told him that skepticism was one of his most important investigative tools, and he would use it to pry away at the Ringling evidence until the truth could be set free. There had been a dangerous mixture of volatile compounds used for waterproofing purposes, and there were cage chutes placed in a position to block the exits. Even the old-timers on the department remembered those aspects of the fire. The kids at the Burns School had asked how such things could have been allowed to happen, and that was the key question.

Rick's hunch that there was more to the story of the Ringling blaze had been born in the dead of night, and his hunch would serve as the basis for questions he intended to ask of anyone and everyone who had even the most remote connection to a long-cooled fire that had suddenly come back to life. Rick reminded himself that 168 souls had perished on a summer afternoon at the circus, and they deserved to be remembered. If, after inquiring about the blaze, he came to the conclusion that an accidental cause was the only explanation, he would find a way to honor their memory in private. He decided to begin his quest where the kids had started—at the newspaper.

As with every new investigation, Rick was motivated to learn everything that could be learned about the Ringling blaze. The *Courant* news morgue had archived hundreds of stories about the circus fire, with the oldest articles portraying the aftermath of the blaze and its effects on the city. There was no doubt that the tragedy had changed the life of the community, and Rick could empathize with the agony of those who tried to escape without injury or death. He had witnessed the gruesome effects of heat and flame over the course of his career, and there was no question that the July 6 fire had all the earmarks of a thundering furnace of destruction.

Death has always been a core element of the firefighting profession. Before Rick's involvement in the Ringling circus case, there had only been one child whose memory kept him awake at night. While working as a line fireman, Rick's ladder company had responded to a house fire. As he made his way through the burning building, he heard a little girl screaming in terror. She was hiding in her bedroom closet, hoping the flames would not reach her. Rick crawled through darkened rooms, calling to the frightened child, moving steadily toward her voice, but the smoke was thick and blinding, and it slowed his progress. Seconds before he could reach her, the ceiling collapsed, silencing the terrified voice in the darkness. The memory of that child, and the guilt Rick felt over his inability to save her, stayed with him for years. In a dream that haunted him, he imagined the fear on her face, and he berated himself for having taken too much time pulling on his boots, too much time entering the building, too much time crawling through the smoke. He never told anyone about the pain he felt. He simply lived with it, waiting for the memory to fade like an old photograph. Years later, another child's face would haunt his dreams.

As he pored over the published news record, Rick could feel his instincts churning. His pit bull tendencies were about to reveal themselves, and they would force him to gnash and tear at the circus case until he found what he needed. During his earlier search of fire department files, Rick had been surprised by the fact that there were no pictures of the worst blaze in city history. In the *Courant* morgue, however, there were hundreds of photos. Most were gruesome in the black and white tabloid style, while others captured the fear and shock of those who had come through the flames and survived, or who had watched as others—including their loved ones—died in misery. The most heartbreaking pictures were those of children in hospital beds, innocent victims doing their best to smile while being treated or fed during their recovery from the trauma they had suffered that day.

Rick soon discovered a copy of the photo of Little Miss 1565—the photo that had circulated around the country and around the world in an effort to identify her—and he was instantly captivated. Those who had seen the child's picture had always said she was beautiful, even in death, and they were right. With her eyes closed, she appeared to be sleeping. Her blonde hair was curled and brushed away from her face, as if someone had placed the strands in that position in one last gesture of tenderness. Her face showed some signs of crush trauma, but she was not burned in the way so many others had been. Only a minor char mark along her left cheek muted the beauty of her face. Despite her injuries, the innocence of Little Miss 1565 remained intact. Holding her image in his hands for the first time, Rick could not tear his eyes away from her, and he decided then and there that the photo would stay with him as he searched for more details of the blaze.

EIGHTEEN

In the five years since he had become an investigator, Rick had analyzed hundreds of fires, the results of which had led to dozens of arrests. He had become a respected expert in criminal and civil proceedings, as well. His hunches in those cases had always been right, so he was compelled to follow his instincts about the Ringling blaze, even though it had happened decades earlier. He knew there had to be more information than that which he had already uncovered, and he promised himself that he would find it.

As he delved deeper and deeper into the mystery of the child's identity, Rick came to the conclusion that the only way to find her would be to symbolically return to the 1944 fire itself, learning all he could about the blaze so he could understand how Little Miss 1565 had been lost. He viewed her as a symbol of cultural innocence that had vanished and could never be regained. Her morgue photo captivated him, and he kept it with him all the time, never fully escaping the thought of her.

Although he was not aware of it at the time, Rick had begun a spiritual quest from which there was no turning back. He was seeking something much deeper than a name for a lost child. Since he had always been a man of action, he would not have been inclined to see the grand spiritual plan before beginning his search for Little Miss 1565. The desire to find her crept into his life like a flame, slowly and steadily burning its way into his heart. She had come into the world as we all do, alone. Sadly, she had died the same way. Her life, and all the promise that it must have held, had been taken from her in a fiery climax to an afternoon at the circus. Others had tried to find her, but they had failed. Rick wanted to succeed, and he knew that to do so would require diligence and commitment, perhaps even obsession. Someone else might have been able to turn away, telling themselves that no one cared anymore, but Rick wanted to tell the world that she had been here, and that she mattered—if only to him.

His interest in Little Miss 1565 quickly became something more than just another case, and just another investigation. He soon began to hear the voice of a child, a spirit voice, calling to him when he least expected it, at all times of the day or night. Over time, thoughts of the fire became more and more vivid, as if it were happening in the present, and he became haunted by the child who had become its tragic symbol. Rick's first instincts told him that the voice could not be real, so he did his best to deny it. For a while, the voice would disappear, but it would always return, urging him forward, promising to guide him, erasing his fear, eroding his resistance. Soon, she was fully in his life, shifting his priorities and beliefs, strengthening his resolve until he contradicted his instincts and agreed to follow her. As disturbing as the voice was, Rick found the supernatural call irresistible and fascinating, a symbolic quest for a lost child who wanted to be found. She became his secret, a secret shared with no one.

One of the painful thoughts that spurred Rick's interest in Little Miss 1565 was that she had died so young, so alone. As time went on, he tracked down and eliminated each of the main theories of 1565's abandonment. The initial search required that Rick interview scores of survivors and witnesses to the blaze. In the process, he learned that she was not a Ringling family member, since no circus troupers died in the fire. She was not a runaway, because her photo had been sent all around the world, and no one had responded to say that she belonged to them. And she could not have died with her entire family, since no homes or property had been abandoned or unclaimed by anyone who had been at the circus that day. As his search continued, the mystery of Little Miss 1565 began to haunt him.

The inquiry that Rick had initiated on a hunch quickly began to take up most of his off-duty time—along with a good portion of his own money.

A Matter Of Degree

Every time he came across a piece of information, regardless of where he found it, he would pay for copies to be made. The balancing act necessary to sustain a full-time job and a part-time investigation wore on him, but he still found the time to sift through the regional libraries, including those in Hartford, Wethersfield, East Hartford, Enfield and West Hartford. During most of those visits, he found little or no information he could use. When his attention shifted to the state library in Hartford, however, he began to uncover important state records, documents suggesting that something had gone terribly wrong on July 6, 1944.

The Connecticut State Library had compiled the most complete archive of Ringling circus fire documents ever assembled, a vast collection of public files and clippings that had never been analyzed before. Although the collection was still in its infancy as Rick's inquiry progressed, he found a massive array of material to examine. There were dozens of boxes containing hundreds, if not thousands, of pages of state police files, along with exhaustive hospital records intended to provide an accurate assessment of the treatment rendered during the tragedy. Rick also located detailed witness statements, all of which were taken in the first hours after the deadly blaze in an attempt to determine the fire's point of origin. As he leafed through the statements, he was struck by how consistent the witnesses had been when they claimed to have felt monstrous heat at their backs before the appearance of flames. Rick instantly noted the importance of those assertions, given that he believed the fire had to have been radiant by the time it broke through the sidewall canvas, and the archives offered testimony in support of his assumption.

As the hours went by, Rick pored over the files. He had no intention of examining all of the material, since the sheer scope of the existing collection would have made analysis an impossible task. Rather, he found himself fascinated by the age and power of the files, a virtual reincarnation of the people who had lived through the Ringling circus fire of 1944. He was symbolically transported to that time and place, and he wanted to gain an introductory sense of what they had experienced, and how the events had been interpreted. He knew it would take months for his understanding to gestate, months for any real meaning to rise from the words that had been inscribed within those pages. For now, he chose to revel in the details, hoping for an insight.

The material was a jigsaw puzzle with millions of seemingly unrelated pieces, each having an intrinsic connection to the others, from which Rick would have to extract meaning. As he contemplated the task before him, he discovered a cluster of state police documents that bore little significance to the more formal reports he had previously found. The new pages appeared to be dialogs, conversations that had been saved for the record. More careful analysis revealed that they were transcripts of conversations between State Police Commissioner Edward Hickey and a variety of law enforcement officials from other parts of the country. Apparently, Hickey recorded his phone calls, an avant-garde action for a state official to have taken at that time. Images of Watergate flashed through Rick's mind, but he rejected the possibility that anything sinister lay at the heart of the recordings in the Connecticut archive. Instead, he began to photocopy the material, bundling the selected pages into chronological sequence so he could independently refer to the record as time allowed.

News accounts from the period had also been mixed into the state library archive. Some of the articles reported that the Ringling officials who had been bound over on the night of the blaze had been declared criminally responsible for the deaths of 168 people. For Rick, this was stunning news. If there had been criminal culpability, there had to have been a trial, and reports of the trial would have been published in both the *Hartford Courant* and the *Hartford Times*, the competing papers of the day. Rick had little hope of discovering archive materials from the *Times*, since the paper had stopped publishing well before he began his inquiry. When he returned to the *Courant* morgue, he knew what stories he needed, and he knew when those stories were likely to have been printed. He was stunned to learn that the *Courant* had few recorded articles about a trial of anyone connected with the Ringling circus. There were numerous stories about six circus employees who had been charged with manslaughter and who had later been sent to prison, but there was no record of a trial.

Rick fought the impulse to display his amazement at this news, doing his best to maintain an investigator's game face. A criminal proceeding of some kind had to have taken place in order to sentence six men to prison, but no thorough record of that proceeding could be found. There seemed to be no logic to the sequence of action in the immediate wake of a horrific fire. Hints of confusion and suggestions of impropriety were beginning to reveal themselves wherever he looked, and he would need time to understand their implications. As if it were an afterthought, the clerk added that he had come across a story from 1950 that described a confession made by a former Ringling roustabout who had been arrested in Ohio on arson charges, and he offered the article for review. Rick's pulse began to race. The circus puzzle had suddenly become more complex than he could have envisioned, impeding resolution, but each piece fueled his desire to uncover additional information, especially information that had not been previously examined or properly understood. The hunch that had awakened him in the middle of a wintry night had led him along an investigative trail that should have long since grown cold, a trail capable of revealing secrets buried in the ashes of the past.

    With news of a confession fresh on his mind, Rick returned to the state library to do a more thorough search of their files. With the assistance of a cooperative clerk, Rick obtained the legal document, a partially faded copy of a transcribed confession that read like fiction. For six solid weeks, Ohio investigators had listened to the stories told by a twenty-year-old drifter, and those stories had horrified them. The young suspect offered gruesome facts and insights about fires and crimes committed over the course of his troubled life, fires that arose primarily in New England from 1938 to 1946. By his own account, he had gone beyond the use of fire in his roster of crimes. Seasoned as Rick was, he found the details of the arrest and confession terrifying in their declarative truth. He was compelled to read the complete interrogation file word for word, taking himself deeply into the moment, as if he were one of the investigators on the case as it unfolded.

    While investigating a grain elevator fire that occurred on April 12, 1950 in Williamsport, Ohio, investigators arrested a 24-year-old man named William Graham on suspicion of arson. During his initial interrogation, Graham broke under pressure and implicated an intimate acquaintance named Robert Segee in a string of arsons in Circleville, a fact that provided a legal basis for questioning Segee. Graham astonished Arson Chief C. R. LaMonda and his investigators by asserting that Segee had set the 1944 Ringling circus fire in Hartford. The nervous suspect reinforced his claim by stating that Segee had worked and traveled with the circus at the time of the tragedy. Graham's statement captured the attention of LaMonda and his team, who asked where Segee could be found. Graham told his interrogators that Segee had recently left Columbus, and that he was living with his brother in East St. Louis, Illinois.

Armed with that information, Deputy Sheriff Carl Radcliff and Arson Inspector Russell Smith contacted Pickaway County Prosecutor Guy Cline and filed a request for the extradition of Robert Dale Segee. Cline completed the legal documentation on May 16, and he accompanied Radcliff and Smith to Illinois the next day. On May 17, they traveled to the home of Lewis Segee III, where Robert was said to be living. However, Lewis told the officials that Robert had recently moved back to Ohio. Suspicious of this claim, the investigators canvassed the neighborhood and found Robert living with a friend less than a mile from his brother's home. The Ohio officials had the legal right to extradite Segee, even if an arrest became necessary, but they decided instead to request his cooperation in an active investigation. To their amazement, the docile young man willingly agreed to return to Ohio with them.

Segee was taken to the Columbus Police Department on the morning of May 19, and the initial line of questioning centered on the tragic fire that had virtually destroyed the Ringling circus on July 6, 1944. Within minutes, Segee revealed that he had set a string of fires in both Circleville and Columbus. Then he stunned the investigators by admitting that he had set the Ringling circus fire in Hartford, and that he had done so at the urging of a dream figure he called the "Red Man," who threatened to burn him if he did not set the blaze. Segee remembered that the Red Man had appeared minutes before the circus fire began, and that a match had been placed to the oil-soaked tent, and that "the flames shot all the way up to the big top."

As sensational as those revelations were, Ohio officials knew they would require additional study, so they kept the information to themselves. They were experienced arson investigators, and they recognized the possibility that the young man in their custody could well be exaggerating his role in the circus blaze—if he had played any role at all. Indeed, he could be nothing more than a talkative suspect who courted the attention of investigators by exposing fantasies of arson. But they also recognized that Segee might be telling the truth—and that he might even be insane. Since the strange kid with an odd demeanor had confessed to arsons in Ohio, they had no choice but to hold him. Meanwhile, Cline sent a wire to the corporate offices of the Ringling circus seeking confirmation of Segee's claim of employment.

On the afternoon of May 19, Radcliff and Smith drove Segee to Circleville. In the company of Fire Chief Talmer Wise, Segee guided the investigators to three specific sites where he claimed to have set fires in barns and garages in June and August 1947. Convinced that Segee had committed these crimes, the investigators took him to the Justice of the Peace in Ashville, where he was charged with one felony count of arson, one felony count of attempted arson, and one misdemeanor count of malicious destruction of property.

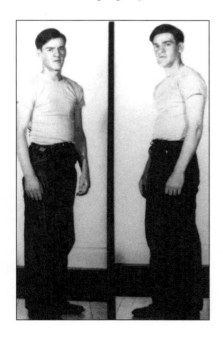

Official booking photos of Robert Dale Segee after his 1950 arrest in Ohio.

PHOTO COURTESY OF THE CONNECTICUT STATE LIBRARY

Segee pleaded guilty to all three charges. As a result, he was placed under a $10,000 bond on the felony counts of arson, then he was bound over for a Special Grand Jury hearing. In addition, he was fined $500 and given thirty days in jail on the single misdemeanor charge. The sentence was suspended for ten days so that Segee could be given physical and psychological examinations. Pending the outcome of those tests, he was held at the Franklin County Jail.

After Segee's confession, Ohio Fire Marshal Harry Callan was convinced that his office had solved the circus fire case. The evidence that he and his investigators had already gathered made it clear that Segee possessed uniquely detailed information about the Hartford fire, information that only the arsonist would know. As a Ringling employee, Segee would have had both the means and the opportunity to have committed the crime, and his long-standing history of arson offered a possible motive for having set the fire, so his confession had profound merit.

Within hours of Segee's court appearance, Connecticut State Police Commissioner Edward Hickey received a call from a UPI wire reporter named Bill Clark, who was seeking comment on a developing story. Clark informed Hickey that Ohio officials were questioning a twenty-year-old former circus worker "in connection with the Hartford fire." Clark indicated that the suspect had not "admitted anything" about his involvement in the blaze. Although Clark's tip was rock solid, it would take another six weeks before he discovered that his source had failed to mention that Segee had already confessed to the Ringling fire by the time news of his arrest began to leak.

Clark told Hickey that Ohio State Fire Marshal Harry Callan had promised that there would be "a story by the first of the week," once the initial investigation was complete. Clark's request for comment had taken Hickey by surprise, so he tried to buy some time. Hickey said he was reluctant to comment to the UPI, especially since he had "not made any arrest for anybody setting the [1944] fire." Instead, he asked the reporter to contact Fire Marshal Callan to determine if it would be beneficial for Hickey to "send a man out there" to inquire about Segee. The reporter promised to call Hickey with an update.

Having successfully deflected the press, if only for a short time, Hickey immediately contacted Fire Marshal Callan's office and spoke with Deputy Commissioner Ward in an effort to get an update on Segee and the status of any ongoing investigation. Ward then spoke with Callan on Hickey's behalf and reported that it had been confirmed that Segee was a Ringling employee at the time of the fire, but the Ohio "probe [was] not far enough along" to justify Connecticut investigators making a trip to Columbus to interview Segee. Ward stated that Callan had promised to contact Hickey as soon as there was enough information to warrant further inquiry from Connecticut authorities.

Seconds later, Hickey called Hartford Police Chief Michael Godfrey, but the chief was out of the office. Hickey left a message indicating that he had spoken with Ohio officials who reported that Fire Marshal Harry Callan was "holding [a young suspect] for questioning, but [Segee had] not said anything about the Hartford circus fire," nor had he made any admissions about his involvement in the 1944 fire. Like the wire service reporter who first contacted him, Hickey did not know that Segee had already confessed to the circus blaze.

When news of Segee's arrest broke in the Ohio papers and around the country as a result of the UPI wire reports, attorneys representing the Ringling circus responded with indignation. They had asserted in court that there was "a strong probability" that the tragic 1944 blaze was a deliberate human act, but their pleas for a more thorough investigation had gone unheeded. James Haley and his attorneys were certain that the outcome of the original legal proceedings in Hartford would have been far different if the damaging evidence about Segee had been uncovered at the time.

On May 21, less than two days after he received the call from the UPI, Commissioner Hickey sent Connecticut State Police Captain Paul Lavin and Hartford Police Captain Paul Beckwith to Columbus in an attempt to interview Robert Segee. The written record revealed that Hickey ordered his men to make the trip in absolute secrecy, with no contact with either press or radio.

As the Connecticut investigators made their way to Columbus on the morning of May 22, Dr. Rimelspach conducted a complete physical examination of Segee at Ohio State University Hospital. A basal metabolism test and an electroencephalogram were administered, then pituitary x-rays were taken. At the conclusion of the exam, Segee was found to be in excellent physical health, with no apparent brain wave abnormalities reflected in the EEG.

Early that afternoon, Pickaway County Prosecutor Guy Cline received confirmation from attorneys representing the Ringling circus that Segee had been employed as a member of the lighting crew from June 30 to July 13, 1944. The news bolstered the information Segee had provided about the Hartford fire that claimed 168 lives just six years prior to his arrest in Ohio. Hours after Segee's circus employment was confirmed, he was taken to the Alfred Willson Children's Center in Columbus, where he was introduced to Dr. Bernard Higley, the staff psychologist who had been assigned to conduct the court-ordered mental examination. Dr. Higley estimated that it would take from ten days to two weeks to complete his study.

From the beginning of their work together, Dr. Higley gained Segee's confidence and cooperation by promising to help him find treatment for the psychological problems that had plagued him since his youth. Higley reported that, because of the trust that existed between doctor and patient, Segee willingly revealed the nature and circumstances of crimes he committed as a juvenile, but he "used his intelligence" to limit the disclosure of details relating to arsons committed after the age of eighteen. Higley speculated that Segee must have been aware of the legal risk posed by such admissions, despite the fact that he had already pleaded guilty to three Ohio arsons. Segee's conversable manner led Higley to conclude that there was no reason to doubt the truthfulness of the statements made during what would become a month-long examination.

By any measure, the personal and psychological revelations offered by Segee were both sensational and astonishing. Segee began his discussion with Dr. Higley by stating that he had come from a family of drifters, and that he had continued a nomadic existence since striking out on his own. Segee also confessed a secret he had held since childhood, a secret that had tormented him all his life. He said he had been haunted since his youngest years by a terrifying dream image, a fiery male figure "with fangs and claws dripping with blood, and with red hair on his chest and flames coming from the top of his head." Segee called this figure the "Red Man," and claimed that he appeared in his dreams for a single purpose—to order him to set fires.

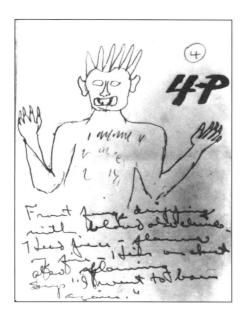

Segee's original line drawing of the nightmare figure he called the Red Man.

PHOTO COURTESY OF THE CONNECTICUT STATE LIBRARY

Sometimes, the Red Man would appear with a flaming red horse, and the horse would chase Segee, trying to run him down. The horse would race like the wind, but his hooves would never touch the ground. Segee went on to assert that the Red Man often spoke to him in his dreams, saying "I want to burn again." The confessed arsonist added that his dreams became so terrifying that he refused to go to sleep because he was convinced he would die. Instead, he roamed through the night, following the orders he received from the Red Man.

The flaming red horse that chased Segee in his dreams.

PHOTO COURTESY OF THE
CONNECTICUT STATE LIBRARY

Maintaining his professional composure, Dr. Higley asked Segee to describe the kinds of crimes he committed while under the influence of the Red Man. The cooperative patient readily obliged, astonishing the psychologist by claiming to have killed a nine-year-old girl named Barbara Driscoll in 1938. They had been childhood playmates in Portsmouth when Segee was just eight years old. He and Barbara had gotten into an argument and she began to call him names. Segee was angry and hurt, so he took a walk along the Piscataqua River. Barbara decided to follow him, calling him names all the while. Segee told Dr. Higley that he "blacked out" moments later. When he recovered, he knew he "must have killed the girl" because she was lying in a pool of blood nearby. Segee "found the rock [he] struck her with," but he did not throw it into the river. Instead, he threw away the small hatchet he had been carrying. He remembered that he had never been so frightened in his life, and that he had been plagued by the memory of the murder ever since.

Over time, Segee tried to convince himself that he had not killed Barbara, and that an older man had committed the crime instead, but he could never escape the painful recollections of the murder. Segee told Dr. Higley that he set the Diamond Match Lumber Company on fire shortly after the little girl's death, in an effort to "burn out the bad memories" associated with the crime. He also reported that an older man was later arrested and charged with Barbara's murder.

Segee went on to describe dozens of wharf fires that he had set in both Portsmouth, New Hampshire and Portland, Maine in the six years following Barbara Driscoll's death. He asserted that the commercial piers in Portland were his "fire area," and that he felt comfortable roaming along the docks lined with warehouses. Segee told Dr. Higley that the Salvation

Army used one of those warehouses as an office and storage facility. Segee added that he and his friends often pitched pennies in the alley adjacent to the facility. One day, he watched from the alley as a Salvation Army officer and a young female co-worker had sex in front of their office window. As part of his continuing confession to Dr. Higley, Segee stated that he went into the Salvation Army building the next night and set the headquarters on fire, using kerosene and wood shavings as his fuel. He reported that he had set the building on fire in response to the sexual activity he had seen there the day before. Segee claimed that the actions he had witnessed triggered memories of his own "sexual relations with different other little girls, and that was a bad memory that had to be burned out."

Dr. Higley soon came to the conclusion that sex and fire were inextricably linked in Segee's mind, and that their linkage had frequently proven lethal. Having gained the trust and confidence of the young suspect, Higley encouraged Segee to reveal the core motives for his behavior. The psychologist even promised to intervene with Ohio authorities in an effort to avert criminal punishment and obtain the psychological treatment necessary to ameliorate Segee's illness. In return, Segee offered a complete history of his crimes. He elaborated on the psychic connection between sex and fire, and he confessed that long-simmering inner rage had led him to commit additional murders in the years after Barbara Driscoll's death. Segee told Dr. Higley that, when he was seven years old, he was often beaten by his father for having engaged in childish "sex play" with little girls in his neighborhood. When his father discovered these acts of youthful experimentation, he would go so far as to burn his son's hand over an open flame. Segee recalled that vicious penalty when he explained that the memories he attempted to burn out as an adult pertained to frustrating sexual experiences with women, most of whom left him "unsatisfied" and ready to start fires.

Segee revealed that, while living in Portland in 1943, he would often have sexual encounters with teenage girls from town. In many instances, Segee would invite the girls to the wharf area, where he would lead them to empty buildings or warehouse businesses whose employees had already ended their workday. Going deeper into his past, Segee revealed that "there had been quite a little sex play with different girls" within one particular warehouse on the Central Wharf. He told Dr. Higley that, over time, the building itself came to represent the memories of those sexual encounters, and that he ultimately "wanted to burn out [those] memories." Segee confessed that he had set fire to the building one afternoon, and that he had hoped to escape without being seen. However, he was discovered by a watchman, who quickly cornered the startled arsonist. Unwilling to be captured, Segee "jumped toward him and grabbed him on the throat and knocked him down," then he "tightened [his] fist" until the watchman lay still. Although Segee was never implicated or arrested in connection with the crime, the memory of that day had plagued him ever since.

Over the course of Segee's month-long examination, he confessed to multiple arsons in New England and Ohio, and he confessed to four murders, two of which were said to have been committed before he was twelve years old. As an experienced psychologist, Dr. Higley was accustomed to wild ravings and elaborate fantasies from patients who conflated fact and fiction in an attempt to describe the nature and extent of their inner torment. Segee's revelations, however, carried the distinct ring of truth because they contained foundation elements relating to time, place, names and circumstances—the telling details that psychotic patients would most likely exclude—so Dr. Higley soon came to believe that Segee was sane.

Of all the details the strange young suspect provided, those that Dr. Higley found most disturbing pertained to the Ringling circus fire of 1944, a tragedy with which Dr. Higley and his peers were familiar. Given the powerful information obtained during the early stages of his examination, Dr. Higley came to the conclusion that Ohio officials should send Inspector Russell Smith to New England for the purpose of corroborating the details of Segee's confession to multiple arsons and the murder of four innocent people.

NINETEEN

When Connecticut detectives Lavin and Beckwith arrived in Columbus on the morning of May 22, they immediately made their headquarters at the offices of the Ohio Highway Patrol. The OHP superintendent assigned Sergeant Joseph Seryak to assist Lavin and Beckwith while they conducted their inquiry. During an initial conference with Arson Chief LaMonda, Lavin learned that Segee had mentioned the circus fire while being driven from Dr. Higley's office to the County Jail. LaMonda indicated that Segee was anxious about "what the Connecticut authorities would do if he admitted to setting the circus fire at Hartford." In his initial report, Lavin wrote that he and Beckwith had expressed their interest in meeting with Segee, but Chief LaMonda denied access to the young suspect because of the ongoing court-ordered psychiatric evaluation. Lavin's report included few details of his investigative activities, except to cite requests for a review of information previously compiled by Ohio authorities.

The Connecticut officers returned to Hartford on May 24 and delivered a brief verbal presentation to Commissioner Hickey in his office at 100 Washington Street. In a more detailed report written the next day, Lavin asserted that much of the difficulty in obtaining the full cooperation of Ohio investigators was due to the fact that Segee was still undergoing a psychiatric evaluation by Dr. Higley at the Willson Children's Center, and that Ohio authorities had stated that their inquiry would not be considered complete until the evaluation was submitted and reviewed. Lavin wrote that, while he and Beckwith were in Columbus, Chief LaMonda provided confirmation that Segee had worked for Ringling from June 30 to July 13, 1944 and that "the circus [experienced] three fires during that period." Inspector Smith had shown the Connecticut detectives the investigative report that had been compiled as of the date of their visit. Finally, when Lavin and Beckwith requested the opportunity to interview William Graham at Pickaway County Jail in Circleville, Fire Marshal Callan agreed to make arrangements for that interview.

In a second report to Hickey written that same day, Lavin inexplicably claimed that Fire Marshal Callan and Inspector Smith had actively obstructed the Connecticut inquiry—despite the reasonable level of cooperation provided by Chief LaMonda and other officials, as described in Lavin's first report. Lavin asserted that the Ohio team wanted "to conduct their own investigation into the Hartford circus fire," and to "get the credit [for] breaking the Hartford case as well as the cases in their own jurisdiction." Lavin also reported that Colonel George Mingle, Superintendent of the Ohio Highway Patrol, offered to intervene with the Governor in order to secure more cooperation for the Connecticut officers, but Lavin "respectfully declined due to [Hickey's explicit] instructions" to avoid publicly revealing their investigation. Lavin also reported that, as Hickey had ordered, their entire inquiry was "conducted quietly, without incident as to publicity from press or radio."

On the morning of their return to Hartford, Lavin and Beckwith met with Alice Peterson of the Traveler's Aid Society. They explained their interest in Segee's travel record from 1944, and Peterson promised to obtain the file for them, although she made it clear that the records were intended to be kept "strictly confidential." The next day, Mrs. Peterson provided the files for Case No. 417A dated July 13, 1944. The record indicated that Segee appeared at the Traveler's Aid office to request a travel pass back to Maine. He was accompanied by Earl Hackett, another Ringling worker who had signed on in Portland a week earlier.

In a document supporting the travel application, Mary McCarthy, the Society clerk, described Segee as "shy but friendly, dirty, no friends," and she wrote that his stated reason for being unable to afford his own way home was that his "pay had been held up due to the circus fire." Segee had assured Ms. McCarthy that "he intended to return home to continue his schooling in the fall," and that he knew "his mother would be worried about his welfare." The Traveler's Aid office in Portland contacted Segee's parents to confirm reimbursement, then Segee was given an advance of $5.76 for train fare and was allowed to return home at Society expense.

In a report to Commissioner Hickey dated June 6, Lavin wrote that he received a phone call at his home from Joe Seryak shortly after seven o'clock on the night of May 29. The cooperative Ohio officer had called to report that Segee had been brought to Highway Patrol headquarters that afternoon by Chief LaMonda, and the suspect had been printed and booked. LaMonda told Seryak that Dr. Higley's examination of Segee was progressing well, but the psychiatric profile would require ten more days. LaMonda gave Seryak some information about fires that had been set in Portland, Maine and Dover, New Hampshire, but he did not provide any details about those fires. Even more important, Seryak stated that Inspector Russell Smith had told him he was "leaving for the east to investigate [Segee's] background."

While speaking with Seryak, Smith had mentioned that "a circus fire started in the toilet section [of the main tent] in Hartford." Smith believed there was a good chance of breaking the Connecticut case, as well as the Ohio cases for which Segee had been arrested, and he was certain that his trip would provide corroboration of Segee's confession. For a brief moment, Rick Davey could not believe what he had read, so he forced himself to review the passage again. In a seemingly innocuous sentence, Captain Lavin had disclosed an astonishingly important fact—that Segee had revealed the point of origin of the Hartford circus fire, and that he had done so within two weeks of his arrest in 1950.

Rick knew that Inspector Smith had not yet investigated the circus fire, so he could not have read the witness reports that suggested the point of origin. Segee must have told Smith that the fire had started in the toilet tent, and his description of the location matched the witness reports to the letter. Those witness statements were taken by the Connecticut State Police and entered into evidence during Hickey's 1944 investigation, so the facts were known years before Segee's confession. Yet, in his report to Hickey,

Lavin made no special mention of Smith's comment. Rick recognized right away that only the arsonist would have known where the fire had actually begun. The corroborative witness statements added to the credibility of Segee's claim, so his statement should have alerted Hickey to the fact that he was a valid suspect. Nevertheless, no action was taken by either Lavin or Hickey, and Rick could not begin to comprehend why. He read on, hoping that the reasons for Connecticut's inaction would soon reveal themselves.

Following Hickey's orders, Lavin and Beckwith left for Dover, New Hampshire on the afternoon of May 30—one day after Lavin received the phone call from Seryak. In a meeting with Police Chief Andrew MacDaniel on the morning of May 31, the Connecticut detectives learned that Robert Dale Segee had no arrest record in Dover, but "the entire Segee family were considered to be mental defectives." In a subsequent meeting with Fire Chief Edward Knott, they were told that there had been a warehouse fire in the vicinity of the former Segee home on July 16, 1944—three days after Segee returned to Portland—and there was no known cause or origin for the blaze.

Lavin and Beckwith left Dover for Scarboro, Maine at 1:30 on May 31. In a mid-afternoon meeting with Portland Police Captain Edward Kochian, the Connecticut detectives learned that Inspector Russell Smith had visited Kochian only hours earlier. The Ohio investigator had requested information about a series of waterfront fires in Portland. Smith had also met with Fire Chief Oliver Sanborn and had obtained a list of fires in the vicinity of the Segee home during the time they lived in Maine.

While in Portland, the Connecticut detectives also interviewed Police Captain Douglas Steel, who told Lavin that an attorney friend named Richard Chapman had once called Steel to inform him that "he had observed a fire at the circus when it played in Portland about a week prior to the Hartford fire." Steel mentioned that Chapman had told him about the rope fire in July 1944, after the deadly blaze in Hartford, but no formal witness report was ever prepared. Intrigued by the information, Lavin decided to contact Chapman at his home. In a brief interview, the attorney recalled that his circus seat was "in the reserved section on the right of the main entrance, somewhat nearer the main entrance than the midway of the tent." Chapman went on to state that, "just before the [matinee] performance started, he noticed a rope hanging from the top of the tent, and he believed [the rope] had a loop at the bottom of it, and that the loop was smoldering." Chapman reported the pending hazard to an usher. Moments later, "the rope was lowered and the fire was stamped out." Chapman added that he believed the rope was "close enough to the tent top to set it afire." In the days and weeks following the Hartford tragedy, no law enforcement officials ever interviewed Chapman about what he had seen, so he thought no more about the rope fire or its potential for disaster.

According to Rick Davey, those comments should have been enough to lead Hickey to conclude that Segee was most probably a dangerous menace to the Ringling circus in 1944, and that he should have been interviewed more thoroughly by Connecticut investigators in 1950. Chapman's seat was near the southwest toilet area, exactly where Segee said he had set the blaze. Other circus workers—including seatmen Gwinnell, Ryan, Mitchell and Todd—had all testified that the flames first appeared on the sidewall canvas in the southwest bleacher section, near the main entrance. There had been three fires in the week since Segee first hired on, so Chapman's report should have been considered valuable when it was first received, and it should have been given credence when Lavin learned about it in 1950. Despite the fact that evidence was accumulating to suggest that Segee was a viable arson suspect, Connecticut investigators took no action in the weeks after his confession.

While accompanied throughout the day on June 1 by two Maine State Police troopers, Lavin and Beckwith were forced to trace the steps taken in Portland by Russell Smith. The persistent Ohio investigator had previously visited the sites of more than a dozen fires in the vicinity of Segee's former home in an attempt to corroborate the claims made in Segee's confession. The Connecticut detectives were later assured by Fire Chief Sanborn that any information gleaned from Smith's subsequent inquiries would immediately be sent to Commissioner Hickey.

By early June, little more than a week into Dr. Higley's examination, the press obtained information suggesting that Ohio law enforcement officials believed Segee's confession. In a front-page story, the *Circleville Herald* went so far as to call Segee the circus arsonist, openly linking him to the 1944 tragedy. When Connecticut State Police Commissioner Hickey was first informed about Segee's capture and confession, he told the press that he did not believe Ohio authorities had "enough on the suspect at present with regard to the circus fire here." Hickey did not intend to act on what was asserted to be a sudden break in the Ringling case. The transcript suggested that Hickey had been in a defensive state of mind, an impression that continued to intrigue Rick Davey as he pored over the records—especially in light of the ongoing secrecy with which Connecticut officials had conducted their inquiry.

On the afternoon of June 2, Lavin returned to Dover, where he spoke with Chief MacDaniel again. MacDaniel reported that Inspector Smith and Portland Assistant Fire Marshal George Morse had met with him on June 1, while Lavin was in Maine. Smith was said to have been "interested in a sex murder of an eight-year-old girl [Driscoll] that had happened in Portsmouth" years earlier. MacDaniel also reported that Smith had uncovered "information about two fires at the Segee home on Middle Road in 1937," fires that had been discovered in a closet and then extinguished by his sister.

Once again, Lavin was following in the footsteps of Inspector Smith, who had gotten to each and every law enforcement office ahead of the Connecticut investigators. MacDaniel told Lavin that Smith was on his way to Portsmouth to continue his inquiry into the Driscoll murder. Lavin concluded his inquiry without going to Portsmouth, returning to Hartford on the afternoon of June 2. In a subsequent report to Hickey, Lavin wrote that Chief MacDaniel had obtained assurance from Portsmouth Police Chief Lynche that any information gathered by Smith during his New Hampshire inquiry would be sent to Connecticut at the earliest possible moment.

On June 3, Hickey received another call from Bill Clark of the UPI, who asked what Connecticut authorities intended to do about Segee. Once again, Hickey stalled, saying that his investigation was continuing. In reality, no true investigation into Segee's confession had yet begun. At 12:30 that afternoon, Hickey sent a telegram to Callan, requesting "copies of all statements made by Segee relative to the Hartford fire." Two days later, Hickey called Callan and demanded to know how news releases about the Segee investigation were making their way into the press. Callan disavowed any knowledge of the leaks, saying that Segee was still under the care of a psychiatrist. If any word had leaked out, Callan asserted, it must have come from state authorities in Circleville, where Segee was first arrested. During that same conversation, Callan announced that one of his own investigators was in New England conducting an inquiry into Segee's background—a fact that Hickey had already discovered. Hickey angrily stated that Smith was traveling in Maine and New Hampshire, but not in Connecticut. Hickey claimed that he had learned of Smith's itinerary from officials in New Hampshire and Maine. He did not reveal that he had never spoken directly with any New England officials other than his own investigators.

Callan denied that Smith had been asking about the Connecticut case while traveling through northern New England, and the documentary record made it clear that Callan was correct. Smith had been sent to inquire about the criminal history of Segee, as compiled in New Hampshire and Maine—an appropriate investigative inquiry. In a statement that read like a warning, Hickey told Callan to "make it clear to your man in Maine and New Hampshire that he is not to be concerned with the Hartford fire." However, if Smith's inquiry revealed any information that might be valuable to Hickey, he wanted Callan to send it to him as quickly as possible.

Hickey complained that, as a result of Smith's work, "the newspapers in Maine and New Hampshire were asking [Hickey] a thousand and one questions," and he responded by declaring that Smith was not authorized to investigate Segee on behalf of Connecticut officials. Hickey told Callan that he was "after information so [he could] investigate it," but the record indicated that he did not order aggressive action to gather that information. Hickey ended the conversation with Callan by explaining that he had sent his own men to Ohio secretly because he "didn't want the press hammering that Connecticut was interfering with [the Ohio] investigation."

To Rick Davey, a seasoned investigator, Hickey's claim did not ring true. In the wake of a rising tide of evidence, Hickey did nothing to investigate Segee's past. Instead, he complained to Ohio. From Rick's point of view, Hickey seemed angry because the New England authorities were asking why Ohio had chosen to investigate the Ringling circus fire and

Connecticut had not. Hickey was furious because Inspector Smith was inquiring about a young man who might well have been involved in a deadly blaze, but Hickey did not assist the Ohio investigator in his inquiry. Instead, he sent his own men north, but his men simply shadowed Smith rather than develop independent information that might have furthered a Connecticut prosecution.

Captain Lavin wrote a separate report to Hickey on June 6, 1950. As Rick Davey reviewed its contents, he was led to question its purpose. Using language that was both aggressive and suspicious, Lavin described the movements of Inspector Smith while in New Hampshire, as if the Ohio investigator had somehow become a criminal suspect. Lavin wrote that "Smith had requested two officers to assist in the investigation" of the Portland fires to which Segee had confessed. Captain Kochian told Lavin that he had assigned Inspectors MacDougal and Kearney to guide Smith through the city. Kochian promised that his men would "keep him advised of [Smith's] every move." When the Portland Inspectors returned to their headquarters, Lavin and Beckwith "interrogated them" and learned that Smith had visited the sites of all fires to which Segee had confessed.

Lavin also reported that Smith's arriving flight had been delayed because of fog, and that he had taken a taxi from Boston to Portland, and that he was registered at the Eastland Hotel in Portland. Lavin wrote that "Smith further admitted [to the Maine investigators] that he was going to spend most of his time that day at the offices of the *Portland Telegram* newspaper morgue for information about the fires." Through the assistance of Captain Kochian, Lavin also learned that Fire Marshal Callan had contacted the editor of the *Telegram* in order to enlist support and assistance for Smith while he conducted an inquiry for the State of Ohio. Lavin was assured by Kochian that "the Portland Department and the officers assigned...would [provide] any and all information that Russell Smith might secure in Portland," and that the information would be sent to Hickey as soon as it was received.

As in his other reports to Hickey, Lavin wrote that the Connecticut investigation was "kept 100 percent confidential, and no member of the press or radio [was] advised" of their presence in Maine. Lavin assured Hickey that Chief MacDaniel would advise Hickey about "the entire set of movements of this Russell Smith" as the inquiry progressed. Lavin also asserted that he and the officials with whom he had spoken believed that Smith was a threat to Connecticut because he appeared to be more interested in "[breaking] the fires in the New England states" than he was in solving the cases for which Segee had been arrested. Ironically, Lavin never described any direct investigative action that he and Beckwith had taken in an effort to research Segee's background. As Rick Davey reviewed the written record, he found it curious that Captain Lavin seemed obsessed with the actions of Inspector Smith, rather than dedicating himself to the task at hand: investigating Segee. Rick believed that Connecticut detectives had missed Smith's real purpose: the corroboration of Segee's guilt. Instead, they turned their attention to seemingly extraneous details that had no relevance to a legitimate inquiry into a suspected arsonist.

In mid-June, Lavin received a supplemental memo from Captain Kochian. The Portland officer wrote that, in the fall of 1943, Segee was judged to have an IQ that ranged between 60 and 78, results that would lead modern educators to consider him mildly retarded. Segee's mental age was determined to be nine years and ten months, although he was nearly thirteen years old when tested. Segee failed all subjects in the sixth grade, and later left school permanently. Kochian added that "our friend [Inspector] Smith was in last Tuesday" and said he was "making wonderful progress" in the Segee inquiry. Kochian wrote that, if Smith was making progress, he was doing so without the assistance of the Portland Police Department—a veiled assurance of ongoing cooperation with Connecticut officials. Smith seemed to be a thorn in their side, as if he were intruding into a case that should have been left alone. Rick was led to conclude that obtaining the truth about the Hartford circus fire was apparently not the issue for New England law enforcement officials in 1950. Rick wanted to know why, and it became clear that he would need to review the entire Hickey report on the blaze in order to determine the truth. Only one thing stood in his way: he had no idea where the report could be found.

Twenty

The information obtained during Inspector Smith's inquiry confirmed that Segee had lived in the area where most of the Portland and Portsmouth fires had been started, and that he had both the means and the opportunity to commit the crimes to which he had confessed. Smith even obtained news clippings that lent credence to Segee's claims of murder. In a March 16, 1943 story, the *Portland Evening Express* reported that police had identified the body of a man who had been found in the "smoke-filled cellar" of a commercial building at the conclusion of a two-alarm fire of questionable origin. The victim, a 48-year-old man named Reid McLaughlin, lived in the basement of an equipment company located on the Portland waterfront, just as Segee had described. During his investigation, Smith learned that the location of the fire-ravaged building was 123 Middle Street, only a few blocks from the Segee family apartment.

As Rick Davey read on, Segee's own words soon came to life, lending even more credibility to his admissions. On June 24, Dr. Higley conducted an interview with Segee in the presence of Inspector Smith and Dr. B. W. Abramson, a Columbus psychiatrist who had studied under Sigmund Freud. During questioning, Segee provided pencil and crayon sketches he had drawn in an effort to describe the nature and content of the dreams that had recently tormented him. Among the pictures of canoes, deer, Indians and eagles, Segee had also drawn a picture of the Red Man, complete with a flowing headdress outlined in black and colored red. Once again, Segee said he had been haunted by recurring visions of the Red Man throughout his life, and each time the fiery figure appeared he would say "I want to be born again," a claim that Dr. Higley interpreted as an expression of Segee's psychological urge to set fires. Sometimes, the Red Man and the flaming horse would appear together in Segee's dreams. He said that their appearance "would please [him] for a split second," then he would become frightened and try to run away, but they would always chase after him.

During that same session, Segee claimed that his dreams had always come to him "as a chain of events, like a roll call," and he said he had experienced recurring images that reminded him of the circus fire in Hartford. Some of his drawings reflected the frightening images he saw in his circus dreams. One frequent nightmare involved the face of a woman who "came up out of the flames, with fire all around her." Segee said the fire woman would stare at him, crying "You are the cause of that."

The female dream image that triggered Segee's guilt over the Hartford circus fire.

PHOTO COURTESY OF THE
CONNECTICUT STATE LIBRARY

When Segee woke from his nightmares, he would be left with intense feelings of guilt, and those feelings had stayed with him until after he admitted that he had set the Ringling fire in Hartford. As the session ended, Dr. Higley presented Segee with a hypothetical question.

Dr. Higley: Suppose I was a magician and I could grant you anything you wanted. What would you want?
Segee: To be cured of these dreams and cured of ever thinking of doing any of these things so that I could live a good clean life.

On the afternoon of June 25, Segee was questioned again by Inspector Russell Smith. Their discussion was witnessed by an Arson Bureau secretary named Rosemary Cutler, who later transcribed her notes for the record.

Smith: Have you been crying, Robert?
Segee: No, sweating.
Smith: From your thoughts?
Segee: Mostly. I wanted to be able to give you a good story today, but I haven't been able to piece things together. I didn't sleep much, and when I did, I kept having terrible dreams.
Smith: Is there anything about tattoos that bother you?
Segee: Yes, a little.
Smith: Do they remind you of the circus fire?
Segee: Yes, but since I told you and Dr. Higley about the circus fire they don't seem to bother me anymore. I had Indians again in my dreams last night. I don't know why I dream about Indians, unless it is because my father is part Indian. In these dreams I see the Indians burning, scalping and murdering.

As Inspector Smith continued the interrogation, Segee revealed that the Portland Pier was his "fire area," and that he had set "about 25 fires in Portland on the piers and docks" when he was younger. With that fact established, Smith probed deeper, hoping for confirmation of Segee's arson methods.

Smith:	Did you roam around much at night?
Segee:	That is when I roamed around the most.
Smith:	Even when you were nine and ten years old?
Segee:	Sure. My parents thought I was in bed. I would get up after they were asleep. I got thinking too heavy about things so I would get up and roam around. I could get up and get away from the house awful quiet without being heard.
Smith:	Here is a fire at 43-45 Market Street?
Segee:	That hits.
Smith:	Here is a fire at 127-25 Commercial Street, which was a two-alarm fire?
Segee:	I didn't set that fire, but I think I know who did. His name is Jackie Cooper. He and Dickie Manchester both used gasoline, the same as I did.

As the questioning continued, Segee admitted that he had also set several fires directly on the docks, as well as a number of fires on the other side of Portland, which he claimed was "out of [his] fire area." He also confessed to a revenge arson in 1941, an act of retaliation against a Portland couple who had said insulting things about Segee's mother and father.

While reading through the 35-year-old interrogation records, Rick Davey was struck by the level of detail that Segee had provided during his discussion with Inspector Smith. Streets and cross streets were mentioned, along with the names, ages, body style, hair color and eye color of his female acquaintances, as well as the names and addresses of the restaurants and theaters he and his girlfriends had visited during their brief encounters. Segee revealed himself to be a dangerous fire starter with practical intelligence, the kind of arsonist that offered the greatest law enforcement challenge.

Like Rick, Inspector Smith had been impressed with Segee's recollection of the details associated with his arson activities. In an effort to satisfy himself that the information relating to arsons committed in Ohio was accurate, Smith decided to take Segee on a tour of the Columbus fire areas described during the previous interrogation. Rosemary Cutler accompanied the men, transcribing their conversation during the trip. In her notes, Cutler wrote that Smith introduced the subject of the Hartford circus fire while driving along Parsons Avenue in Columbus.

> Smith: The big fire at the circus, how did you set it?
>
> Segee: I could have set it any number of ways. They had tents covered with gasoline and oil to keep the rain off. Even the slightest bit of fire would take hold of it very quickly. I don't know why I set it.
>
> Smith: Are you satisfied in your own mind that you set the Hartford, Connecticut circus fire?
>
> Segee: Yes, but I don't remember how I set it.

During the next phase of the investigation, Inspector Smith and Dr. Higley jointly questioned Segee at the Alfred Willson Children's Center in Columbus at four o'clock on the afternoon of June 26, 1950. Their focus that day was the Hartford tragedy, and Segee provided a complete history of the terror he had wrought over the course of his six-day career with the Ringling show. The interview provided even more detail than Smith had obtained one day earlier.

> Smith: First we want to talk about the Ringling Brothers circus fire. What was the incident that happened before the fire, involving the girl?
>
> Segee: I don't know the woman's name. She was thin and she had a big tattoo of a spreading eagle on her back, which reached from the inside tip of her shoulder blade to the tip of the other shoulder blade. The eagle was brown and the tips of the tail feathers were red and black. It had a small black streak on the neck and the rest of the head was white. The eyes and bill were pink.
>
> Smith: How did you meet this girl?
>
> Segee: Me and my other buddies were talking on the circus grounds. She came over and asked my buddy to get her a

bucket of water. We got the water and brought it over to her tent and the one fellow took the water in and pretty soon he came out and told me to come in. She was naked when I went in. She had a mat on the floor and she was down on the floor but there was a bed in the room. I stayed in there for a little while and came back out again. I never saw her or the boy that took me with him after that. This was the same day of the fire in Portland.

Although Inspector Smith's initial question pertained to the fire in Hartford, Segee had gone farther back in time, reporting events that took place in Portland one week earlier.

Smith: How did you know there had been a fire?
Segee: Once it happened [the news] spread all over. I was questioned just a little bit about it. I don't know who questioned me, just a man in plain clothes. It was shortly after the fire when I was questioned. The incident with the girl happened in the late morning, and the fire happened in the afternoon.
Smith: Do you recall seeing the fire?
Segee: It's just a blank in my mind, everything was hazy. I can just remember striking a match.
Smith: Do you know where the fire was?
Segee: I think it was the rope on the big top.
Smith: Who do you think was responsible for that fire?
Segee: I think I was.
Smith: Do you feel pretty sure that you were?
Segee: Yes.
Smith: Did you stay there with the circus that night?
Segee: No, I went home that night. That was the first night in Portland.
Smith: How long was the circus in town?
Segee: About two or three days. From there, we went to

	Providence, Rhode Island. I rode on the coaches on the same train with the circus.
Smith:	What happened when you first arrived in Providence?
Segee:	It was pretty much the same procedure. We rushed to set things up, then we went into town, after we had breakfast. I met a nice little girl down there and I went with her to her home. I didn't get much satisfaction out of her and shortly after that is when the other fire occurred.
Smith:	When you started back to the circus, what happened?
Segee:	I felt very nervous and upset and unsatisfied and I got to thinking about other things, like dreams that I have had. I don't remember exactly when I did get back to the circus, but when I came to myself I was in my own department. During the time of blackout, I remember again striking a match which caused a small blaze.
Smith:	Did you see anything?
Segee:	Yes, I saw a red man. The red man had long fangs and claws and his chest was covered with fiery chest hair and fire was coming out of the top of his head. The fiery man was gone when I came to, back in my own department.
Smith:	How did you feel? Did you wonder if the fire had been put out, or what effect did it have on you?
Segee:	I wasn't very much interested about it. The thing I wanted to do was burn out a lot of bad memories I had. I never did get along with my foreman in the circus anyway.
Smith:	Were you questioned about this fire?
Segee:	I was only questioned slightly, but it was by a different man.
Smith:	You didn't know who these men were?
Segee:	He just asked me where I was at the time of the fire. They never came right out and asked me if I set the fire. I suppose if they would have asked me if I set the

	fire I would have told them.
Smith:	Where was the fire set?
Segee:	On the flap of a tent, but I don't remember where.
Smith:	How long did you stay there?
Segee:	We stayed a short time, and then I guess the second or third day we moved out again and went to Hartford, Connecticut. We were at least eight hours late and that was really a rush to set up.
Smith:	Was there an afternoon show that day?
Segee:	I believe we were too late for that, but there was an evening show. I worked up on the spotlights during the evening show. I also met a girl in Hartford. I think it was the following day after we got to Hartford.
Smith:	Were you on duty the next morning?
Segee:	No. I met the girl downtown. She lived a very short distance from the circus grounds. I don't remember much detail, but I remember that I went home with her. I got to know her and had intercourse with her, but it was not satisfactory. The show had just started when I got back to the circus. I was still nervous and upset and, as far as I know, I thought I just laid down and went to sleep, and then there was the strike of the match again, and then the red man came.
Smith:	Did you see any flames?
Segee:	Just a small flame and then it turned into this red man again, and then the red man became a red horse, and then I remember somebody shaking me. And when I came to, I was standing on my feet and I ran in and tried to help with the people.
Smith:	What were your feelings when you came to?
Segee:	I was afraid. I had a funny feeling. I was excited and afraid, and I never had that feeling before. After that I ran in the tent and tried to help the other people, and I remember trying to pull one of the bodies out, and it was such a bad sight, and I just collapsed there.

Smith:	What did you think after the fire was out and you saw the fallen tent?
Segee:	That is when I first had bad dreams about all those people. I kept having bad dreams about those people.
Smith:	Did you see any flames?
Segee:	Just a small flame and then it turned into this red man again, and then the red man became a red horse, and then I remember somebody shaking me. And when I came to, I was standing on my feet and I ran in and tried to help with the people.
Smith:	What did you feel about it?
Segee:	I actually did feel at first that I was responsible for it, but as the years went on I tried to tell myself that I wasn't. But lately, when I have thought about it, I feel that I am fully responsible.
Smith:	Do you dream about the fire?
Segee:	Yes. I just see a big flash and a lot of people in the dark with just their faces showing, and the flames are coming up all around their faces.
Smith:	Do they say anything to you?
Segee:	Yes. They keep saying "You were responsible." And then the red man and the red horse appear and then the woman, and she keeps saying "You are responsible."

Later that evening, a more elaborate interview with Segee was conducted for the purposes of obtaining a detailed confession that could be used in a future legal proceeding. Participants included Fire Marshal Harry Callan, Arson Inspector Russell Smith, Arson Bureau Chief Charles LaMonda, Guy G. Cline, Prosecuting Attorney of Pickaway County, and Dr. Bernard Higley, all of them in the presence of stenographer Ralph Benedetti. The third and final inquiry would lead to criminal charges and a prosecution of Segee.

During the final interview, Segee formally confessed to multiple murders, along with dozens of wharf fires in New England, and he provided what he believed were logical reasons for his behavior. The young arsonist was compliant when asked to recount the sequence of events during his week of employment with the Ringling circus in 1944. One last time, Segee stated that he had hired on in Portland and had become a member of the lighting crew. He went on to describe how he had "blacked out" after unsatisfactory sexual encounters with young girls in Providence and Hartford, and how the Red Man had ordered him to set fires in each city. In every instance, he remembered striking a match and passing out. When he regained consciousness, a fire was raging.

Segee said that, soon after the fire in Providence, rumors began to circulate "like wildfire" among Ringling workers. Some employees were convinced that wartime saboteurs might have been responsible for the fires, but Segee knew that the Red Man had ordered him to set the fire, and he had obeyed. The immense scope and lethal effects of the Hartford blaze changed the content of Segee's nightmares. He had never killed with fire until the July 6 tragedy, and the memory of what he had witnessed as the inferno raged had taken its toll on the confessed arsonist in the years that followed. He told his interrogators again that he had recurrent dreams in which the faces of victims trapped under the Big Top on July 6 rose out of the flames, and all of those victims cried out that he was responsible.

As Dr. Higley had previously stated, Segee was in no way reluctant to discuss the circumstances of crimes he committed while he was a juvenile—even the catastrophic blaze in Hartford—but he became much more evasive when asked for the details of arsons committed while he lived in Ohio, crimes for which he could be tried as an adult. In every case, however, Segee ascribed either emotional injury or anger as the basis for his urge to set the fires to which he had confessed. As he had done from the beginning, Segee asserted one last time that the memories he had attempted to burn away were "sexual memories." With their questions answered, Fire Marshal Callan and Inspector Smith brought the interview to an end by inviting Segee to include additional comments for the record, but the troubled arsonist declined.

> Callan: Robert, is there anything else you want to tell us at this time that we haven't asked you?

Segee:	All I can say, Mr. Callan, is there has never been any promises made that I just—I can go to a place where I can be cured.
Smith:	Now, Robert. Do you still have some things on your mind that are still bothering you?
Segee:	Yes, Mr. Smith, but I can't get the answer to them myself. I just have silly dreams. I have to try to get the answer before I give it to you.
Callan:	Now, Robert. During the time that you have been in custody, have you been treated alright?
Segee:	I have had friendship, sir.
Callan:	And this statement that you have made [has been] made of your own free will, is that right?
Segee:	Yes, sir.

The official Ohio record made it clear that Segee had not been coerced into confessing his crimes. In fact, he had been given every opportunity to refuse to sign the confession statement, but he willingly agreed to cooperate with law enforcement officials nonetheless, most probably because Dr. Higley had promised to provide treatment for Segee's psychic crisis. His comfort with Dr. Higley allowed important facts to flow freely over the course of the examination. When coupled with the corroborative details obtained by Inspector Smith, the confession record was explosive. The document confirmed Richard Chapman's description of the Portland circus fire on the tent rope, a fire that Segee acknowledged setting, and it also revealed that the investigation undertaken by the Connecticut State Police in 1944 had been cursory at best. Rick believed that the 1950 record contained more than enough information for Commissioner Hickey to have pursued Segee as a suspect, yet nothing was done. So, the disturbing question that had begun to haunt Rick rose once again: Why?

After obtaining his young patient's confession, Dr. Higley was faced with the responsibility of preparing a report of his psychological findings. When he compiled his results, Dr. Higley asserted that Segee had not had a happy childhood, and that he showed an extreme hostility toward his father, who had often severely punished him with fire. The Red Man was a dream figure who represented Segee's father, the "monster" who triggered the anger that became "the unconscious motive for setting fires."

According to Dr. Higley, Segee was sexually impotent, a psychological fact upon which "the framework for hostility toward his father" was established. The psychologist wrote that sexuality was "the central core of [Segee's] crimes," and that "frustrating sex experiences and accompanying hostility set the stage for fire to burn out the memory" of those experiences. Segee's "sexual maladjustments made him vulnerable to conditioning to fire," and his deep-seated feelings of anger and resentment were so severe that they could "only be satisfied by setting a fire." In essence, fire served an intrinsic emotional purpose, becoming a "destroyer of bad memories." Over time, Segee came to rely on the power of fire to eradicate psychic pain.

Dr. Higley wrote that the young arsonist was exceedingly effeminate, and that "homosexual relations with Bill Graham [the man who first implicated Segee in the Ohio arsons] came nearly to being the missing part of the jigsaw puzzle" of Segee's violent behavior. His crayon drawings had revealed "a homosexual angle to the scenes of violence, and three of his four admitted homicides involved perversion in some form." Despite the often brutal aspects of the murders to which Segee had confessed, Dr. Higley did not believe the young suspect was a sadistic killer who mutilated his victims for sexual pleasure. Instead, the psychologist went on to speculate that "violence released tensions which, in an abnormal way, gave [Segee] satisfaction," just as setting fires had always done. Dr. Higley believed that the murder of young Barbara Driscoll "may have been the first in a series of violent acts to destroy memories" that could not be contained.

In describing Segee's crayon drawings, Dr. Higley noted that the pictures were "rationalizations of guilt and frustration [which supplied] a motive for his admitted crimes, both arson and homicide." The psychologist believed that the drawings "[made] his admissions more plausible." Dr. Higley added that, although he had diagnosed Segee as a "typically neurotic" individual who was not psychotic at the time of his examination, "the potentials for a later psychosis [were] definitely present" in his profile. Dr. Higley asserted that Segee "had the opportunity to commit the arsons and homicides" to which he had confessed, and his behavior during the psychological examination often suggested that he was aware of the legal risks posed by his most recent crimes in Ohio.

Dr. Higley declared that Segee was "a sex-conditioned arsonist" whose psychiatric record "[pointed] toward impulsive behavior of a dangerous nature." The psychologist went on to assert that Segee's behavior was "of a type seldom discovered," and that there would be extraordinary diagnostic value in further evaluation of his condition. Dr. Higley reported that Segee himself had stated many times that "it [would not be] safe for him to be at-large, and that he [wanted] to be cured" before being allowed to live in society. Dr. Higley agreed with Segee's self-assessment, and he recommended that the confessed arsonist "be held at Lima State Hospital for further study and observation, and for treatment, if that is possible."

Rick Davey found the 1950 psychological evaluation very disturbing, but something Dr. Higley wrote near the end of his report troubled Rick even more. The Ohio psychologist had worked very hard to establish and maintain Segee's trust and cooperation during the month-long evaluation. Then, little more than a week into the initial phase of the study, "publicity regarding [Segee's] confession broke in the national press." Dr. Higley wrote that the young suspect was "questioned by Eastern authorities regarding crimes he admitted committing in their cities, especially the circus fires." A distraught Segee later told Dr. Higley that "these officials confused him with threats to take him back East if he admitted these fires. They tried to influence him not to trust [Inspector] Smith or [Dr. Higley]. Segee became so mad that he disposed of clothing [Smith and Higley] had obtained for him, and which he badly needed."

Dr. Higley wrote that Circleville authorities had allowed eastern investigators to treat Segee aggressively because they wanted to "obtain his written consent for the use of his [crayon drawings] by *Life Magazine*." The psychologist could not comprehend the apparent irony found in the sudden decision by Circleville officers to "become sympathetic with Eastern authorities efforts to discredit [Segee's] story while arranging for its [national] publication." Dr. Higley was incensed by the fact that his efforts to uncover the basis for Segee's mental condition, and his simultaneous attempt to find an appropriate and effective form of treatment, were subverted by law enforcement officials who had issued idle threats of prosecution.

According to Dr. Higley, such "disturbing and petty jealousy [should have had] no place" in the investigative process. Because law enforcement officials from the east had profoundly interfered with the progress made by Dr. Higley during the psychological evaluation, "[Segee's] resentment and hostility toward his father were temporarily, and for no good reason, directed at those [who were] working for a favorable outcome." The psychologist went on to assert that, "if this could happen in a week in Circleville, then this hostility could as easily be turned against society with dangerous effectiveness." With that specific possibility in mind, Dr. Higley recommended that Segee be held at Lima State Hospital for prolonged evaluation and treatment.

Rick Davey concluded that the "Eastern authorities" referenced in Dr. Higley's report must have been Lavin and Beckwith, the investigators secretly sent to Columbus by State Police Commissioner Hickey. As reluctant as Rick was to admit the possibility that Connecticut officials had engaged in an active cover-up, the evidence was leading him to that conclusion. The record suggested that the investigators knew much more than they had reported. If they had conducted an open and objective investigation, there would have been little need for the secrecy to which Hickey and his operatives seemed committed. Rick had spent countless hours going over the documents he had uncovered, but no acceptable reason for a cover-up had revealed itself. He would have wanted to ask Hickey and his Connecticut investigators about their actions, but they had long since died. Rick would have to decipher their motives from the documents the lawmen left behind.

TWENTY ONE

By the end of June, Ohio Fire Commissioner Harry Callan publicly declared that Segee had confessed to the Hartford circus fire, and to other fires that made the young man a sensational suspect. Pickaway County Prosecutor Guy Cline simultaneously released the details of his own investigation into Segee's claims, announcing that the former Ringling roustabout had attempted to set the circus on fire three times during the week leading to the lethal Hartford blaze. During their respective press conferences, Cline and Callan told the media that Segee was ordered to set fires by the dream figure he called the "Red Man." Callan said that the records relating to the Segee case would be "made available to any local authorities who might request them for aid in prosecuting Segee," but he added that no such authorities—including those in Connecticut—had requested extradition of the arson suspect.

On July 1, Fire Marshal Callan sent Hickey the complete file of evidence relating to the investigation of Segee that had been gathered by Ohio officials. The file included "black and white drawings made by Segee," along with other pertinent materials. The only file missing, Callan stated, was the psychological profile of the suspect that was still being compiled at the time.

The next day, news began to leak from Dr. Higley, who declared that, although Segee was not insane, he needed treatment rather than imprisonment. "I don't think society has a right to expect punishment in this case," Higley asserted. "Segee is very anxious to be cured of his ailment." The psychologist stated that he had "analyzed more than 100 insane persons," but Segee could not be placed into any established category of mental illness. Dr. Higley had never seen a case such as Segee's, and he quickly became convinced that the young arsonist was not psychotic. Rather, he concluded that Robert Dale Segee was a deeply troubled young man who could serve as a psychiatric beacon, guiding the way toward a revised form of treatment for arsonists in the future. Dr. Higley's professional intentions were never questioned, but Ohio authorities soon judged Segee far more harshly.

On the morning of July 3, Hickey received the packet of Ohio evidence, and shot an angry letter back to Callan, whom Hickey believed had withheld evidence until the last possible moment. He accused Callan of denying Hickey the "ordinary courtesies of interstate cooperation" during the investigation. According to Rick Davey, Hickey seemed unduly focused on professional courtesy when, in fact, he should have addressed the scope and quality of his own investigation.

Later that same day, Hickey sent a secret memo to Col. Mingle of the Ohio Highway Patrol, and he enclosed a copy of his reply to Fire Marshal Callan. In the memo to Mingle, who had previously cooperated with Hickey's men, the commissioner complained about having been "sucker shot" by Callan during the Ohio investigation of Segee. Hickey also revealed that Callan had "sent some of [his] investigators to Maine and New Hampshire" to inquire about Segee's assertions of arson in his home states. Being careful not to disclose that he had previously told Callan not to allow Inspector Smith to expand his investigation to include a crime allegedly committed in Hartford, Hickey simply went on to state that "at no time was any contact made here in Connecticut."

In a press interview on July 4, Hickey declared that he had found "nothing new" in Segee's confession. He went on to assert that he had been aware of the prior Ringling fires in 1944. Hickey bluffed reporters by saying that there was "no psychiatric report" from Ohio on which to base a new investigation of the Ringling circus case. Hickey did not reveal that, during his original investigation, he had never established the connection between Segee and the chain of suspicious fires experienced by Ringling in the week prior to the Hartford tragedy. The 1950 Ohio confession revealed that Segee had joined the circus on the day of the Portland fire, and that he had been reprimanded and humiliated by a supervisor on July 6—an event that could have provided a motive for revenge. The confession established the connection necessary to consider Segee a suspect in the circus fire, but Hickey downplayed the importance of the document.

Rick Davey's reading of the record led him to the conclusion that, if Segee's incendiary background had been discovered and examined in 1944, he would have become a suspect in the case. If he had been implicated, there would have been a mitigating atmosphere in the courtroom as the case against the circus employees progressed—if such a case were even filed. With that in mind, Ringling would have mounted a more vigorous defense, introducing facts and circumstances that might have created reasonable doubt. Without a conviction, liability for death and injury claims most likely would have been divided between Ringling and the City of Hartford. Although the press should have been skeptical when Hickey announced that he had found "nothing new" in Segee's 1950 confession—especially since reporters had been dogging the story for months—no hard questions about Hickey's investigation were ever posed, and the opportunity to resolve the circus fire case vanished once again.

On July 5, Callan called Hickey and continued to deny that his office was responsible for any leaks to the press. Callan repeatedly asserted that the leaks must have come from the prosecutor's office in Circleville, an assertion that Hickey refused to accept. Of vital importance to Rick Davey were statements made by Callan during the conversation regarding the conduct of Lavin and Beckwith, Hickey's investigators. Callan denied that Segee was "confined to an insane asylum" at the time the Connecticut detectives traveled to Ohio, and he asserted that "[Hickey's] men did not correctly report" their findings. Hickey then declared that he believed his men, but Callan stated that he did not. "The fact of the matter is, the boy was confined in the County Jail, and they knew that," Callan countered.

Hickey denied that his men were ever told where Segee was being held, but Callan said they had been fully informed. Furthermore, the transcript showed that Hickey never mentioned Lavin's initial report—written and submitted six weeks earlier—which supported Callan's assertion that the detectives knew exactly where Segee was being held. As the conversation continued, Fire Marshal Callan went on to claim that Hickey's men "came out [to Ohio] like two mummies," and they refused to offer any information about the state police investigation into the Hartford circus blaze. Hickey said that his men had no information to offer, which led Callan to address the issue of the original investigation directly. He angrily stated that Hickey had "made an investigation of the fire" in 1944 and that Hickey "certainly had some information" to offer Ohio authorities while Lavin and Beckwith were investigating Segee.

To Rick Davey, the record suggested that Hickey could not admit that his actions were intended to do two things: quietly acquire information that could dispose of Segee as a suspect, and take the strongest offense with Ohio officials in order to create the impression that a vigorous Connecticut inquiry was under way, all the while maintaining secrecy about the fact that virtually no such investigation was being done. A strong offense appeared to be the best defense, but Rick was still unable to assign a motive for Hickey's conduct.

The July 5 transcript also revealed that, by the time Hickey received Callan's call, he still had not read the report on Segee that Callan had provided. When Hickey acknowledged that fact, Callan could not believe his ears. Hickey had not displayed the usual conduct of a law enforcement professional, and Callan was confused. Hickey had steadily complained about Ohio leaking information to the press, but he had not even expended the effort to read and understand the nature of the allegations against the suspect. The only portions of the report that Hickey had read were those that had been printed in the Eastern press. Ironically, the conversation with Callan degenerated when Hickey repeatedly claimed that the *Hartford Courant* had been allowed to interview Segee and Ohio officials, leaving Hickey to learn of their interviews when they were published in the morning paper. Rather than undertake his own investigation, Hickey complained that Callan had begun an inquiry into the confessed arsonist in the deadly Hartford circus fire. Callan saw no logic in Hickey's argument.

Each state had grounds to conduct an inquiry into Segee's confessed crimes, but only Ohio had an active case pending. According to Rick

Davey, Hickey appeared to have sealed the Ringling circus case, a case that should have been reopened for the sake of truth and historical accuracy. Although he had not yet uncovered Hickey's reasons or purpose, Rick was not surprised that Callan could not understand a demand for "the ordinary courtesies of interstate cooperation." Those words amounted to a euphemism for an assurance of secrecy from a fellow law enforcement official, an assurance that would have allowed Hickey to insulate himself from the public exposure of what Rick had come to believe was an investigative failure in 1944. Hickey's fury with Callan derived from the fact that Ohio was consistently releasing information to the press, and that the information was making its way to the public, a process that Hickey sought to block. Later that day, Commissioner Hickey told a less-than-demanding press corps that, although he had received an extensive report on Segee from the Ohio authorities, he was "not accepting Segee's statement because there [was] no corroborative evidence to indicate the truth" of his confession.

On July 11, Maine arson investigator Guy Moors arrived in Columbus to interview Segee and review the details of his confession. The interview was set to take place at the Lima State Hospital for the Criminally Insane, where Segee was undergoing the first of two additional sixty-day psychiatric evaluations. The Maine inquiry was triggered by Segee's confession of the strangulation death of the watchman who had been found dead in the smoldering ruins of a warehouse that Segee claimed to have set on fire in March of 1943.

At 11:45 on the morning of July 13—two days after his interview with Segee—Inspector Moors called Commissioner Hickey, who recorded the conversation. Speaking cryptically, Hickey asked whether Moors had seen Segee, and Moors reported that he had met with the young suspect. Hickey then asked if the investigator had talked with him alone. When Moors said he had, Hickey stated that Ohio officials "wouldn't let [Hickey's men] see him at any time." An obviously-puzzled Moors said he was told by the confessed arsonist himself that Connecticut investigators had interviewed him. Hickey claimed that Segee was mistaken, but Moors went on to say that Segee had told him "there were two men, and he was led into the Sheriff's office when he was confined to the jail."

Before reading any further, Rick Davey paused to absorb the truth behind the conversation. Moors had confirmed that Segee was initially confined in the Pickaway County Jail, and that he had been made available for an interview with Connecticut detectives—just as Fire Marshal Callan had previously asserted in his conversation with Hickey. To Rick, those facts suggested that either Captain Lavin had been less than forthright in his reports to Commissioner Hickey—or Hickey knew far more than he had acknowledged.

The July 11 transcript also revealed that, as the conversation progressed, Moors told Hickey that the man got up and introduced himself to Segee, then said "We are from Connecticut, and we would like to interview you in regard to the fire." Hickey responded by asking Moors whether the men identified themselves as Connecticut State Policemen, and Moors said they did not. Although Hickey had already received reports from Lavin and Beckwith about their secret trip to Ohio, and although he knew that only one Hartford reporter—not two—had spoken with Segee at the jail, Hickey told Moors that the men who questioned Segee must have been "newspaper reporters from one of the Hartford papers, but it was not our investigators."

Hickey inquired about the suspect, and Moors said "He has intelligence, but he's tough." Hickey then asked if Moors had obtained a copy of "the doctor's report," which Hickey described as "mighty important." Moors stated that he was not given a copy of the report, but that it would be sent to him soon. Rather than requesting the report directly from Ohio officials, Hickey asked that Moors send him a copy for Connecticut records.

Rick Davey found Hickey's conduct very strange for a law enforcement official. In light of all the other evidence, Hickey could have shown cause to conduct an inquiry into Segee, asking for cooperation from the State's Attorney's office in the form of a request for extradition. There would have been much to consider, even if Segee were later proven insane. At the very least, a report to the people of Connecticut could have been created, putting the probable cause of the tragic blaze on the record once and for all. Instead, Hickey remained silent.

After his indictment in June 1950, Segee was ordered into the care of psychiatrists at Lima State Hospital for the Criminally Insane for several more months of clinical evaluation. As part of their analysis, a group of psychiatrists led by Dr. Louis Seidenberg placed Segee into a sleep-like trance through the use of sodium amytal, a truth serum. While under the influence of that drug, Segee made detailed statements that corroborated his initial confession to Dr. Higley. According to Dr. Roy Bushong, Superintendent of Lima State Hospital, Segee described the fiery dream figures that ordered him to set fires, but he denied any involvement in the strangulation slaying of Mona McBride, an Ohio crime in which Segee was considered a suspect. Whenever the subject of the Ringling fire in Hartford was introduced, he became "highly emotional" and repeatedly screamed that he "didn't kill anybody." Dr. Bushong added that Segee's "dreams were symbols of his fear. Tensions built up by fear were relieved only by setting fires," which were prompted by "an urge that seemed almost uncontrollable."

By the end of October 1950, Lima State Hospital officials reported that they accepted Segee's confession as accurate and they found that he had an obsessive-compulsive impulse neurosis. Segee had been declared sane, a fact that left the confessed arsonist open to criminal charges from New England to Ohio, according to press accounts. Days later, Segee was returned to Circleville, where he pleaded guilty to the arson charges for which he had previously been indicted. On November 3, Segee formally requested leniency as he stood before the court, but Judge William Radcliff sentenced him to two consecutive terms of two to twenty years, the maximum sentence under Ohio law. If his behavior were exemplary, Segee would become eligible for parole in forty months.

The psychiatric report had stated that Segee was "capable of committing serious crimes" in the future, a fact that influenced Judge Radcliff's sentencing decision. Despite the incriminating effect of Segee's confession, the psychiatric findings, and the Circleville sentencings, no criminal charges were ever filed against him in Connecticut, and no request for extradition to New England was ever received by Ohio authorities. Rick remained troubled by that fact.

The record suggested that Hickey appeared to be relieved when Segee was sent to prison in November 1950. Two weeks after the confessed arsonist was sentenced, State's Attorney Albert S. Bill requested investigative information about Segee in an effort to determine whether he might be subject to prosecution in Connecticut. Responding to Bill's request, Hickey sent a memo in which he stated that the suspect had recently been convicted in Ohio. Hickey went on to write that, since Segee was fourteen at the time of the circus fire, the blaze would have come under the jurisdiction of Juvenile Court. Hickey included numerous supporting documents, among them a brief article from the July 4, 1950 *Courant* that described an interview with Segee conducted at Pickaway County Jail on July 3. During the interview, Segee attempted to recant his statements. For Rick Davey, nothing in the article implied that it had been reporters from Connecticut who had inflamed Segee against both Dr. Higley and Inspector Smith. Although Hickey had asserted that it must have been press reporters who had met with Segee, Dr. Higley's final report suggested otherwise.

Commissioner Hickey and Col. Mingle of the Ohio Highway Patrol continued to cooperate secretly throughout the rest of the year. On December 21, Mingle forwarded a copy of a supplemental investigative report, along with "some newspaper clippings reporting the results of the sanity tests" and subsequent conviction and sentencing information relating to the Segee case. The report described a November 21 post-conviction interview conducted by Highway Patrol investigators. During the interview—the purpose of which was to determine whether Segee could have been considered a suspect in the murder of a Massachusetts man—he recanted his earlier confession and stated that "all the fires and homicides he is accused of committing came about as a result of his telling about his startling dreams and vivid imagination," rather than on any actual facts or experiences.

Segee described his activities on the day of the Hartford fire, adding new layers of conflicting details. He claimed that he and two of his buddies from the circus went into town to see *The Four Feathers*, a British film about a presumed coward who must prove himself in battle. Segee stated that he and his friends returned to the circus grounds after the Big Top had burned down, and that they were denied access to the Barbour Street site because police had roped off the area. He claimed that detectives later questioned him and his companions, but they were released after a brief interview.

Segee's responses stood in direct conflict with the free confession he had offered months earlier. If his interrogators had checked the facts, they would have learned that *The Four Feathers* had been screened in 1939—five years before the Hartford circus fire. A review of the complete record would have shown that Segee was openly dissembling, since his account did not provide for the burns he had received on his arms in the aftermath of the blaze. Even his family and friends in Portland had told investigators that Segee had returned home with obvious burns in the days after the blaze. His revised story did not match the evidence previously gathered, but Segee provided enough fragments of truth to throw the Ohio Highway Patrol off the track.

Interestingly, the OHP investigators had also questioned Segee's parents at their home in Columbus. Their daughter, Roselyn, whom they called Penny, was present for the interview, which took place a few months after Segee confessed to one of the deadliest crimes in American history. As might be expected, the family asserted that they had never known Robert to set any fire deliberately, "whether at home or anywhere else." Perhaps because they were aware of Segee's prison term in Ohio and the possible legal peril in Connecticut, his parents offered what they might have hoped would serve as an alibi for murder. Robert was known for his "vivid dreams, bordering on hallucinations," but his family swore that he could not have raped and murdered young Barbara Driscoll in Portsmouth. Penny was baby-sitting the younger Segee children that night, and Robert was home in bed, sound asleep. It did not seem to matter to the Segee family, or to the OHP detectives, that Robert had previously declared that his ghoulish dreams always made him afraid to go to sleep—especially during his younger years, when he might have needed the protection of a baby-sitter.

In July 1951, less than one year after Segee was sentenced, news accounts began to suggest that he would seek a parole hearing in September. In response to those reports, Prosecutor Guy Cline announced that he would make an appearance before the parole board to oppose Segee's release. In addition, the *Columbus Dispatch* reported on July 15 that Judge Radcliff had submitted a memo to the parole board at the time of Segee's sentencing. Aware that the law allowed for parole consideration after forty months, Radcliff wrote: "If you can believe one tenth of what this man admits he has done, he should never again be released upon society." The *Dispatch* article went on to report that "lawmen in Hartford, Connecticut have taken little interest in [Segee's] confession," despite the scope of his revelations, and that "his case...was virtually ignored by New England authorities."

TWENTY TWO

Despite widespread interest in Segee's admissions of guilt from press and public alike, Hickey continued to insist—even as late as March 1952—that "the Ohio report contained nothing new," and that "there [was] no evidence in Connecticut to warrant taking any interest in this person." Rick Davey found the commissioner's use of the phrase "in Connecticut" linguistically intriguing. He could not help but wonder why Hickey had said there was no evidence of Segee's guilt *in Connecticut*. The phrase kept churning in Rick's mind, suggesting latent meaning. Given the absence of any real investigation by Hickey into Segee's explosive admissions, the only evidence that corroborated his confession was compiled by Ohio law enforcement officials, not by Connecticut detectives. Rick knew that Hickey had been given an official copy of the Ohio investigative report, which incorporated Segee's formal confession. He had also received a copy of Dr. Higley's psychiatric report, which told a consistent story from beginning to end about a troubled young man who had brought the flames of hell to Hartford on a summer afternoon in 1944, taking 168 lives in the process.

From Rick's point of view, it was an insult and an outrage for any Connecticut official to have offered what amounted to an alibi for a confessed arsonist. Even more outrageous were Hickey's published statements asserting that, because Segee was only fourteen at the time of the fire, "his conduct would [be considered] juvenile delinquency and not constitute a crime in Connecticut." Rick was instantly reminded of those who had died in the Ringling circus blaze. He knew that anyone who remembered the fire—survivors, families, and successive generations alike—would share his belief that a crime had been committed in 1944, even if the man originally charged with the responsibility to investigate the deadly blaze had chosen to disregard the evidence of Segee's guilt. The people of Connecticut might have appreciated the vindication that would have come from an attempt to address the wrong that had been committed by Segee, even if his imprisonment were not possible.

In 1955, near the end of Segee's fourth year of imprisonment at Mansfield State Reformatory, he was examined once again by Dr. Louis Seidenberg. This time, he was declared to be a paranoid schizophrenic, so he was returned to Lima State Hospital for a new course of treatment. Two months later, he was formally paroled. Segee remained in Ohio for the next five years, but he ultimately rekindled his incendiary habits—just as authorities had feared. In March of 1960, he was taken into custody by Ohio sheriffs, who brought him to Columbus State Hospital for examination after he became a suspect in a new string of arson cases. After clinical evaluation, he was returned to Lima State Hospital, where he remained for one year.

In March of 1961, Segee was released into the care of his family on a trial basis. Just six months later, however, Dr. Harry Luidens, the Ohio mental health commissioner, reported that Segee had surrendered himself to officials at Columbus State Hospital, claiming to be afraid that he "might harm someone" unless he received treatment. Segee's voluntary commitment bolstered Judge Radcliff's previous assertion that the convicted arsonist was a danger to society, and that he should not be set free. In light of everything Rick had read, he believed that his re-investigation would not be complete without a consultation with a respected psychiatric professional who could offer a current comment on Segee's condition, as it was described in the Ohio record.

In a detailed interview, Dr. Eugene Nedelsky, an Ohio psychologist who once worked with Dr. Luidens, indicated that he agreed with the original psychiatric findings presented by Dr. Luidens and his peers at Lima State Hospital in 1950. Dr. Nedelsky stated that it was probable that Segee was sane but mentally ill, an apparent paradox that many laymen would find hard to comprehend. "There would be no cure for the young man's condition," according to Dr. Nedelsky, "but he could be stabilized with the use of drugs" that would induce a remission of his illness. Dr. Nedelsky asserted that, without the consistent use of such drugs, Segee's condition would regress, making him more likely to commit the same kinds of aggressive crimes that had led to his initial arrest and prosecution.

Rick could not accept the fact that the State of Connecticut had done nothing in the wake of the information obtained about Segee in 1950. He was led to question Hickey's motive for inaction, and he knew that the only way to ascertain why the commissioner behaved as he did was to undertake a complete review of the original circus fire investigation, seeking clues to Hickey's conduct in the process. This time, Rick would begin with the official source of the documents that had triggered Hickey's 1950 inquiry—the State of Ohio.

The authorities in Columbus were stunned to learn that the Connecticut State Police had made the Segee confession a part of the public record in 1987, and they expressed their hope that the file would not be further reviewed or released, since it was always intended to remain confidential. Their reaction surprised Rick, who asserted that the information was important to the history of Connecticut, and to his inquiry into the Ringling tragedy. He could not imagine that the file would do any harm to a convicted arsonist who must have long since died. Rick's comments were met with prolonged silence. Then, to his amazement, he learned that Robert Dale Segee was still very much alive.

At first, Rick did not know how to respond to the news that Segee had survived for 45 years after the Hartford circus fire. So many thoughts and emotions flew through his mind at once that he could not select one from another, a form of confusion that left him momentarily unable to speak. He felt an immediate and compelling need to meet with Segee in order to confront him with questions that only the arsonist could answer, but Rick was professional enough to know that he could not act without reasonable deliberation—precisely because he believed Segee was guilty, a bias that might lead him to make a rash investigative error. So, he brought himself under control and vowed to gather additional details about the deadly blaze, ensuring that his facts were indisputable. Then he would travel to Ohio for an interview—interrogator and accused coming to grips with the facts at the same moment, in the same space.

In order to confirm Dr. Higley's claim of law enforcement interference, former Pickaway County Prosecutor Guy Cline was contacted at his home. During the interview that followed, Cline stated that Dr. Higley had worked diligently to establish a rapport with the young arson suspect. Cline went on to say that Higley was correct in his assessment that "Eastern authorities" had disrupted Segee's psychological condition, thus impeding the progress of the investigation. Cline also recalled that "officials in Connecticut reacted badly" to the news of Segee's arrest, denying Ohio investigators the cooperation they sought. The retired prosecutor stated that Connecticut police officers had traveled to Ohio for the specific purpose of interviewing Segee, and he confirmed that they had indeed been allowed to meet with the suspect while he was held at the Pickaway County Jail—a fact that Commissioner Hickey had always denied. "There would have been no reason for us not to allow the interview," Cline stated. He also recalled that, after the fateful meeting, Segee refused to cooperate with Dr. Higley, and he expressed distrust toward Inspector Smith, the Ohio arson bureau investigator.

Cline's corroboration of the interview with Segee added to Rick Davey's suspicion that an active cover-up was under way in 1950, but the reasons were still unknown. From Rick's perspective, the threat of retribution presented by Connecticut State Police troopers must have led Segee to the conclusion that silence would be his best defense against a charge of arson in the Ringling case. Under no circumstances could he allow himself to be extradited for purposes of an investigation. Like many other states, Connecticut used the M'Naghten Rule to define the sanity of criminal defendants. According to that common-law test, an accused person "must have had the mind, capacity, reason and understanding to have enabled him to judge the nature, character and consequences of the act charged against him, and that the commission of [the act] would justly and properly expose him to punishment; and that, in committing the act, he was not overcome by an irresistible impulse arising from mental disease." In essence, the M'Naghten Rule required complete mental impairment in order to shield a defendant from judicial punishment, a standard that was considered overwhelmingly stringent. Since Segee had been declared sane, he would not be protected from criminal liability under M'Naghten if he were extradited and charged in Connecticut.

Segee must have recognized that his best chance for salvation lay in Dr. Higley, who had promised to find his young subject the counseling necessary to make the fiery demon disappear, so he reestablished their professional rapport. Of course, the confessed arsonist could not have known that there was never any real risk of extradition to Connecticut, and he could not have known that Commissioner Hickey did not intend to reopen the circus fire case that had led to the conviction of six Ringling employees. With protection from prosecution foremost in his mind, Segee recanted his statement of guilt in connection with the Hartford circus fire. By doing so, he provided the means by which Connecticut officials could publicly refuse to consider his case. In that sense, Lavin and Beckwith's jailhouse interview had accomplished its true purpose.

Driven by the desire to confront Segee, Rick was more compelled than ever to find the Hickey report in order to begin a thorough analysis of the evidence that had been gathered in 1944. His daily activities as a member of the Hartford Fire Department had become mundane and tedious when compared to the thrill of returning to a 45-year-old case as notorious as the Ringling circus fire—especially since he had come to suspect that the official story was inaccurate, and that there was much more to the deadly blaze than had ever been revealed.

Several years had intervened since Rick's first visit to the Connecticut State Library. In that time, much more material had been added to the circus fire archive. Rick had to navigate carefully, trying not to retrace the path he had previously forged through the collection. His first important discovery was a new cache of fire photos that provided more detailed evidence of the fire ground and the effects of the blaze on the human beings who had been caught in the jaws of the beast. The photos also offered new views of the areas within the Big Top that were said to represent the point of origin. Because visual evidence acquired at the time of a 45-year-old blaze was the next best thing to having walked the fire ground, Rick vowed to pay special attention to the photographs as he continued his analysis.

As he scoured the state library archive, Rick also found state police reports that included additional witness statements, many of which were taken from Ringling workers and performers who had claimed that the flames had appeared on the sidewall canvas on the southwest corner of the main tent. Rick noted that the reports were consistent with those he had already reviewed, but they also offered something even more important—a vivid description of the heat felt at the backs of spectators who were seated in the upper rows of the blue bleacher section, the area where flames were first identified. Although some investigators might have ignored such details, Rick knew that grass fires did not radiate heat in the manner described by the Ringling witnesses, none of whom said they had seen flames at ground level. In some reports, witnesses asserted that cigarette burns had penetrated the sidewall canvas in prior circus seasons, but no flames had ever grown out of such damage. When considered together, those facts tended to confirm Rick's belief that the Ringling blaze was dangerously radiant.

Rick was deeply troubled by published newspaper accounts reporting that the fire had started from a cigarette carelessly discarded into the grass at the base of the bleachers. When he compared that claim to the witness statements, he could not force them to correlate. He was hounded by the fact that no one had seen any evidence of smoke, and he knew that a grass fire always smoldered before it began to flare. Rick had become aware of a scientific analysis of the ignition capacity of a lighted cigarette, and he had examined it carefully. The scientist who conducted the study on behalf of the FBI reported in 1977 that "cigarettes appear to be marginal causative agents because of the relatively low temperature of the surface of the burning cigarette and their slow rate of heat release." Since the Ringling witnesses saw no smoke at ground level, the cigarette study led Rick to question the official cause of the fire.

The state library archive contained another report that lent credence to Rick's emerging theory of deliberate ignition. Written and presented by the

National Fire Prevention Association in July 1944, the report claimed that, "once the [Ringling] fire started, it was impossible for firefighters to reach the scene in time to prevent a tragedy." The report suggested that there would have been little chance to save the tent or prevent additional deaths "even if the entire fire department had been stationed at the circus grounds" that day. Given Rick's own analysis of the blaze, he was inclined to agree with that assessment.

The NFPA found that "the canvas ignited supposedly from an accidental fire at a spot close to the main entrance at a time when the wind from the southwest [pushed the flame] through the tent." Rick had experienced phantom sounds during many fires over the course of his career. He believed the witnesses who reported a roaring wind had experienced a physical phenomenon called the chimney effect, so he rejected the premise that aggressive winds had fanned the flames. He was intrigued, however, by the report's inclusion of the phrase *supposedly from an accidental fire*. In Rick's mind, the phrase suggested that NFPA investigators might have harbored a suspicion that the blaze had been set, and that they had not been able to acquire the information necessary to declare the actual cause.

Rick's close examination of the archival photographs had revealed that the grass at the base of the bleachers had not been burned, and there did not appear to be any combustible material that would have promoted a fire at the time the matinee began. Modern scientific studies had determined that the ignition of a grass fire was not possible at humidity levels higher than 23 percent. As an artifact of its time, the NFPA report seemed reasonable, but the description of weather conditions made it clear that the agency's opinion about the cause of the Hartford blaze was less than reliable. From Rick's perspective, however, all other elements of the report paled in comparison to the declaration that the exterior men's room tent was the fire's point of origin, a claim that agreed with all of the witness accounts—and with Segee's 1950 confession.

Rick reminded himself that many witnesses had also reported the extreme heat of the day. It was possible that the afternoon of July 6 had been so hot and dry that the grass was more combustible than usual, but the only way to know for certain was to obtain an official weather report and make a comparison of temperature, humidity and other combustion factors. After weeks of prodding, he received a copy of the complete report from the National Weather Service, which was a division of the Department of Agriculture in 1944. *(See Appendix)*

The report listed all of the salient weather conditions that occurred over the course of the day. The humidity at sunrise was a staggering 62 percent, but it fell to 41 percent by one o'clock and held steady until well after sunset. A high temperature of 88 degrees was first recorded at one o'clock, and the temperature did not change until five, when it fell to 85 degrees. As the circus matinee began, the temperature was 88 degrees with 41 percent humidity, a recipe for sticky misery—far too humid for a cigarette to ignite a grass fire.

Rick learned that, throughout the afternoon, a mild breeze came from the north. Although several witnesses and investigators claimed that strong external gusts of wind had driven the flames across the tent top, worsening the effects of the blaze, the report indicated that the wind never exceeded ten miles per hour at any time during the fire, with an average hourly velocity of less than seven miles per hour throughout the day. As Rick had surmised, the wind that survivors had reported was the chimney effect, a draft created by the fire itself as it drew oxygen from the atmosphere in order to feed the flames that devoured the circus tent. The Weather Service report gave Rick the information he needed to verify that the humidity level exceeded that which would allow a grass fire to ignite, and that winds could not have driven the flames across the tent top. Taken together, the elements of the weather report added to Rick's opinion that the circus fire had not been an accident.

Despite the weather report and the FBI study asserting that grass would not ignite in extreme humidity, Rick was still not satisfied. Before he came to a final conclusion about the true cause of the Ringling fire, he wanted to be certain that grass would not ignite in conditions similar to those described on July 6. Through the summer of 1990, Rick conducted multiple burn tests in various levels of humidity. In keeping with the FBI's findings, he could not trigger a grass fire in less than 42 minutes, if at all. Prior to ignition, there was always smoldering, the evidence of which was smoke. Professional assessments, coupled with Rick's informal experiments, consistently called the official state findings into question, all the while supporting the witness accounts compiled at the time of the blaze. Had there been a smoldering grass fire on July 6, someone in or around the tent would have observed smoke before the flames appeared, but no one ever did. When carefully considered, Rick's newly-compiled evidence made a strong case against accidental ignition, and he could not understand why the State of Connecticut had not come to the same conclusion in 1944.

Armed with that information, Rick returned to Segee's mindset, asking himself how the confessed arsonist would have set the Hartford blaze. Given Rick's close examination of the published circus layout, he knew that the area in and around the contiguous men's room tent offered the concealment necessary to initiate a fire that would later become radiant, burning higher on the sidewall and into the tent without impediment. He also knew that, in every fire, there was always evidence that he never expected to find, and each new piece would bring him closer to the truth. There would be a time when he could declare his opinion about the true cause and origin of the Ringling blaze. For now, there was more research to be done.

The Connecticut State Library had grown accustomed to Rick's periodic visits, and they accommodated his many requests for information from their archives. They could not have known that they were cooperating in a definitive analysis of the original investigation of the Ringling circus fire, or that the records in their archive would contribute to a change in the public perception of the blaze. During a review of the collection in the fall of 1990, Rick uncovered the final report of the inquest conducted in July of 1944. A total of 55 witnesses were called to appear before Coroner Frank Healy, and he issued his findings on January 11, 1945. The coroner found that Ringling did not provide adequate firefighting equipment, and that the water hoses owned by the corporation and coiled on the water trucks were not capable of attaching to municipal hydrants, some of which were located as close as 300 feet from the main tent. As a result, the hoses and wagons "were absolutely useless" in battling the blaze. Healy reported that there had been "numerous fires on the sidewalls of the main tent during the 1944 season," and all of those fires had been reported to management. As Rick studied the inquest findings, he noted that Healy ignored the fact that none of the earlier sidewall fires ever resulted in a conflagration such as the fire experienced in Hartford on July 6.

Healy wrote that a Ringling employee "saw fire running up the side wall" near the main entrance to the tent. He added that water thrown from buckets had "failed to stop the fire from climbing" toward the tent top. The fire had apparently gained so much strength and intensity by the time it was first observed that no attempts to extinguish the flames were successful. The fire jumped over the sidewall vent near the top of the tent, then "spread over the top with such rapidity that the entire tent was consumed." From Rick Davey's point of view, logic and recent history—as well as firefighting experience—should have suggested that the Ringling fire was uniquely powerful and furiously radiant at the moment of its discovery, but no state official saw fit to investigate deeply enough to uncover the true cause of the blaze.

To his credit, Coroner Healy found that "the heat was so intense that many people fainted and others were burned to death." Although there were no autopsies conducted on the victims, it could be assumed that superheated air seared their lungs and caused suffocation. The temperature of more than 1500 degrees would most certainly burn flesh, even without the touch of flame to human skin.

Healy cited the inadequate number of fire extinguishers in Ringling's possession, and he noted that too few charged units had been placed around the main tent that day. He asserted that the availability of such fire extinguishers "would have averted the calamity," but Rick believed that fire extinguishers would have had no significant effect on a [radiant] fire of the type that had apparently destroyed the circus that day. Like the NFPA investigators, Healy also wrongly asserted that "there was a high wind blowing which served to fan the fire after it started." Rick's discovery of the Weather Service records had proven that there was no wind strong enough to fan the flames that destroyed the circus on July 6.

Healy castigated the circus for not having made a more diligent and vigorous effort to obtain fireproofing material for their canvas. He also included language that could have been read as an attempt to protect the

City of Hartford from future claims. He cited the fact that the Hartford Fire Department had not been "requested to furnish equipment [and was never] notified" that the circus had arrived in town. As a result, Chief King "had no equipment or firemen on the circus grounds." In seemingly gratuitous language placed deep within his report, Healy found "no legal duty on the part of the Fire Department, Police Department or Building Department of the City of Hartford to make an official inspection of circuses under canvas." Rick Davey had spent his entire career protecting life and property. As a professional, he believed that the city had a moral—if not legal—obligation to safeguard its citizens, especially during a crisis that would prove to be the worst tragedy in the community's history.

Fortunately, Rick's spirits were buoyed when he discovered the testimony of a fire professional who had been called to the inquest. Commissioner Hickey requested that New York City Fire Marshal Thomas Brophy come to Hartford for a formal review of the evidence gathered in the wake of the circus fire. When Brophy later testified before Coroner Healy, he stated that he had been Chief Fire Marshal since 1915, and he had been investigating the cause and origin of fires for almost forty years. Healy quickly established that Brophy held the credentials to be considered an expert in his field, and he testified as such. As Rick read the record, he found it ironic that Brophy's testimony was less definitive than either Hickey or Healy might have wanted it to be. They had invoked Brophy's experience as foundation for the acceptance of his testimony, but it was his investigative experience that led Brophy to craft his answers carefully and objectively.

Brophy's review of the blaze had been complicated by the fact that Hickey and his men had trampled through the fire ground while collecting evidence, contaminating the scene. Much of that evidence had been removed from the site and delivered to state police headquarters at Hickey's command—an investigative risk that should never have been taken. Brophy had been required to compile his findings primarily from photographs, and from an examination of the remnants of the Barbour Street fire scene.

When asked for his opinion of the cause of the blaze, Brophy indicated that his opinions were based on an examination of the fire ground, and on the scant evidence provided to him by Commissioner Hickey. Brophy's review led him to state that "it is possible that the fire may have been caused by smoking carelessly, either by a cigarette or an open match flame." However, Brophy went on to testify that he did not know what the physical conditions of the site were at the time of origin, "nor do I know whether or not there was any combustible material near the point of origin at the time of the fire." His answer suggested that there could have been other unknown elements of ignition of which Brophy would not be aware, a factor that made it impossible to declare the absolute cause and origin of the blaze. Not the most effective testimony for authorities seeking a definitive cause for the deadly fire.

As his testimony progressed, Brophy's professional objectivity continued to reveal itself. When asked to declare the temperature of the blaze, he would only go so far as to state that "it must have been intense" because of extensive evidence of charring along the northerly path of the fire. Healy had been given a report by Hickey asserting that a charred seat jack was evidence that the fire had started at the base of the bleachers, so he questioned Brophy with that point of origin in mind. However, Brophy countered by suggesting that it was also possible, in his opinion, "that a piece of sidewall might have dropped to that point." Although he did not state that secondary ignition had caused the charring of the jack in evidence, his answer implied that it had. Brophy then went on to state that he did not know "how long the fire was burning at the bottom of the jack," nor did he know whether or not the bottom of the sidewall had been draped across the jack prior to ignition.

In an effort to re-direct Brophy's testimony toward the seat jack as a cause rather than an effect of the sidewall ignition, Healy asked whether or not the sidewall would "take fire if the jack was fired first." Brophy said it might, but he added that he believed "there was something else outside of the wooden jack that was first ignited. I don't believe that a match or cigarette could ignite that wooden jack." Rick Davey read Brophy's testimony as a devastating blow to the state's theory of accidental ignition—and as confirmation of Rick's own opinion about the cause and origin of the Ringling blaze. He was pleased that someone of Brophy's professional stature would not compromise the integrity of his investigative findings, even under the demands of a legal proceeding. Rick's only regret was that no questions about deliberate ignition had been posed during the inquest, making it impossible to discern Brophy's opinion of arson as the cause of the deadly blaze. Of course, an open consideration of arson could have foiled any opportunity to focus blame on the Ringling circus.

Healy must have recognized that he was losing control of the testimony, so he asked Brophy about cut grass and wood shavings lying on the ground, and whether or not they could contribute to a fire of great intensity on the seat jack. Without introducing the issue of smoldering time or the emission of smoke prior to ignition, Brophy said it was possible "if there was sufficient combustible material at or near" the base of the jack, but the presence of such material had never been determined.

According to Brophy, the City of New York would have been far more stringent than the City of Hartford in its policy of granting permits for circus performances, and flameproof canvas would have been required before a permit was issued. He went on to state that his "chief function [was] to investigate the cause and origin of fires," and that he had no role in the enforcement of permit regulations. When asked by Healy whether or not fireproof material was available for purchase without government restriction at the time the Ringling circus was preparing for the 1944 performance season, Brophy said he had "no knowledge concerning fireproof materials or liquids." Seconds later, Healy dismissed Fire Marshal Brophy.

Twenty Three

Rick was understandably elated after having read the inquest findings, since his own investigative assumptions about the cause of the circus fire were supported by Fire Marshal Brophy's testimony. However, when he stumbled upon the most vital document of all—a worn copy of the State Fire Marshal's report from January 1945—Rick believed he had struck the mother lode of official records. Bundled within the same box as the inquest findings, Hickey's report seemed rather brief, running a meager eighteen pages. Given the scope of the Hartford tragedy, Rick had envisioned a more detailed presentation. Regardless of its size, the importance of the document as a historical and evidentiary artifact took precedence as he began to read.

Presented on January 11, 1945—the very same day the inquest findings were issued—the state police report echoed many of the statements found in the coroner's report. Commissioner Hickey had called 146 witnesses during his investigation of the fire. Over the course of the inquiry, he learned that the fire department had not inspected the circus before the first performance, nor had any firefighting equipment been stationed on the Barbour Street grounds. Nevertheless, the police chief had issued a permit—despite the fact that Ringling had not provided a certificate of insurance for the two-day performance. Rick's heart began to race with the realization that the City of Hartford had opened itself to charges of negligence by failing to ensure the safety of spectators, a fact that must have disturbed municipal authorities when news of the fire first broke.

Hickey went on to report that flames burst through the sidewall without warning, spreading rapidly up to the Big Top and across the entire canvas, sending napalm flame onto terrified people below. Rick was able to empathize with the fleeing spectators, even though the horror of their experience was modulated by Hickey's use of understated language. Witnesses consistently cited the southwest corner of the tent as the origin of the flames. Rick took special notice of the fact that Hickey had testified about the blaze during his own investigation, since he had attended the circus on July 6, and his testimony agreed with the other eyewitness descriptions.

As Rick continued his review of the report and the supporting testimony from the original investigation, he became concerned by the fact that the evidence collected in the wake of the blaze had been transported to the state police building for inspection. Rick instantly recognized that the removal of evidence from the Barbour Street fire ground could have been a fatal flaw in the state investigation. Based on an uncorroborated report from a Hartford police officer, Hickey had concluded that the fire originated in the grass at the base of the wooden supports, beneath the blue bleacher section in the southwest corner of the tent. Flames then devoured the sidewall canvas and spread to the Big Top itself. As a result of an examination conducted by a former state trooper with no experience in arson investigations, Hickey's conclusions made little sense to Rick Davey. From his perspective, the evidence suggested something radically different.

Rick was particularly impressed by the testimony of Kenneth Gwinnell, a Ringling usher who reported that "a cigarette would have smoked for awhile, but this [fire] came all of a sudden, and it was evidently a match." Gwinnell could not have known that his statement about the absence of smoke would become vitally important nearly fifty years later, when the true cause of the circus fire was being reconsidered. When Hickey compiled his report, he cited Gwinnell's assertions, then wrote that there had been a dozen fires on the sidewall canvas during the 1944 season, but all were "quickly extinguished." According to Rick, that fact suggested that experienced circus personnel would have considered a blaze on the untreated sidewall canvas an uncommon, if not impossible, event. Yet, Commissioner Hickey came to the conclusion that the accumulated evidence "[did] not disclose this to be the act of an incendiary."

Hickey had declared the blaze an accident and, from Rick's point of view, he had done so on the basis of faulty logic and an inaccurate reading of the evidence presented from reliable witnesses. Although Rick believed that negligence had contributed to the extent of the blaze and exacerbated the loss of life, he also believed that the evidence and the testimony strongly suggested that the Hartford circus fire was the result of deliberate ignition, not an accident.

The first element that contributed to Rick's assumption of arson was the fire's brief duration. From the moment flames first emerged, the blaze had required no more than ten minutes to reduce the Ringling circus to smoldering rubble. Rick knew that it was virtually impossible for such a destructive conflagration to have arisen from a simple grass fire, especially a grass fire allegedly ignited by a carelessly discarded cigarette. Eyewitnesses and survivors testified that they had not seen smoke prior to the appearance of flames, and scientific evidence had determined that smoldering was a prerequisite for any grass fire. The furious heat experienced by spectators in the southwest bleachers gave evidence of the radiant nature of the circus fire, which had to have grown stronger and more violent before flames broke through the sidewall canvas.

The evidence of flame growth led Rick to conclude that the fire started outside the tent and moved inward. The sidewall was consumed as the blaze made its way toward the Big Top, indicating that a large fire with a radiant base served as the engine of growth. Ringling workers testified that they had tried to quench the flames by tossing several buckets of water, but the unstoppable fire raged onward. Rick believed that an external blaze drove the flames up to the tent top, devouring the sidewall in the process. Witnesses who stated that a flame about the size of a grapefruit or a basketball first emerged high on the sidewall had all made the assumption that that was the point of origin. However, they were actually observing the effect of an angrily radiant fire that had penetrated the canvas from the outside.

Once inside the tent, the flames moved upward rapidly, spreading out along the canvas in a V-shaped pattern. Witnesses later described their puzzlement over the fact that such a small fire could have generated such extreme heat, but the apparent incongruity made perfect sense to Rick Davey. Experience told him that an external fire served as the source of pre-emergent heat, and the rapid pace of the flame spread offered proof that the fire was large and powerful long before witnesses first observed flames.

Rick paid special attention to Commissioner Hickey's description of the point of origin. Although he correctly indicated the general area of ignition as the southwest corner of the main tent, Hickey inaccurately asserted that a grass fire had ignited the bleacher jack, causing the fire to spread to the sidewall canvas. Rick's exhaustive evaluation of the archival photographs revealed that the grass at the base of the support jacks remained unburned after the destructive blaze, and that the area of charring on the bleacher jack was approximately fourteen inches from the ground. The photographs clearly demonstrated that the damage to the jack could not have been caused by a smoldering cigarette. As a result, Hickey's official conclusion was most likely invalid.

Rick came to believe that the damage to the bleacher supports had been caused by another combustible material that had fallen onto the wooden jacks from above, and New York Fire Marshal Brophy's testimony during the inquest strongly supported that conclusion. The jacks and bleachers had been treated with several layers of highly combustible oil-based paint that would instantly flare and spread in the presence of fire, a process that would have enhanced the killing effects of the circus blaze once secondary flames reached the bleacher seats. Brophy and Davey had each read the evidence the same way, albeit nearly fifty years apart, and their interpretation called the official state finding of accidental ignition into question. Even the NFPA report, which was completed six months before Hickey's report was presented, had declared that the exterior toilet tent was the most logical point of origin for the blaze. Rick was left to wonder why Commissioner Hickey had not agreed.

Unable to answer the many questions that had arisen about Hickey's conclusions in 1945, and unable to find the motive for his conduct in 1950, Rick decided to re-read the final report in hopes of finding clues that would lead him to the truth. This time, he based his assessment on the belief that Hickey had made a rush to judgment, accepting the assertion of a police officer that a careless spectator had triggered the deadly fire by tossing away a lighted cigarette. That claim formed the basis for Hickey's theory of ignition, and he had clung to his theory—despite the fact that the careless smoker was never found, and despite the fact that police never questioned or identified the man who reported that he had seen someone dispose of a burning cigarette. Rick knew that tunnel vision was a professional hazard for arson investigators, a subjective bias that could impede the discovery of the truth. From his point of view, an apparent lack of objectivity had led Hickey to assert a cause that did not cohere to the evidence.

As Rick continued to analyze Hickey's report, something that should have been unimportant rose from the pages, taking Rick by surprise, a fact that would prove so vital that it would place the entire investigation—and Hickey's actions in 1950—into perspective. Near the end of the document, Hickey had written that William Caley and John Cook, two Ringling seatmen who were regularly assigned as fire watchers under the southwest bleachers, "were required to perform other duties, [and to] leave their posts and go to the opposite side of the tent to set up the animal chutes in the northwest corner." Hickey added that Caley and Cook "were also required at the end of the animal act to...disengage the cages and remove them from the exits. During their absence [from the southwest corner], no substitutes were on duty under the Blue Bleachers."

For Rick's purposes, that one page of the state report presented a pivotal piece of information. He had previously concluded that the point of origin was in the southwest quadrant, and he believed that Segee had set the fire in the men's room tent, just as the suspect himself had inadvertently revealed to Inspector Smith in 1950. Rick knew that the rookie roustabout had the psychological profile and a probable motive—revenge against the boss who had slapped and humiliated him—as well as the means to start the blaze, but he wanted to prove that Segee also had the opportunity to do so. Hickey's report provided evidence of that opportunity by asserting that Caley and Cook left the southwest section completely unguarded during the early portions of the show. As a member of the crew, Segee would have known that the seatmen's absence would grant him all the time he needed to start a radiant fire in the men's room—a separate unit staked within inches of the main tent—and to do so without being discovered. Once ignited, the blaze could have grown stronger, feasting on canvas fuel, becoming more and more dangerous and deadly as the matinee progressed.

The deeper Rick delved into the old files, the more validity could be given to Segee's confession—and the more sense could be made of Hickey's actions. The commissioner had been entrusted by the State of Connecticut to obtain the truth underlying the circus fire, and he had declared the blaze an accident. By asserting the negligence of the Ringling corporation, he exonerated the City of Hartford, thus eliminating the necessity for liability payments to victims and survivors—despite the fact that a Board of Inquiry had found evidence of municipal negligence during their own investigation. Ringling had paid millions of dollars in settlement payments on the strength of Hickey's investigative opinion. Along the way, the state sent six circus men to prison without a trial.

Rick's investigation had revealed that the Ringling corporation was vastly underinsured in 1944, leaving virtually no chance that the circus would be able to compensate victims and survivors in proportion to their pain and suffering. Ironically, Ringling's lack of insurance exposed the Insurance City to immense financial risk. With that risk in mind, a formal trial was out of the question because a trial would have required a detailed defense, a process that was certain to shed light on the Board of Inquiry's findings of municipal negligence. Such a defense would assuredly introduce the possibility of arson, especially since expert testimony had not conclusively eliminated deliberate ignition as the cause of the July 6 blaze. The fact that the city had failed to fulfill its civic duty to protect the people of Hartford prior to Ringling's performance heightened the inherent possibility that the city might be required to make its own settlement payments to the victims of the blaze.

The circus employees who had been charged with manslaughter were defended by a highly political Connecticut attorney, and they had been sent to prison in 1945 on a plea of no contest—without mounting a defense. In the wake of the sentencing decision, the Ringling corporation decried the outcome of the judicial hearing, but the sentences were not rescinded. Once the circus defendants were sent to prison, a badly wounded community came to the conclusion that the time had come to heal, and the devastating effects of the tragedy began to subside. There would always be memories, especially of the children who died. Those memories might not fade away completely, but they would surely lose some of their sharp edges over the course of time. As the healing process began, no one in the city of hope could have predicted that the community's wounds would be reopened without warning six years later.

In 1950, Segee confessed to having set the Ringling fire, and the implications of his confession were vast. Rick's examination of the evidence made it clear that Commissioner Hickey and his team had botched the original investigation by not having found Segee in July of 1944. Hickey must have known that the public embarrassment, and then the backlash, that would follow an announcement of his failure would be devastating, a response that he would not have wanted to endure. The archive material suggested that he was determined to torpedo the arsonist's confession and its legal and public relations implications in Connecticut. Some might even have asserted that state authorities had to have ignored Fire Marshal Brophy's testimony in order for the coroner to offer a definitive finding of criminal liability solely against Ringling at the conclusion of the inquest.

In the days after Segee's confession, painful memories of the circus fire cut their way into the conscious life of the city once again. Hickey knew that Segee was said to be crazy and dangerous, a combination powerful enough to have incited the national press. If the people of Hartford came to believe that he had told the truth—if he had actually set fire to the Ringling circus on July 6—then the demand for retribution would be undeniable. Any revelation of Hickey's investigative failure would be so shocking as to engender immense public reaction that might reopen old wounds and trigger a political reprisal against state and city officials who had been entrusted to uncover the truth about the tragic fire. City officials would have to explain their own negligence in the hours leading up to the catastrophe, and Commissioner Hickey would have to explain why he had failed to question or arrest Segee during the 1944 investigation. All at once, Hickey was faced with a revival of the crisis he had controlled six years earlier. This time, however, the threat was even more powerful, and he had to find a way to end the problem once and for all.

Immediately after Segee's confession, Hickey secretly ordered two detectives to Ohio. When they met with the confessed arsonist, they threatened him with prosecution in Connecticut, thus disrupting the psychiatric process that Ohio authorities had set in motion. According to Dr. Higley's report, the detectives made every "effort to discredit [Segee's] story," rather than objectively consider the evidence against him. They warned him that, if he continued to assert that he had set the Ringling blaze in Hartford, he would become subject to extradition, perhaps even prosecution. Segee took their threats seriously, and he quickly recanted his confession. By doing so, he gave Hickey the ammunition he needed to quell any demand for a prosecution in Connecticut. When Segee was later convicted in Ohio, Hickey was able to put the risk of a trial aside for a second time, protecting himself and those who had empowered him.

Rick realized that the financial risk to the City of Hartford in 1950, coupled with the fact that the 1944 investigation had been a failure, created a demand for concealment after Segee confessed. The truth would have rekindled the pain and suffering of those who had endured the tragedy, and it would have posed an additional risk of inciting the indignation of a new generation of media, journalists removed by age from the period of history in which the fire had occurred, men and women who might ask the crucial questions that a more malleable press had not asked in 1944. The truth about the Ringling circus fire was simply too dangerous, so it had been concealed by Hickey. As a veteran arson investigator with a consistent record of successful arrests and prosecutions, Rick had seen this kind of response before: defensive actions taken in the hope of escaping retribution. More often than not, avoidance failed. In the circus case, however, it appeared that Commissioner Hickey had dodged the media bullet.

Twenty Four

Rick Davey had not begun his inquiry into the Ringling circus fire with a suspicion that an investigative conspiracy had occurred. As with every other investigation in which he had participated, he had trusted that law enforcement authorities had properly fulfilled their responsibilities in 1944. After nearly two decades of service as a member of the Hartford Fire Department, Rick had developed a reputation for his commitment to justice. However, his findings in the Ringling case tore away the ethical and legal moorings to which he had been tethered throughout his career.

Shock and sorrow commingled in Rick's spirit as he contemplated the implications of his findings. The evidence he had accumulated over eight years led him to the conclusion that he had been metaphorically betrayed by the system to which he had dedicated himself. In 1950, a young man confessed to the deadliest blaze in Connecticut history, but Commissioner Hickey—the man charged with the responsibility to investigate the circus fire—chose to ignore the evidence of the arsonist's guilt. Rick felt compelled to publish the information relating to Hickey's effort to conceal the truth about Segee's role in the Ringling tragedy, but he could not envision a way to explain Hickey's decision to the people of Hartford. Ironically, Rick had even begun to wonder whether anyone would care about his findings if he revealed them.

He had undertaken a re-investigation for the specific purpose of restoring a lost child's identity. After eight years of effort, Little Miss 1565 was still lost, and Rick was no longer certain that he would find her. For the first time, he wished that the outcome of his inquiry had been different, and that he had not found evidence of impropriety by Commissioner Hickey. A statement from Rick confirming that the Ringling fire had been an accident would be so much easier to present, since it would conform with the pre-existing perception that there had been no secrets to conceal, no ramifications attached to the truth. As in so many cases, the truth about the Hartford circus fire was relatively simple, but its meaning was sadly complex: an admittedly guilty man had been allowed to go free in order to ensure that a flawed investigation would never be reopened, and mistakes would never be revealed.

Having come so far in his inquiry, Rick did not know how much farther he would be willing to go. He realized that he might have to live with his secrets for the rest of his life, never revealing what he had learned, but that was a burden he would be willing to carry. From his most private perspective, he had failed to fulfill his one true mission—the quest for a child who should never have died so young, or so alone. Little Miss 1565 was still lost, still unknown, and Rick was no longer confident in his ability to find her. For now, there was nothing left to do but escape—and he was not quite sure if he would ever return to the city, or to the department he had served for so long.

Rick was conscious of having left Connecticut, and he was conscious of having arrived in Virginia Beach, but the miles he had covered between those two points had left no impression at all. It was as if he had been asleep during the journey, remembering only his departure and arrival upon awaking. The metaphor seemed appropriate, given that the last few days had seemed surreal, as if he were moving through another man's nightmare. He needed a respite from the disappointment he had experienced during the aftermath of his investigation. The air in Virginia was crisp and clear, and the sky was cloudless and brilliant blue. For the first day or two, Rick tried to convince himself that his trip to the south was intended to be a true vacation. He had done all the things that any interested tourist would do, but he had experienced events from an emotional distance, seeing but unseen, hearing but unheard, a man suspended between two worlds, as if he were a ghost who had become trapped between the life that had been and the life that would be.

Each day was born with the quality of mourning. As the hours wore on, anger and frustration would make their way into Rick's conscious mind, propelling him forward, temporarily displacing the sorrow that rose from his self-perceived failure. Feelings of betrayal cut through him relentlessly, leaving a trail of emotional questions that demanded answers that would not come. Those questions led him to wonder whether his failure to achieve justice would ever allow him to face his family again—or to face himself without regret, without ridicule. The spirit voice had gone silent, and Rick had abandoned his quest.

As he walked along the beach on the third day, he paused to consider the child. Her spirit had turned to him for help, calling out over the course of eight years, and Rick had hoped that he would have the courage and ability to persevere until he uncovered her identity, setting her free after being imprisoned in anonymity for so long. He had expected the circus fire case to be the crowning feature of a successful career. Instead, his quest for Little Miss 1565 had become the only investigation that had ended in failure, and that fact gave rise to his sorrow and regret.

Rick had no idea whether an apology would mean anything, especially since the child to whom he would offer it had died nearly fifty years earlier. Standing alone on the beach, he openly stated how sorry he was that he had not kept his promise, and that he had not accomplished his mission, a mission begun with confidence and purpose. Moments later, he berated himself for being so foolish as to believe that a spirit voice could have guided him as his mission progressed, or that Little Miss 1565 might hear his plea for compassion and forgiveness. Only children believed in such fairy tale nonsense. If there had been any validity to the theory of spiritual intervention, he would not have failed in his attempt to find the little girl in the first place.

As Rick drifted back toward the hotel, he thought he felt someone touch his arm. When he turned around, no one was there. Seconds later, he heard a voice in the wind, and it seemed to be whispering to him. Certain that his state of mind had allowed him to imagine the entire episode, Rick returned to his room. Sleeping through the night was impossible, so he lay awake, staring into the space that closed around him. He listened to the ocean and watched the curtains sway as a soft breeze made its way into the room. In the darkness, Rick thought he heard the voice again, a child's voice whispering a message of encouragement: "I'll show you the way." This time, there was no denying the presence of the voice as it called, and Rick interpreted the message to mean that the time had come to regain his confidence and resurrect his commitment.

Although he had only been gone a few days, Rick had recovered his lost hope, and he wondered how he had ever sold himself a ticket to self-pity, and why he had allowed himself to give up in the face of adversity. Little Miss 1565 was the reason he had begun this mission in the first place, and she would be the reason he would complete it. There was no longer any room for failure or indecision. Regardless of whether or not the people of Connecticut ever learned about the actions of Commissioner Hickey, they had a right to know who the lost child really was. Rick vowed to return to Hartford and focus on the little girl to whom he had become devoted, the spirit whose voice had called him to his mission of the heart.

Having rekindled the desire to identify Little Miss 1565, Rick reexamined the state police files that had been archived at the Connecticut State Library. While sifting through Commissioner Hickey's transcripts and correspondence, Rick found a letter from a woman named Emily Gill. She had written to Hickey on July 20, 1944 to express her gratitude for his "help and cooperation in the search for [Emily's] niece, Eleanor Cook." She went on to thank the commissioner for the assistance provided by State Trooper Sam Freeman in the hours after the circus fire. Working together, Gill and Freeman "took the names of the little girls who had not been identified and checked the funeral homes, in case of misidentity." Emily wrote that they had also "checked the little girl who answered to Eleanor's description, and found her to be the Mystery Girl."

Rick was instantly intrigued by the reference to the child he had come to know as Little Miss 1565, and he readily accepted Emily's description of her as the "mystery girl," especially since her identity was still unknown more than 45 years after the date of the letter. Rick was even more intrigued by Emily's assertion that the little girl at the hospital bore a striking resemblance to her niece, and that the missing child's name was Eleanor Cook. Although he would never be able to explain why, Rick was struck by a bolt of investigative intuition. He began to suspect that Little Miss 1565 and Eleanor Cook were the same child—despite the fact that Emily Gill had claimed that the unknown victim at the armory was not her niece.

Over the course of several weeks, Rick hunted through dozens of listings and regional directories dating to 1944, but he could not locate Emily Gill, nor could he find anyone who knew her. As a career investigator, he knew that law enforcement officers were always required to create written reports after every assignment. Emily's reference to State Police Trooper Freeman gave Rick hope that Freeman might have filed a report at the conclusion of the search for Emily's missing loved one, but he was unable to find any such report.

Rick promised himself that, as his re-investigation advanced, he would search through the state police files for any documents that might shed light on the actions Freeman had taken. For the time being, he turned his attention to the medical casualty reports from 1944, hoping to find a meaningful reference to Emily Gill. Once again, he found nothing that would lead to the woman who had actively sought her niece in the hours after the Ringling disaster. However, the casualty reports did reveal one unexpected piece of evidence that made Rick's search worthwhile. Dr. Milton Fleisch consistently reported that 168 victims had died as a result of the circus fire, and he provided a detailed breakdown of those victims by age and gender. In his report, Dr. Fleisch wrote that the "total is one more than the sum of males and females because the age and sex of one victim, who was crushed and torn to fragmentary remains, is not known." Rick recognized that Dr. Fleisch was referring to the unidentified Victim 001, an infant whose death had been described in a previous report written by Dr. Walter Weissenborn, the county medical examiner. Rick viewed the casualty report as definitive, since Dr. Fleisch and Dr. Weissenborn had independently confirmed that Victim 001 was a single human being, a fact that brought the certified number of victims to 168. *(See Appendix)*

Acting on his intuition, Rick continued his search for information about Emily Gill and her missing niece. Since he was seeking the identity of a child he knew to be dead, he paid close attention to the death certificates that had been completed by Dr. Weissenborn in the hours after the Ringling blaze. Of the six individuals who remained unknown through the evening of July 7, three were said to be adults and three were said to be children, and only two of the children were female. All of the victims—except for 1565—were unidentifiable because of the extensive charring that had virtually destroyed their bodies and their humanity. Rick realized that, if there were a mystery girl in 1944, it would have been either Victim 1503 or Victim 1565.

Dr. Weissenborn had completed a Medical Examiner's Report to the Coroner on July 10, the day that the remaining six unknowns were buried. In his report, Weissenborn wrote that the child known as Little Miss 1565 had been taken to Municipal Hospital, where plasma transfusions and other "supportive treatments" were administered. Despite the efforts to save her life, the child died at 6:04 on the evening of July 6 and she was taken to the state armory, where several attempts were made to identify her. The next night, her body was brought to the morgue at Hartford Hospital, where additional attempts to identify her were unsuccessful.

Rick studied all of the photographs and supporting documents relating to Little Miss 1565. He noticed that the morgue tag listed her age as five, and the dental chart created on July 6 indicated that she was approximately six, but Dr. Weissenborn's report stated that she was between six and eight years old. Rick asked himself how experienced professionals could describe the age of a single child in three different ways. The apparent age discrepancies triggered a desire to learn even more about the little girl who had lost her life and her name in the hours after the Ringling circus fire.

News accounts from mid-July 1944 had reported that Eleanor Cook was missing, and they had declared that she was six years old. Those basic facts contributed to Rick's suspicion that Little Miss 1565 and Eleanor Cook were the same child. However, other elements of the story were disturbing because they seemed to violate the laws of anatomy—and logic. Relatives of the missing girl had stated that she was "four feet four," which seemed to suggest extraordinary stature for any child, especially a child of six. Given the family's description of height, the newspaper also stated that Eleanor was "tall for her age." Rick wondered whether or not the family had misspoken, indicating that the child was four feet four when, in fact, they meant to say that she was only 44 inches tall. The difference was much more than semantics.

Driven to confirm or refute the published statements, Rick consulted various physicians as well as medical texts and determined that no six-year-old child of either gender reaches the height of four feet four, or 52 inches. He also found that sixty five percent of six-year-old girls exceed the height of 44 inches, making the remaining thirty five percent shorter than average. In addition, Rick learned that less than twenty percent of girls between ages eight and nine reach the height of 52 inches, thus making them taller than average. Taken together, the medical information led Rick to conclude that the news accounts of Eleanor's height were wrong. She could not have been four feet four at age six, and she was unlikely to be that tall at age eight. If she were eight years old and a semantic error had led her family to have wrongly described her as four feet four when her height was only 44 inches, then she could not have been "tall for her age." Rick determined that, no matter how they were assessed, the age and height statements had only questionable validity.

Rick remembered that the death certificate for 1565 described her as having been three feet ten, or 46 inches—a height more in keeping with an average girl between the ages of six and eight. He also remembered that the medical examiner's report indicated that "a dental chart, x-rays of the skull, teeth and sinuses and a picture of the body" had been sent to the Coroner's office and to the state police in 1944. During Rick's extensive search of the Connecticut State Library archive, he never uncovered x-rays of any kind. Even if x-rays had been found, he was convinced that they would not be state-of-the-art, and that they would therefore be unacceptable for modern forensic purposes. Rick did find the dental chart, however, which had been created by Dr. Edgar Butler in the immediate aftermath of the circus fire. Surprisingly, the chart indicated that 1565 had only two permanent teeth, the lower incisors, as well as additional teeth "at the point of eruption." Rick knew that a child that age should have had other permanent teeth, especially her six-year molars, but the chart listed none. In the absence of x-rays, Dr. Butler's chart seemed rather cursory in its assessments, so Rick did not consider it conclusive.

Perhaps most troubling of all for Rick was Dr. Weissenborn's statement that 1565 had been wearing "a flowered dress and brown shoes" at the time of her death—a description that conflicted with the newspaper's statement that Eleanor Cook had been wearing a "red plaid playsuit" when she attended the circus. Dr. Weissenborn had indicated that 1565's clothing had been sent to the Coroner's office along with the x-rays and the dental chart, but Rick had never found any clothing in the circus fire archives. He had come to doubt the reliability of the age and height assessments for Eleanor, and that doubt had bolstered his belief that she and 1565 were the same child. However, he also began to fear that the clothing discrepancy might derail his identification theory. His only hope was that Eleanor's family had been as wrong about their description of her clothing as Rick believed they had been about her age and height.

TWENTY FIVE

Operating on the belief that Eleanor Cook and Little Miss 1565 were the same child, Rick was eager to eliminate any possible discrepancy about clothing, as described in various published accounts. Ironically, the answer he sought was found in the visual evidence, rather than in the printed word. The post-mortem pictures of 1565 that were taken upon her arrival at the state armory showed the child from various angles, and every shot included a view of her face. Those same photos also provided body views, some of which revealed that she was lying naked on the gurney, wrapped only in what appeared to be a light-colored cotton hospital blanket. Rick instantly recognized the importance of those photographs. If Little Miss 1565's naked body had been covered by a blanket upon arrival at the armory, there would have been no clothing to assist her family when they attempted to make an identification. With that in mind, Rick realized that the family of 1565 would have been required to base their opinion of the missing child's identity solely on her facial features, features that would have changed drastically in the hours after the Ringling blaze.

Rick was simultaneously elated and crestfallen by the photographic discovery. On the one hand, the evidence strengthened his opinion that the published accounts of 1565's clothing were incorrect. That fact also established the possibility that hospital staff or state officials might have assigned the wrong clothing to 1565's body—although Rick believed that a mistake of that kind was unlikely. On the other hand, he worried that he might have fallen into his own well-made identification trap, convincing himself that Little Miss 1565 was recognizable even without the clothing she was said to have worn. That was a subjective opinion that had led many other investigators along the path to failure, and Rick was only interested in success.

Once again, he was compelled to erase the doubts that arose each time he discovered a new piece of evidence. The temperature inside the Big Top at the height of the blaze was estimated to have been 1500 degrees or more. Rick knew that extreme heat shrinks the cartilage in the human body, changing areas such as the nose and ears in ways that are either subtle or striking, depending on the circumstances. The post-mortem photos suggested that Little Miss 1565's ears were smaller and her nose was pugged because of the blaze. In addition, her hair was disheveled and her forehead had been compressed by an injury that had shattered her skull. Those changes in her appearance would have made it difficult, if not impossible, for her family to recognize the child they knew in life.

Rick's obsession with the morgue photo of 1565 drove him to analyze the structural details of her face in an attempt to ensure that passion had not overtaken his professional judgment. The features of every human face are unique. In the case of Little Miss 1565, her most identifiable features were her ears. Most people have rounded ear lobes that slope smoothly around to the cheek, just above the jawbone. In the case of the unknown child, however, her ears were larger than average and the lobes were nearly straight, as if they had been chiseled into an almost linear shape before joining with the cheek.

Rick reminded himself that Little Miss 1565 had been trampled. In the process, her foreskull had been fractured. The injury changed the configuration of her face, giving it a more flattened appearance than it would have had while the child was alive. When linked, the skull injury and the facial changes resulting from the shrinkage of cartilage would have been enough to impede an identification in 1944. Still, Rick believed that he could use the configuration information objectively in order to provide additional data in support of his new theory of identification. He even went so far as to use calipers to measure the distance between the bottom of

1565's nose and the ridge of her upper lip, so he could make a comparison between the unknown victim and Eleanor Cook. Rick realized that he would first have to find a member of the child's family in order to assess photographs of Eleanor in life—as well as 1565 in death—if he were to prove that they were the same child. Of course, he would also have to convince the family that his theory was valid, not just a wild hunch with no basis in fact.

With no end to his re-investigation in sight, Rick's frustration steadily increased. Neither he nor any prior investigator had been able to locate Emily Gill or any member of her family, and the official documents in the state library archive had successfully concealed the last of their secrets. Then, as if to make matters even worse, Rick uncovered a document that threatened to shatter his theory completely. In 1981, Judith Lowe wrote a letter to the *Hartford Courant* asserting that "the time [had] come to set the record straight" about the true identity of Little Miss 1565. Judith was the widow of Ed Lowe—one of the two detectives who had honored the memory of the unknown child each year by adorning her grave with flowers. Mrs. Lowe stated that she wanted to resolve the issues surrounding the child's identity once and for all, perhaps as a belated tribute to her husband and his loyalty to the little girl who had become an important part of his life. Before he died, Detective Lowe claimed that a child named Judith Berman had died in the circus fire and that, in accordance with Jewish religious laws, her body had been obtained and buried before sundown after her death. Lowe stated that, in a case of mistaken identity, the Berman family had selected the wrong body, and that they had left young Judith behind as the unknown victim, 1565.

According to Mrs. Lowe, "the family asked not to be identified, because of the heartache and agony they had already been through." Mrs. Lowe wrote that proof of her husband's claims was "all on record at the Hartford Police Department," since her husband had given his information to then-Chief Paul Beckwith—ironically, one of the detectives who had conducted the secret inquiry into Segee's 1950 confession. When Rick interviewed Mrs. Lowe about her 1981 letter, she stood by her assertions and encouraged Rick to contact the Berman family himself, so the issue could be resolved. Within a matter of weeks, Rick spoke with the Bermans, who vigorously and strenuously denied that Little Miss 1565 was their daughter, Judith. Although their denial could have been interpreted as a negative result because it refuted Mrs. Lowe's claim of absolute identity, Rick viewed the outcome as an additional impetus for his own theory of identification.

As if to confirm his theory, he soon came upon a document that shed new light on the connection between Little Miss 1565 and Eleanor Cook. On July 15, 1944—five days after the burial of the six unknown fire victims—Dr. Lincoln Opper conducted a hair sample analysis at the request of Commissioner Hickey. One of the samples came from Little Miss 1565, and the other came from the hairbrush that had belonged to Eleanor Cook. Dr. Opper, director of the science laboratory at Norwich State Hospital, subsequently concluded that significant microscopic similarities in the medulla and light cortex suggested that "both specimens may have been derived from the same scalp." *(See Appendix)*

The report was an astonishing piece of information that momentarily stunned Rick Davey. After nearly nine years of work, he had finally found definitive scientific evidence—something other than his own leaps of investigative logic—that supported his theory that Little Miss 1565 and Eleanor Cook were the same child. From Rick's point of view, Dr. Opper's findings were as close to an absolute match as modern science would allow. In the 45 years since the report was written, forensic scientists never declared two hair samples an absolute match. Such samples were determined to be either consistent or inconsistent, based on a variety of characteristics such as those analyzed in 1944. Additional identification methods such as retinal scanning had been developed since that time, but it was impossible to employ those methods in the case of Little Miss 1565. The only aspect of the report that troubled Rick was the fact that it had been filed away since 1944, and he was appalled to learn that the Connecticut State Police had never acted on the findings in any way. Within five days of Little Miss 1565's burial, the people of Connecticut could have been given the opportunity to identify her and return her—if only symbolically—to her grieving family. Sadly, that had never been done. Now, in light of what he had discovered, Rick felt it was his duty to continue his quest until he could fulfill the moral obligation that should have been fulfilled by his predecessors.

A Matter Of Degree

Over the course of his re-investigation, Rick had photocopied and compiled thousands of pages of documents, most of which had come from the circus fire archive at the Connecticut State Library. Having reached a plateau in his quest for proof of Little Miss 1565's identity, Rick knew he needed additional material to support his theory. As he had done so many times before, he started his review from the very beginning, poring over each page of the accumulated file in the hope of uncovering vital evidence. Rick had conducted his initial examination of State Police Commissioner Hickey's records with a two-pronged purpose in mind—to find the cause of the fire, and to determine the actions taken by Hickey during the state investigation. This time, he tore through the records seeking clues to Little Miss 1565's identity—and the possible connections to the missing child known as Eleanor Cook.

After several weeks of analysis, Rick discovered a state police report that he had never seen before. Ironically, it was attached to the official report created by Commissioner Hickey in 1945, but Rick had apparently overlooked it during his first examination of the record. The report was simple and straightforward, written by a state police trooper who had been ordered to participate in the search for missing victims of the circus fire on July 7, and who then continued the mission throughout the day on July 8. The trooper's name was Sam Freeman, the same officer who had assisted Emily Gill in the search for her missing niece. Rick had hoped that Trooper Freeman had written a report of his actions during the aftermath of the Ringling blaze, and he was gratified to have found it. As he read, Rick realized that Freeman's report was the document that would seal the identity of the child known as Little Miss 1565. *(See Appendix)*

While searching for her missing niece at Municipal Hospital on the afternoon of July 7, Emily Gill was told by a nurse's aid named Mrs. Brodigan, and by a social worker named Margaret Moody, that a young girl answering Eleanor's description had died around six o'clock on July 6. Emily and her brother, Ted Parsons, had searched the armory that night in an attempt to locate and identify the little girl they loved. When they viewed the body of 1565, they stated that the child was not their niece. On the evening of July 7, Emily made another attempt to identify victim 1565. Once again, she declared that the child was not a member of her family.

Within an hour of that declaration, Trooper Freeman was assigned to assist Emily by making the rounds of funeral homes that had received the children who had died in the circus fire.

The search of a half dozen sites in the capitol area took several hours and lasted into the night. While Freeman and Emily were viewing the children whose deaths had broken the hearts of dozens of Hartford families, the bodies of the last unidentified victims—including Little Miss 1565—were taken from the state armory to the Hartford Hospital morgue. The transfers were completed by ten o'clock. Freeman's report made it clear that he and Emily did not return to the armory at any time on the night of July 7. Even if they had, they would not have found 1565 lying there, and no armory official would have suggested that they visit the Hartford Hospital morgue, since Emily had previously declared that 1565 was not a member of her family. The emotional toll from the search had left Emily exhausted, so Freeman drove her back to the Marshall Street apartment, where she said she would meet other members of her family. Along the way, Freeman asked for a photograph of Eleanor, explaining that a picture of the child might help him gather more information from those who might have seen her in the hours after the fire.

Two men—Sam Freeman and Rick Davey—united by their commitment to justice, separated by the passage of fifty years, became captivated by the photograph of a beautiful little girl whose eyes spoke directly to them, reaching into their hearts, stimulating thoughts of love and loss. Driven by the need to find the little girl and restore her to her anxious family, Trooper Freeman refused to give up his mission. Armed with the photograph, he returned to Municipal Hospital just before midnight on July 7 to continue the search for Eleanor. Most of the nurses who were on duty that night had been relieved, but those who had served during the aftermath of the fire remembered the little girl, and they remembered how beautiful she was—even as death approached. Freeman was unable to reach Mrs. Brodigan, but he called Margaret Moody at her Winsted home. Mrs. Moody told him that his description of the little girl in the photo matched the child who had died all alone on July 6. Just before two o'clock in the morning on July 8, Freeman left Municipal Hospital and drove home for some badly needed rest.

A few hours later, Freeman returned to duty at state police headquarters. As the day shift began, he showed the family photo of Eleanor Cook to police officers who had been assigned to the armory during the identification process on the day of the fire. Two of the officers, John Ring and Charles Casalengo, were certain that the child in the photograph was the same little girl whose body had been at the armory until Friday night, and then transferred to Hartford Hospital. Accompanied by Officer Ring, Freeman went to the morgue and spoke to the medical examiner about the missing child. After seeing the family photograph, Dr. Weissenborn said he believed that Little Miss 1565 was Eleanor Cook.

Freeman's report verified that the unidentified child in the Hartford Hospital morgue on July 8 was Victim 1565. The report revealed that Freeman had obtained confirmations of identity from Margaret Moody, Officers Ring and Casalengo, and from Dr. Weissenborn. With those four confirmations in hand, Freeman contacted the nurse's aid, Mrs. Brodigan, who agreed to come to the morgue to view the unidentified child. When she arrived, the nurse's aid made a positive identification of Victim 1565 and the clothes the little girl had been wearing when Brodigan treated her on July 6. Confident that he had compiled the evidence necessary to certify the identification of the little girl, Freeman decided to contact Emily Gill. He was aware that Emily had twice denied that the child was her missing niece, but Freeman was convinced that the emotional pressure of the moment had made it difficult for the fearful woman to accept the death of a child she loved. Freeman believed that identification was possible and imminent, so he was determined to provide the opportunity for Emily to view Little Miss 1565 for a third and final time.

Although the call from Trooper Freeman offered mixed news for Emily, she agreed to travel to the hospital with him. If the kindhearted officer was right about the little girl in the morgue, then Emily would have to face the reality of Eleanor's death, and she would bring the sad news to her sister and the entire family. If Freeman was wrong about her identity, Emily would have to live with the agony of doubt and uncertainty, most likely forever. Regardless of the personal consequences, she accepted her familial responsibility.

When Emily arrived at the hospital, Dr. Weissenborn was waiting for her. The gangly physician with oversized features and an abrupt manner had been overworked since the circus fire occurred, so his introduction was brief. Dr. Weissenborn explained that he was about to show Emily the body of a child, and that he believed the child to be her niece. All she was being asked to do was to glance at the little girl for the purpose of identification. The words were a mere formality, of course, intended to prepare the woman for the gruesome task that had been set before her. When the sheet was lifted, Emily recoiled. The child on the table appeared to be Eleanor, but Emily remained unsure. This was the same little girl that she had seen at the armory twice on the night of the fire, and she simply could not force herself to state that Little Miss 1565 was her missing niece. Although the physical similarities were striking, Emily said she was reluctant to make an identification because she thought Eleanor had eight permanent upper teeth.

Before reading any further, Rick paused to consider the implications of Emily Gill's claim. She had previously described her niece as a child of eight, and she had stated that the child was 52 inches tall—an anatomical improbability. In the presence of Trooper Freeman and Dr. Weissenborn, Emily also asserted that Eleanor had eight permanent upper teeth. Rick was not an expert in anatomy or evolution, but he knew that symmetry was a necessity in human development. A child with eight permanent upper teeth would also progressively develop eight permanent lower teeth, for a total of sixteen—and Rick's research had revealed that children between the ages of six and eight do not have sixteen permanent teeth. So, he reluctantly concluded that Emily Gill had been incorrect about Eleanor's teeth, just as she had been incorrect about her niece's height.

The report indicated that, as Emily studied the little girl lying naked beneath the sheet, those who witnessed the viewing became aware that she was struggling to maintain her composure. Seconds later, Dr. Weissenborn stepped in to assist her with the identification. Taking his cue from Emily's claim that her niece had eight permanent upper teeth, he opened the dead child's mouth and revealed that she had "four second upper teeth and four second lower teeth," for a total of eight. He also asked if Emily could identify the little girl by the dental work that had been done. Struggling to contain herself, Emily did her best to remember. It still seemed to her that Eleanor had eight upper teeth, not four. Everything else appeared to be right—except for the teeth. In every other respect, Emily was inclined to say that the little girl in the morgue was her niece.

Freeman reported that Dr. Weissenborn encouraged Emily to obtain a dental chart from Eleanor's dentist, but the family was unable to do so because the dentist was traveling in Canada. A distraught and disappointed Emily Gill left the hospital without having fulfilled the responsibility that her family had asked her to accept, but she would not be faulted by those who loved her. They would join in the belief that Honey had been lost, and that the time had come for the remaining family to heal.

Recognizing that Emily had been operating under a severe emotional strain and that she had become indecisive, Dr. Weissenborn declared her "incompetent to identify the body of Eleanor Cook." Rick noted Freeman's language with keen interest. The officer wrote that 1565 was not just any body, it was the body of a specific child—Eleanor Cook—and she had not been identified. Freeman's subtle reference was vitally important because it implied that Emily Gill's indecision had been the only impediment to identification on July 8. Although Dr. Weissenborn had hoped to identify the little girl in the morgue before releasing her for burial, he was forced to list her by the number she had been assigned when she arrived at the armory. In the wake of that decision, Little Miss Fifteen Sixty Five was abandoned to anonymity.

TWENTY SIX

When Rick contemplated the meaning and ramifications of the Freeman report, he began to realize that the evidence he had accumulated over the course of nine years would lead a reasonable person to conclude that Little Miss 1565 and Eleanor Cook were the same child. For the first time since Rick's quest began, he believed that an identification was possible, and that he would be able to bring an end to the mystery of the missing girl once and for all. Before moving ahead, however, he paused to reflect on the work done by State Trooper Sam Freeman. Rick owed a debt of gratitude to a diligent officer who had taken the time to record the events as he experienced them, a scrupulous process that opened the way to the truth about a lost child's identity. There was a touch of sorrow involved, since Rick was aware that Freeman had not lived to see the restoration of Little Miss 1565's name. The truth would have been bittersweet, since Freeman had been forced to close the case on July 8, 1944—even though he was certain that the beautiful little girl in the morgue could have been returned to her family.

Rick's ongoing review of the official records revealed that there were others in the state police community who believed they could resolve the issue of Little Miss 1565's identity, but their efforts had been unsuccessful. In mid-April 1956, a fledgling state police trooper secretary named Anna DeMatteo, a former nurse, compiled a report that she hoped would assist state authorities in making an official identification of Little Miss 1565.

A Matter Of Degree 247

The information contained in the report derived primarily from DeMatteo's friendship with twenty-year-old Donald Cook, with whom she had worked in 1955 at the New Haven County Home, a state facility for orphaned children. DeMatteo could not resist the impulse to investigate, albeit superficially, the information that had come to her through the intervention of fate. Rick recognized that some elements of her convoluted narrative were indeed accurate, while other elements seemed to have little or no bond with the truth. He trusted that the rookie trooper must have had the best intentions, but her report consisted mostly of her personal recollections, rather than real evidence.

During the summer in which DeMatteo and Don Cook worked together, DeMatteo learned that the entire Cook family had attended the circus on July 6, and that Don's mother "had been severely burned about the legs and still bore the scars" from the fire. DeMatteo reported that Don had also mentioned that he managed to escape from the tent that day. Most important of all, Don had stated his belief that "the little girl whose grave is [decorated] with flowers yearly was his little sister." DeMatteo wrote that "Mildred Cook [had] suffered a nervous collapse due to the emotional shock and injuries sustained," and she added that the "home situation was not too ideal" for Mildred and her children.

Laboring under the assumption that Don's brother, Edward, was still alive in 1956, DeMatteo went on to write that "after the fire, the boys were sent to live with relatives" in Massachusetts. She also wrote that she "could not remember the reason Donald gave for his mother's failure to identify the child's body." DeMatteo reported that Don's younger sister was Little Miss 1565, the child who had never been identified. DeMatteo's recollection was based on Don's prior description of the sister he had not seen since the day of her death, eleven years earlier. DeMatteo wrote that the little girl was "about five or six years old" and that she had "long and blondish hair." From Rick's perspective, the description of the child seemed to match that of Eleanor Cook—except for the issue of age.

On April 16, DeMatteo discussed her recollections with her commanding officer, who advised her to contact Lt. Frank Chameroy of the State Police Bureau of Identification. That day, a mutual friend contacted Chameroy's superior, Captain Shaw, who later ordered Chameroy to show

DeMatteo the file photos of Little Miss 1565, as well as the clipping of her hair. Inexplicably, Shaw told her to "keep [her information] confidential for reasons of discretion," adding that a subsequent police review would be done. Shaw's use of such a cryptic phrase caught Rick Davey's eye as he read the file. Knowing how Commissioner Hickey had conducted himself in the wake of Robert Segee's confession six years before the DeMatteo inquiry, Rick found the state police captain's request for confidentiality more than mildly intriguing. He wondered why the state police remained sensitive about the identity of the little girl who had become the symbol of the Ringling tragedy.

Two days after receiving Shaw's memo, DeMatteo presented a three-page report to her supervisor, who submitted the file to a senior officer for review. The case report was then sent to Hartford Police Chief Michael Godfrey for his consideration. On April 23, in a memo addressed to "Mrs. DeMatteo," her supervisor wrote that Chief Godfrey had reviewed the case report and stated that "he personally talked with Mrs. Cook at the time of the fire." Godfrey had stated that Don Cook "must be misinformed because Mrs. Cook did lose a child in the Hartford circus fire, but it was a boy" rather than a girl, and that an "identification [of her son] was made." In light of Godfrey's opinion of the case report, the state police major who had overseen the progress of the review wrote that "the matter can now be considered closed," and he ordered DeMatteo to return the "photographs and other physical evidence" she had been given. With her original investigative plan shattered, DeMatteo took no further action.

Rick had found DeMatteo's 1956 inquiry unfocused in its methods and questionable in its results, so he was not surprised that she had decided to abandon any further investigation after being rebuffed by her superiors. When he read that DeMatteo had decided to revisit the case seven years later, albeit with the same meager result, Rick was astonished. Working with a senior state police trooper named Dunbar in 1963, DeMatteo sifted through the original missing person reports as well as the casualty lists compiled at the city hospitals in 1944. She uncovered the fact that Mildred and Edward Cook had been placed in Room 505 at Municipal Hospital, and she learned that the other children had been listed as missing on the July 6 reports compiled at the Brown School. The address for all three children was shown to be 4 Marshall Street, their mother's address in Hartford.

DeMatteo also learned that, as of nine o'clock on July 10—the morning of the funeral for the six unidentified victims—both Eleanor Cook and Judy Norris were still listed as missing. This fact led DeMatteo to the conclusion that she might finally have the means to identify both 1565 and 1503. As part of her renewed mission, DeMatteo searched the public record in an effort to find Don Cook, the young man who had triggered her interest in the first place. She learned that Don had enlisted in the Army in 1955, shortly after DeMatteo's inquiry ended in failure, but she managed to locate him through a check of motor vehicle records.

Don was living in Collinsville, Connecticut at the time of DeMatteo's second investigation. When she contacted him, he willingly agreed to meet with his former co-worker. During the interview, DeMatteo showed Don the morgue photo of 1565, a picture he had never seen before. He and his family had been shown many photos of the unidentified child, but this one offered more clarity than any other picture. Aware that his mother had already invested nearly twenty years in recovery from the loss of two children and the physical effects of the blaze itself, Don was reluctant to do or say anything that would damage his mother's fragile emotional state. Although he was fairly certain that the child in the morgue photo was his lost sister, he encouraged DeMatteo to meet with Marion Parsons—the aunt with whom the Cook children had lived—for confirmation.

When first contacted by DeMatteo, Marion expressed no desire to see the photo because she was certain that the girl in the morgue was not her lost niece. Prevailing on Marion nevertheless, DeMatteo obtained an interview. When she was presented with the morgue photo, Marion was reduced to tears. She claimed never to have seen the picture before, and she was convinced that she had never seen that particular child during her own visit to the armory on July 7. Recovering her emotions, Marion stated her belief that the little girl in the photograph was her missing niece, and she believed that other members of the Parsons family would agree with her.

DeMatteo then showed the picture to Marion's sister-in-law, Dorothy. At first glance, she agreed that the child in the picture was Eleanor Cook. A few minutes later, however, she changed her mind. The mixed results of the dual interview left DeMatteo without an identification, so the meeting ended. In the hours that followed, a decision would be made by the Parsons women that was consistent with their long-held belief in family unity: they would jointly declare that the child in the photo was not Eleanor Cook. They said that their decision to relegate Little Miss 1565 to continued anonymity was preferable to the emotional damage that would be imposed upon Mildred Cook and Emily Gill if the Parsons women identified the little girl as their niece.

The denial of Little Miss 1565 troubled Rick Davey very deeply. He held a photo of the beautiful child in his hands—the very photo that DeMatteo had shown the Parsons family—and he was unable to comprehend how anyone could reject the possibility of an identification and a restoration of their own flesh and blood, no matter what the reason. Although Rick was suddenly inclined to abandon his examination of the DeMatteo file altogether, he forced himself to continue, if only to be certain that he had not missed a single shred of salient evidence.

DeMatteo's last hopes for an identification of 1565 had been dashed, but she held on to the belief that she could still identify 1503. After all, there were two unidentified children, and there were two young girls on the missing persons listings. Since 1565 had not been identified by the Parsons family, DeMatteo imposed her own pretzel logic on the last phase of her inquiry. Perhaps Eleanor Cook was actually Victim 1503, and Judy Norris was actually Victim 1565. That switch might work, especially since the entire Norris family had been killed in the circus fire, leaving no one behind to dispute an assertion that Judy was Little Miss 1565. DeMatteo also believed that the additional height of 1503 would more closely match the eight-year-old Eleanor—especially since newspaper accounts had previously asserted that she was taller than the average girl her age.

In DeMatteo's original inquiry, she had relied on the accuracy of Don Cook's recollections when she concluded that 1565 was about five or six years old. The state's speculative medical and dental records at the time of the blaze had estimated the age of 1565 as six, and the medical examiner had described Mildred as being twenty when she was actually 38. In 1963, however, DeMatteo declared Eleanor's age to be eight. Rick was led to assume that the listed age for the child was correct, since DeMatteo had the benefit of cooperation from the Parsons family. However, Rick believed that DeMatteo was blatantly wrong in her assumption that the two unknown female victims were similar enough to each other as to be interchangeable. Rick's own analysis of the death certificates refuted that assumption. *(See Appendix)*

In the 1944 missing person report filed for Judy Norris, the child was described as six years old. In contrast, 1503 was described in her death certificate as a nine-year-old female, approximately three feet eleven inches tall, weighing about 55 pounds, with eight permanent teeth, and having "brown hair with a reddish glow." During DeMatteo's 1963 inquiry, she found herself with two unknown children and two identification numbers, and she inexplicably concluded that it was simply a matter of assigning the proper number to the proper child, giving each one a name in the process. However, in order to unify her assumption of crossed identity, she ignored the information listed on 1503's death certificate. Had she studied those details, she might have realized that Judy Norris and Eleanor Cook did not match 1503 in any meaningful way, especially given the extreme charring that had damaged the body.

DeMatteo's sloppy investigative work led to the conjecture that 1565 must have been Judy Norris, even though 1565 was a child of slightly smaller stature than the missing six-year-old. DeMatteo also apparently disregarded Tom Barber and Ed Lowe's failed attempts to identify Little Miss 1565 as Judy. The detectives had spoken with those who knew the missing girl, and every person they questioned categorically rejected the morgue photo of 1565 as a photograph of Judy. Rick came to believe that, if left to her own devices in 1963, DeMatteo would have misidentified Little Miss 1565 as Judy Norris, and she also would have misidentified 1503 as Eleanor Cook.

In contrast, the evidence that Rick had gathered and reviewed over the course of his re-investigation suggested that Judy Norris had been claimed by a family other than her own. That assertion was supported by comments contained in the missing person report filed in July 1944. Judy had been reported missing by her paternal aunt, Mrs. John Holden, who scoured the armory in the hours after the fire. The report indicated that "the [family] dentist accompanying Mrs. Holden insisted that the child was not in the armory." Rick believed that, if Judy had been misidentified, her body might well have been gone by the time those who knew her best began their search for her. The documentary evidence that Rick had analyzed led him to conclude that Little Miss 1565 was Eleanor Cook, and that 1503—a much larger child than either Eleanor or Judy—would always be unknown. As confident as he was, however, he knew he would have to find a member of Eleanor's family in order to prove his theory beyond a reasonable doubt.

In late November 1990, Rick wrote a letter to Don Cook, whose last known Connecticut address was in Unionville. In the letter, Rick explained his interest in the Hartford circus fire, and he described the essence of his nine-year inquiry into the tragic blaze. He also declared his belief that Little Miss 1565 was Don's missing sister, Eleanor. To bolster his assertion, Rick described a photograph he had uncovered that showed three children standing by the front steps of their house, and he asserted that it was a picture of the Cook children in happier times. He closed the letter by inviting Don to contact him. At that point, all Rick could do was wait, and patience had never been one of his virtues.

Twenty Seven

The letter came several weeks later, and it was postmarked from Iowa. Rick frequently allowed mail to accumulate for days before taking the time to open it, so he had no idea what the envelope contained. Given that he had no friends or relatives in the Midwest, he was initially inclined to toss the letter away without reading it, but curiosity got the best of him. He despised junk mail of all kinds, so an unsolicited offer would make its way into the shredder in a matter of seconds. In this case, however, the letter offered the answer that Rick had hoped would come.

Don Cook apologized for having taken so long to respond. He and his family had only recently moved to Iowa, and it had taken some extra time for his forwarded mail to reach him. Don was pleased to have gotten Rick's letter, especially since its contents had intrigued him, and he made it clear that Rick was correct in his assumption that the picture he had come across was a photo of the Cook children. Don remembered the circumstances vividly, including the fact that he was astride his bicycle when the picture was taken. He even went so far as to urge Rick to take a closer look at the photo. If it was the one Don had in mind, there would be a small lunch box in the lower right hand corner.

Without reading any further, Rick raced to his den and retrieved the picture. Just as the letter had predicted, the lunch box was resting on the ground, an artifact that served to validate the photo—and Don Cook's credibility. As Rick read on, he realized that Don had an astonishing capacity to recall the history of his family. Rick wondered whether, because of a tragic awareness of how fleeting the lives of loved ones can be, Don had developed the ability to remember vital aspects of the time they had spent together, trapping what was most precious before it slipped away forever.

As the letter progressed, Don revealed how gratified he was that Rick had undertaken a re-investigation of the Hartford circus fire. Ever since the tragedy occurred, Don was certain that Little Miss 1565 was his missing sister, but he had been consistently unable to convince any state authority to accept his opinion. As it happened, Don was planning a trip back to his hometown in Massachusetts to visit his mother, so he urged Rick to call him in Iowa so they could schedule a mutually convenient meeting. Without hesitation, Rick called the number listed in the letter. Minutes later, he and Don Cook held the first of many long conversations in which Rick's questions would be answered—and the identity of Little Miss 1565 would be restored.

The initial meeting was awkward, as anyone would have expected. Two men who did not know each other had suddenly been thrust into the same space, bonded together by their desire to resolve the mystery of a little girl's identity. Neither man was accustomed to the intervention of strangers, especially when they wove their way into matters of family. Don was an affable salesman from Iowa who preferred to maintain his privacy, while Rick was a wary investigator from Connecticut whose job entailed the discovery of secrets that men would rather not reveal. Both men were instantly aware of the need to suspend their customary conduct in order to gain each other's trust, and to accomplish the mission that had brought them together in the first place—the identification of a beautiful little girl who had died in a tragic and unnecessary fire nearly fifty years earlier. A shared purpose had changed the lives of both men, and that fact made them feel more like friends than strangers when their meeting began.

Don explained that the Ringling circus fire had a devastating impact on his family. His mother had vacillated between hope and despair in the years following the blaze. In addition to a long and excruciating recovery from extensive burns, she was forced to come to grips with the death of one gentle son and the uncertain fate of her only daughter. Over time, Mildred came to accept the finality of her children's death. The fact that Don was the sole surviving child left him with a special responsibility to protect his mother, and he had accepted it. Each year, he would take her on holiday trips—especially for the Fourth of July—so her mind would be occupied, locking out painful thoughts of the fire. Don would also ensure that articles touching on the subject of the circus fire were trimmed from newspapers and magazines before they were given to his mother. Her pain eventually subsided, but her memories grew stronger, emerging without warning, threatening to displace the happiness that she had tried to cultivate in recent years. In order to suppress images of loss and loneliness, Mildred turned to repetitious daily activities and sing-song rhyming games that took her away from her memories long enough for fog to settle over the island of sadness to which her guilt-ridden spirit had been banished.

Rick introduced the issues of interest that he hoped would lead to the identification of Little Miss 1565. He explained that he agreed with Don's opinion that the child was his sister, but several key questions remained, and they had to be answered. He revealed that he had found a state police report written on July 8, 1944 that provided a chain of identifications by those who had treated Little Miss 1565 on the day of the fire. The report made it clear that the child had eight permanent teeth, but her Aunt Emily had disputed that fact. Left with no other choice, the medical examiner had later declared Emily incompetent to make an identification.

Don had never been told about the Freeman report, but he immediately understood its implications. He explained that, unknown to anyone outside the Parsons family, both he and his sister had come down with a disorder called rickets in their early years, the result of a vitamin D deficiency arising from Mildred and Wesley's inability to provide the nutritional support their children desperately needed. As a result, Eleanor's bone growth and tooth development had been delayed. Although she was eight years old at the time of the fire, her six-year molars had only recently come in. She had lost eight teeth in the two years prior to the summer of 1944. Each tooth had been carefully tucked away in its own envelope, and Eleanor had uniquely marked each envelope. As the years went by, no one in the family ever mentioned Emily's attempt to locate her missing niece. The search had ended in failure at the Hartford Hospital morgue. The

Parsons family never obtained a second dental chart because, by the time the dentist returned from Canada, Little Miss 1565 had been buried and Eleanor's funeral had taken place. Additional inquiries about the missing child would have rekindled painful memories, which would have served no useful purpose. Compassion operated against further action, so doubts gave way to resignation.

Years later, Judith Lowe's letter claiming misidentification was discovered by a *Hartford Courant* reporter while he was compiling research for a feature to be published on the anniversary of the circus fire. Hoping for confirmation, the reporter contacted the Berman family, who vehemently denied Mrs. Lowe's assertions. Given the family's denial, the reporter was led to the conclusion that Little Miss 1565 might be the missing Eleanor Cook. With that possibility in mind, he contacted Mildred for her reaction. The elderly woman was aware of the pain that would be inflicted upon her sister if a report of a misidentification were published. Emily would never be able to live with herself if she learned that she had relegated her own flesh and blood to isolation and anonymity in a community cemetery. Although an announcement of misidentification would have brought closure to the case, Mildred pleaded with the reporter to delete the claim from his story. As with so many other family decisions, Mildred's choice protected the living, and that was the Parsons way.

Don's explanation supported Rick's theory of identification, but he was still troubled by the discrepancy in the published reports about the clothes that Eleanor was said to have worn on the day of the fire. Rick was concerned that the conflicting reports might destroy his theory completely, leaving no chance that Little Miss 1565 would be identified. However, Don stated that he and the other children had been with their mother for three days prior to the circus fire, and no one else in the family—including Emily Gill—had seen them in that time. The significance of that statement resided in the fact that Mildred had bought each of her kids some new clothes for the holiday, and they were wearing those clothes on July 6. Given that Wesley had never been able to provide for his family, Mildred took great pride in having purchased clothes for her children. Eleanor might well have owned a plaid playsuit, but she was wearing a flowered dress on the day she died—and only Mildred and the kids would have seen that dress. Even if clothes had been sent to the coroner's office after Eleanor's death, only Mildred would have recognized them. During the period of time in which Little Miss 1565 was being sought, Mildred was in a coma, unable to offer proof that the child who had died alone on July 6 was her daughter.

Over the course of the meeting, Rick was able to compare Don's facial features with those of Little Miss 1565, and he noted some distinct similarities. Their ears seemed a bit larger than average and they shared the same linear ridge along the base of the lobes. A thorough review of family photographs confirmed those similarities, but Rick went even further in order to satisfy himself. He analyzed the last pictures ever taken of Eleanor, using the same caliper measurements that had been applied to the morgue photo of Little Miss 1565. When compared, the feature measurements were identical.

Don was able to put another misconception about Eleanor to rest during the meeting, and he did so voluntarily. He noted that a number of published accounts about his missing sister had asserted that Eleanor's hair had been cut short prior to the summer holiday in 1944. That claim had called the identity of Little Miss 1565 into question at the time, since the child had shoulder-length blonde hair. However, Don distinctly remembered that Eleanor had not cut her hair that summer, and that fact added to his belief that Little Miss 1565 was his sister. When Rick mentioned that Dr. Lincoln Opper, the state scientist who had conducted a hair analysis nine days after the fire, had found that the sample from Little Miss 1565 matched the sample from Eleanor's hair brush, Don was stunned. He had never been told of the analysis before. If he had known about those results, he would have pressed for an identification when Anna DeMatteo interviewed him in 1963.

The reference to DeMatteo's investigation brought Rick to the most important issue of all—height. Eleanor had been described in news accounts as being "tall for her age." During the search for the missing girl, Emily Gill had gone so far as to assert that her niece was "four feet four," a wild claim for which there was no anatomical foundation. Years later, Anna DeMatteo had based her own assumption of Eleanor's height on a combination of Emily's claim and the published reports, and had then attempted to prove her identification theory on the basis of that assumption. Rick, on the other hand, had researched the facts relating to Little Miss 1565 and Eleanor Cook so thoroughly as to be convinced that all previous height descriptions were wrong—with one exception. The death certificate for 1565 listed her height as "three feet ten," or 46 inches, which would easily coincide with a female child between the ages of six and eight. However, the death certificate established a difference of six inches between opposing descriptions, an enormous discrepancy that could not be explained by chance. For Rick's theory of identity to be accepted as valid, he would need proof that Eleanor was not as tall as she was previously said to be.

Don immediately rejected the claims of Eleanor's extreme height. He went on to offer support for Rick's assertion that Eleanor and Little Miss 1565 were one and the same child by stating that his sister was shorter than an average girl her age. Since their younger brother, Edward, had the benefit of proper nutrition from the earliest time in his life, he had not suffered from rickets. Don stated that, because of mildly delayed development, Eleanor was approximately the same height as Edward at the time of the circus fire. In fact, people who were introduced to the children were often surprised that Eleanor was two years older than she appeared. Don even remembered that their neighbor and childhood friend, Ron Tolson, had remarked on Eleanor's stature in the years following the tragedy. Still, Don acknowledged that the published age and height assessments held sway over state officials, extending to DeMatteo during her second inquiry in 1963.

On a hunt for proof, Don gathered a group of family photos from the latter part of 1943, and displayed them for analysis. Several of the shots showed the three children standing together at their home in Southampton, where they were often posed in front of a picket fence that surrounded the property. Don remembered that the fence was three feet high, which helped demonstrate the relative heights of the three Cook children in the late fall of 1943.

In another shot, which served as the family's Christmas postcard that year, the children were digging in the garden. Given the approximate height of the fence, Don estimated that Eleanor stood about 44 inches tall—exactly the height that could have led to a semantic error in Emily's description of her niece—near the end of 1943. As a stickler for accuracy, Don later derived an even more definitive way to determine his sister's height.

Edward, Honey, and Don near their home in Southampton.

PHOTO COURTESY OF DON COOK

The Christmas card picture from 1943.

PHOTO COURTESY OF DON COOK

While studying the photo of himself and his siblings as they stood in front of their home, he noted that there were two steps and several rows of siding which served as the background for the shot. During his stay in Southampton, Don decided to measure the architectural elements in the photo in order to make an accurate comparison of Eleanor's height. First, he measured the two front steps at the Parsons homestead and found that they were seven inches and nine inches respectively, for a total of sixteen inches. He also noted that each row of siding was eight inches high. Since he estimated that the top of Eleanor's head was approximately four inches above the third row of siding, Don added the height of the steps and the height of the siding together and concluded that his sister could not have been more than 44 inches tall in the fall of 1943.

The photo used by Don Cook to confirm his sister's height.

PHOTO COURTESY OF DON COOK

From Rick Davey's perspective, the measurement was a master stroke of investigative work. The calculation disposed of the theory that Eleanor had been tall for her age, and it eliminated the six-inch discrepancy in the reports—a discrepancy that could not have been explained in a child with normal pituitary function. Best of all, it dovetailed with Rick's belief that Little Miss 1565 and Eleanor were the same child. Since the death certificate for 1565 indicated that the child was "three feet ten" or 46 inches at the time of her death, it seemed reasonable to Rick that Eleanor could have grown two additional inches between the fall of 1943 and the summer of 1944. If so, her height would have been identical with that of Little Miss 1565. When Rick combined all the key physical data—facial features, height, teeth and hair—with the stunning revelations about Eleanor's clothing, he became convinced that he had sufficient proof of identity for the State of Connecticut to make a formal change in Little Miss 1565's death certificate, removing a lost child from the darkness of anonymity after 47 years.

Although he endorsed Rick's finding, the discovery was bittersweet for Don Cook. He had been given the resolution that comes with knowledge, but that knowledge was painful—his sister was never coming home. At the same time, he had acquired the responsibility to inform his mother that there was no longer any question about what had happened to Eleanor. As for the events of July 1944, Don accepted the fact that State Trooper Sam Freeman had assembled the necessary links in the chain of identification. Every witness—including Dr. Weissenborn—had agreed that Victim 1565 and Eleanor were one and the same child. However, the legal responsibility for identification had fallen to Emily Gill, whose inaccurate knowledge of her niece conflicted with the medical evidence. With the hope of identification foreclosed by a key member of the Parsons family, there was no other option open to Dr. Weissenborn than to declare that Little Miss 1565 would enter the realm of the spirit without a name.

Having finally resolved the last questions relating to Little Miss 1565's identity, Rick realized that his mission of the heart had been accomplished, so he granted himself permission to savor the moment. Ironically, his joy lasted for a few fleeting seconds, then a strange and unexpected sorrow welled within him, as if the end had come too soon. The nine-year quest that had demanded every ounce of his skill and commitment could now be described in a single sentence.

Her name was Eleanor Emily Cook, and her family called her Honey.

Twenty Eight

By November 1990, Rick had come to the conclusion that he had developed sufficient evidence to treat the Ringling circus fire as an arson, and he believed that the man who had confessed to the crime in 1950 had actually set the fire. He was also convinced that he had collected sufficient information to prove the identity of Little Miss 1565. So, he brought his initial findings to Luis Velasco. In addition to being a trusted friend, Luis was a federal agent working undercover in Hartford. After a detailed briefing on the evidence, Luis expressed his support and suggested that Rick present the case to the Serial Arson and Bomber Research (SABR) team. He explained that the elite federal unit was comprised of superior investigators and behavioral scientists from the United States and around the world, all of them assigned to analyze cases that had been brought to the Bureau's attention by investigators from every level of the law enforcement hierarchy. If the SABR team agreed with Rick's conclusions, they might be able to offer assistance in an advanced investigation—even a prosecution.

Rick had never heard of the SABR unit before, and the thought of making a formal presentation to an elite cadre of FBI investigators sent his heart racing. Nonetheless, he had spent more than eight years developing evidence in the circus fire case, and he realized that the only way to be certain that his conclusions were valid was to expose them to professional scrutiny. If he were proven right, he would have the support of America's

A Matter Of Degree

most prestigious law enforcement organization, lending credence to his assertion that the Ringling fire that had claimed the lives of 168 unsuspecting people was a deliberate act of arson, rather than an accident. Of course, if he were proven wrong, he would suffer supreme professional humiliation, something he had always sought to avoid.

Rick had a solid belief in the strength of his evidence and the validity of his conclusions, so he agreed to present his case to the SABR unit—despite the risk to his ego. Days later, Luis made the initial contact through the Justice Department's National Center for the Analysis of Violent Crime (NCAVC) in Quantico, Virginia. After learning of Rick's investigation, Special Agent Gordon (Gus) Gary of the Bureau of Alcohol, Tobacco and Firearms (ATF) was assigned to schedule and coordinate the formal review. Within two weeks, an invitation was issued for Rick to appear before the federal team in early January 1991.

As the date approached, Rick finalized his preparations—and confronted his own rising anxieties. He had compiled hundreds of photos that he intended to use for illustration purposes, and he knew they would be more easily examined and understood if placed in sequence and enclosed in special jackets. Shortly before the trip to Quantico, Rick selected some albums at a photo store and placed them on the counter. When the cashier announced the total, Rick was stunned to hear that the price was exactly $15.65. For several long seconds, he stared in silence, contemplating the meaning and effect of that number. Although he had not heard the voice of the lost child's spirit for some time, Rick interpreted the cost of the albums as a sign of her presence in his life, a guiding force that would lead him to conclude his mission.

```
        RITZ   CAMERA




000165 10 0980 11-13-90      8496
422150474  ALBUM/FR1    14.49 T
           SUBTOTAL     14.49
0001          TAX        1.16
10   CASH 1 TOTAL 1     15.65
1 AMOUNT TENDERED       20.00
           CHANGE        4.35


          THANK YOU
```

Days later, an unexpected event intervened, disrupting the well-made plan for the SABR review. Tensions escalated between the United States and Iraq, and Operation Desert Shield became Operation Desert Storm. Full-scale war had broken out in the Persian Gulf, and all American military forces and federal law enforcement agencies—including the FBI—were placed on heightened alert. Over the course of the next four weeks, Rick's presentation was postponed five times. Finally, the long-awaited meeting was confirmed for February 28.

Luis Velasco and Detective Tom Goodrow accompanied Rick to Quantico, and they drove onto the Academy grounds after ten o'clock on the night before the presentation. The emotional pressure had risen steadily throughout the trip, making Rick far too nervous to sleep, so he pored over his files until well after two the next morning. Three hours later, he was awake and anxious once again, certain that the seeds of a massive migraine had been planted deep within his nervous system.

The FBI Academy was the inner sanctum, the Mecca for investigators from around the world. When Rick and his team arrived shortly after eight o'clock, Agent Gary was waiting for them. Gus Gary was an affable man, and he did his best to make the Connecticut contingent feel comfortable as he led them through the entrance hall, across the FBI logo embedded in the stone floor, then onto an elevator that carried them down four stories, into what was described as the dungeon of the building. Eleven behavioral science professionals—the same types of forensic specialists who had consulted on the recent production of *Silence of the Lambs*—were waiting for Rick when he arrived, all of them crowded around a conference table that took up most of the floor space in the cramped office where their high-level work was performed. In the days before the meeting, Rick had allowed himself to fantasize that the FBI's professional accommodations would equal the scope of the talent gathered for the presentation, so the restricted and cluttered space took him by surprise.

The tension soared as the time came for Rick to make his presentation. He was afraid of having forgotten something during his investigation, of having made a simple mistake that would prove he had not yet earned the right to present his findings to investigators of this caliber. He wondered if they could see his hands trembling, or hear his heart beating. Every time he licked his lips, he worried that they would discover that his mouth had gone as dry as a desert.

A Matter Of Degree

Over the course of seven hours, Rick described the results of his nine-year inquiry. He illustrated his briefing with still photographs and more than 200 slides that offered graphic proof of his conclusions. As the presentation continued, members of the SABR team asked questions about fire propagation, progression patterns, and weather conditions. In every instance, Rick was prepared with an answer that satisfied his interrogators. When his briefing turned to the issue of Robert Segee's confession and the probability of arson as the cause of the tragic blaze, the team members imposed even more scrutiny on the evidence. As each aspect of the case was presented and dissected, Rick soon noticed that the team members became more animated, and that their statements of approval and agreement were offered more vigorously, all of which made Rick more confident of the outcome.

At the conclusion of the Quantico presentation, numerous members of the SABR team congratulated Rick on his presentation and expressed agreement with his findings. Some of them suggested that an arrest of Segee was still possible, despite the age of the case. They even went so far as to propose a reenactment of the circus, to be staged specifically for Segee, a plan that would require the use of elements such as banners, posters, a tanbark, sawdust, and march music, all designed to trigger the arsonist's memories and lead to a final confession.

Rick was elated by their reactions, and he enjoyed basking in the warmth of their professional support, but he felt a moral obligation to inform the SABR team that he had discussed the Ringling case with a newspaper reporter in Hartford, and that the story of his findings had already been prepared and was set for imminent publication. The importance of Little Miss 1565's identity was newsworthy in and of itself, but the revelation that the tragic fire might well have been an arson rather than an accident created a compelling public interest that had to be served, a historic and journalistic necessity to inform the people of Connecticut about what had been learned during Rick's re-investigation.

The federal investigators were somewhat surprised to learn that a story was likely to be published, but they understood the importance of the case. If the Ringling circus fire were proven to have been a deliberate human act, it would be the oldest arson case to be broken by the FBI, and a credit to the Bureau if they were to solve it. That was one of the more intriguing aspects of the investigation, and the SABR team was eager to add the circus case to its roster. They asked Rick if it would be possible to hold the story for thirty days, giving the team enough time to put their confession plan into effect. Rick understood their request, and he offered to contact the reporter in an effort to forestall publication, but he made it clear that he had no power over the media, so he could not promise that the editors of the *Hartford Courant* would agree to a postponement.

As he led Rick back to the lobby, Gus Gary congratulated him in even greater detail on the strength and effect of his presentation. Agent Gary assured him that he could expect to receive a letter of commendation which would cite the depth and accuracy of his investigation of the Ringling case, and he added that letters would be sent to superior officers in Hartford, as well. Then he confirmed the importance of the case once again, and he urged Rick to do all he could to postpone the newspaper article. Agent Gary even went so far as to offer to speak with the reporter directly, so he could explain the team's plan and underscore the importance of a postponement.

With the SABR unit's support firmly in his mind, Rick sailed back to Connecticut, more confident in his findings than ever before. He had gained the approval of the nation's most elite cadre of investigators, and their proposed plan of action might even lead to an interrogation of the man who claimed to have set the Hartford circus fire. Rick was certain that the cooperation of a key federal agency would only make his presentation of the case more viable to state officials in Connecticut, and he was eager to inform them of his accomplishments.

When Rick returned to his office, he immediately placed a call to Lynne Tuohy, the *Hartford Courant* reporter to whom he had given the story. Rick told her about the success of his FBI presentation, and he asked for an additional thirty days before publication. Lynne understood the reason for the request, but she had invested a tremendous amount of time in research and drafting, and the article was prepared to run. More and more people were learning about the story every day, so there was an increasing chance that word might leak out in an uncontrolled way, an even more damaging prospect than publication. In one final attempt to win a postponement, Rick encouraged her to call Agent Gary for more information. Ultimately, the decision to delay publication would rest with Lynne and her editor.

That afternoon, Rick brought the news of his successful FBI meeting to Fire Marshal John Vendetta. To Rick's surprise, John remained calm and collected when he heard that the SABR team had developed a plan with which to interrogate—and perhaps even arrest—the man who had confessed in 1950. John had risen to the highest levels of the Hartford Fire Department because he was an intelligent and experienced professional who was known for his self-control, but Rick had expected a more emotional reaction—if only because of their friendship. Although John was pleased with the report, Rick could tell that he remained distant, even doubtful about the outcome of the FBI's involvement. Rather than press the issue, Rick simply asked for two days of vacation time so he could recover from the grueling effects of the trip to Quantico.

Before leaving his office, Rick received a call from the Connecticut Medical Examiner's office. Dr. Wayne Carver had taken two full weeks to review and analyze the entire case file, but he had agreed with Rick's identification of Little Miss 1565. Don Cook had signed and submitted the documentation necessary to confirm that the unidentified child was his sister, so the Medical Examiner reported that he would soon issue a revised death certificate in the name of Eleanor Emily Cook. Coming on the heels of the FBI's promise of action, the news of Eleanor's formal identification sent Rick's spirits soaring. Unfortunately, his elation was short-lived.

Early the next morning, he received an urgent call from Lynne Tuohy, who said that a leak had made its way to the CBS affiliate station in Hartford, and they were preparing to report that there would soon be a break in the circus fire case. In the wake of that information, *Courant* editors had decided to move the publication date ahead, rather than risk any further postponement. Lynne was in the process of a massive rewrite, and the piece was scheduled to run on Saturday, March 9.

Rick's much-needed vacation ended with Lynne Tuohy's phone call. The publication announcement also ended any hope of satisfying the SABR team's request for more preparation time, so Rick was certain that Gus Gary and the other team members would be disappointed, if not disturbed, when the story ran. Rick called John Vendetta to report the new information, and they jointly decided that a conference should be held with high-level state and city officials. Within hours, a meeting was scheduled for Friday, March 8—less than one day before publication of the *Courant* story.

Aware that the news of Eleanor's identification was about to break, Rick felt an obligation to inform Mildred in person, so she could prepare herself for the ramifications of the story. With Don's assistance, Rick scheduled one and only one emotional meeting with Mildred immediately prior to the announcement of the findings in the circus fire case. Rick rehearsed the words he would use to introduce himself, and he agonized over how he would explain the fact that he had found Mildred's daughter—and taken away her privacy in the process. From the first moment they were together, however, Rick and Mildred were suspended within shared thoughts, as if they both knew that they had been brought together by an unseen hand, for a specific reason that did not have to be identified, so the need for words soon evaporated. In the months and years to follow, their relationship would grow, leading Mildred to think of Rick as one of her own children, a surrogate son for an old woman who had lost one little boy before he had the chance to become a man.

Mildred had kept many souvenirs of her life with Eleanor. During her meeting with Rick, she showed him scrapbooks, photos, and report cards. As he came to know the child whose spirit had already entered his heart, Rick was surprised to learn that Eleanor had missed a total of 39 half-days of school during the 1944 academic year. Despite excessive absences for illness, the little girl did exceedingly well in all her subjects. On June 3—just one month before the trip to Hartford—Eleanor and her brothers participated in a school recital. Don and Edward sang folk tunes from France and Germany, while Eleanor appeared in the first half of the show to sing *Morning Song* and *French Child's Song*. She and Edward were among a handful of students who had actually composed original melodies for the performance.

It seemed to Rick that, along with an interest in the arts, Eleanor had inherited her mother's stoic disposition. She had cut her finger while playing alone one day, but rather than cry and run for her mother, she held back her tears and placed her finger under cold water to stop the bleeding.

When Mildred found her in the kitchen, Eleanor was keeping herself calm by reciting a simple prayer she had learned in Sunday School.

God is my help in every need, God does my every hunger feed.
God walks beside me and guides the way, every moment of my day.
God is my health, I won't be sick, God is my strength, unfailing, quick.
God is my all, I cannot fear, since God and Christ and Love are near.

As their meeting ended, Mildred acknowledged hoping for nearly fifty years that Eleanor would simply "appear on the doorstep one day, without warning" and explain that she had not died, that she had just been lost, and that their life could go on, just as it had before their trip to the circus. The truth about Eleanor's loss would have wounded Mildred's sister, Emily, but her death had placed the elderly woman beyond the point of emotional injury. Although the imminent publicity surrounding Little Miss 1565's identification was certain to focus on Eleanor, Mildred wanted to be sure that Rick would not forget about Edward, her "sweet little boy," because she had grieved for him, as well. She had chosen to remember both of her lost children at Center Cemetery in Southampton. After promising to visit Mildred again in the future, Rick left the old woman to her memories—and her sorrow.

Twenty Nine

With the added confidence gained from his successful presentation to the federal team, Rick believed that his conference with state and city officials would go equally well. Among those in attendance on March 8 were Chief State's Attorney John Bailey; Dr. Wayne Carver, State Medical Examiner; Dr. Edward McDonough; Hartford Police Chief Ronald Loranger; Assistant Police Chief Jesse Campbell; Hartford Fire Chief John Stewart; Deputy State Fire Marshal David Paige; Fire Marshal John Vendetta; Detective Tom Goodrow; and Luis Velasco, Rick's ATF contact. Given the extent of Rick's inquiry into the circus fire case, he was convinced of the accuracy of his evidence. As a professional, he had no choice but to reveal the truth as it had presented itself to him throughout his nine-year mission. Still, he was aware that there could be personal consequences in his decision to publish his findings. He had engaged in a private re-investigation, then he had consulted with a federal agency and the State Medical Examiner to confirm his results and to obtain a formal change in the death certificate for Little Miss 1565. Now, his conclusions in Case No. 91-7600 would be presented to the highest-ranking law enforcement officials in Connecticut.

Despite some reluctance, Rick accepted the risk inherent in the meeting. He began by announcing that he had undertaken a new inquiry into the Ringling circus fire of 1944, and that the *Courant* was about to run a multi-page feature on his findings in the case. Simply stated, he had solved the mystery of Little Miss 1565's identity, and he had determined through professional analysis that the fire was most likely a deliberate act of arson, and he was convinced that the man who had confessed to the crime in 1950 was the same man who had set the deadly blaze. Within an instant, the mood in the room changed drastically. Assistant Police Chief Campbell demanded to know why Detective Goodrow had become involved in such an inquiry, spending department time and money on a cold case nearly fifty years old. In his own defense, Goodrow was able to state that he had only been involved in the case for a couple of months, and that he had participated while he was off duty, not on assignment.

While Campbell cooled down, State's Attorney Bailey asked whether Rick envisioned a formal prosecution of the suspect. Before Rick could answer, Detective Goodrow asserted that there was no formal plan for a prosecution, and that it would be up to Bailey to determine whether a legal proceeding were even possible. Rick Davey and John Vendetta were stunned by Goodrow's response, since it had actually been their hope that a prosecution of Segee would be considered—if only as a vindication of the public injury that the City of Hartford and its people had endured in 1944. Goodrow's unexpected declaration made that possibility more remote.

Rick could sense that some resentment had made its way into the room as the presentation continued, and the fact that a story would be published at dawn the next morning only increased the tension. Rick believed that the unspoken question of why he had not collaborated with state and city officials was running through the minds of the men gathered at the conference table. Fire Marshal Paige alluded to it obliquely when he stated that his office had never been informed that Rick had undertaken an investigation. He went on to imply that Rick was grandstanding for the benefit of his own ego, and that he was doing so at some expense to the State of Connecticut.

Controlling himself as best he could, Rick asserted that he had contacted Fire Marshal Paige's office three times to announce his inquiry, but he never received a reply. Furthermore, he knew that his actions had triggered the interest of the State Fire Marshal because one of the department's investigators later visited the Connecticut State Library to examine the files from the original 1944 State Police investigation—the very same records Rick had reviewed. The investigator had also written a departmental memo briefing the State Fire Marshal on the status of Rick's private inquiry. Fire Marshal Paige was about to respond, but John Vendetta intervened, stating that he was convinced beyond a reasonable doubt that the Ringling circus fire had been an arson. John went on to confirm his belief in Rick Davey, and in the accuracy of the findings he had presented. An irritated Paige then promised that, in order to protect the State of Connecticut from any public embarrassment caused by Rick Davey, he would simply review the findings and declare that the official cause of the Ringling blaze was undetermined, bringing an end to the inquiry once and for all.

It was becoming evident that tempers were about to flare, so the medical examiner seized the moment. Dr. Carver stated that, unless anyone in the room possessed evidence that would cast doubt on Rick Davey's claim that Little Miss 1565 was truly Eleanor Emily Cook—a claim with which Dr. Carver agreed—he was prepared to issue a revised death certificate that afternoon. Once the Medical Examiner's challenge was issued, the room fell silent and the conference came to an end. Minutes later, Fire Marshal Paige excused himself and returned to his office in Meriden.

While speaking with a reporter after the official meeting, State's Attorney John Bailey expressed shock that "Segee was never interviewed" by Connecticut authorities after the confession in 1950. "That is beyond my comprehension," he added. Bailey also promised to review the case to determine if any recourse was available to the state, but he knew that there was no established arson-murder statute in Connecticut at the time of the fire, and that fact made it unlikely that a prosecution would take place.

Prior to publication, Lynne Tuohy contacted Robert Segee at his home in an attempt to obtain the convicted arsonist's reaction to Rick's findings in the Ringling case. True to form, Segee denied any involvement in the circus blaze. "I didn't set that fire," he asserted. "It was an election year that year and I was had. I can't talk to you about this. It would destroy my life, all the life I tried to build since then. You go dragging up that stuff, I'll start suing." When Rick learned of Segee's comments, he was not surprised that the old man had recanted once again. Although he knew that Segee was referring to the Ohio election of 1950, Rick found the denial exceedingly ironic. The very same statement could have applied to the race for the governor's office in Connecticut that year, since the political figures who had supported Commissioner Hickey were concerned about their own election prospects. As it happened, John Lodge, the Republican candidate, lost the election. Rick could not help but wonder whether the outcome would have been even worse if the Republican regime were belatedly blamed for having botched the original investigation into the deadly circus blaze of 1944.

On the morning of March 9, the *Hartford Courant* ran Lynne Tuohy's story as a front-page news feature under a banner headline, with two additional pages in the body of the paper. The attention of America and the world was suddenly focused on Rick Davey's investigation and his solution of the fifty-year mystery surrounding the identity of Little Miss 1565. There was widespread public admiration for Rick's selfless nine-year quest for the truth, a personal mission that had all the earmarks of a mythical hero's journey. Media from around the world quickly swarmed the Hartford Fire Marshal's Office seeking opportunities to interview Rick. He appeared on the CBS *Morning News, The Today Show, Inside Edition* and numerous other programs in the weeks following the announcement, and articles were published in the *New York Times, Newsweek, Life Magazine* and *Reader's Digest*. The immense media attention took him by surprise. He was always a reluctant participant, refusing far more interviews than he accepted—especially those requests from celebrity journalists who sought to exploit the case, or Eleanor herself. Rather than trolling for his own personal glory and fame during each interview, Rick discussed the honor of having restored a lost child to her family.

When a somewhat stunned Mildred Cook was asked by news crews and print reporters for her maternal reaction to her daughter's identification, she answered honestly. "I think I'm relieved. I'm not really sure how I feel." She later told her son Don that she was eager to "take Eleanor out of the limelight, once and for all." Meanwhile, the public reaction to Mildred was strangely mixed. Many people expressed their sympathy for the ordeal she had endured, and for the loss of two precious children, while others were incensed by what they perceived to be her reserved reaction to an intensely emotional discovery. A media-bred audience seemed to want much more from her, and they were inflamed when their desires were denied.

Those who judged Mildred could not have known the degree to which she was still suffering over the loss of her children. The unexpected restoration of Eleanor's identity was simultaneously wonderful and heartbreaking for Mildred, who was suddenly faced with the loss of a precious and intangible commodity: hope. She told reporters that she had resorted to mind games and memory tricks to cheat painful reality out of the opportunity to intrude upon her, as it had so many times over the years, often without warning. She had convinced herself that Eleanor was not dead, and that she would come home one day. Strange as such a notion might seem, that was the hope that Mildred had harbored. With the symbolic return of her daughter, her hope was taken away.

In the days following Eleanor's identification, Mildred became distressed by the fact that the public was being introduced to her in a way that might lead them to think she was an unfeeling human being. She wondered if she had appeared unemotional during her television interview—despite Rick Davey's attempt to prepare her for media attention—and she hoped people would understand that she had "cried so many times over the years that there weren't very many tears left," especially when she was in public view. Mildred felt "only relief that the mystery had finally been solved" and that her daughter had been returned to her.

Sixty-year-old Robert Segee, wizened beyond his age, gained a different sort of notoriety after Eleanor Cook's identification was announced. Unlike Mildred, he seemed unconcerned about public opinion. The convicted arsonist appeared on *Inside Edition* in the same feature piece that focused on Rick Davey. Through a friend at the CBS affiliate in Hartford, Rick was given an advance peak at Segee's performance. When the show was fed via satellite, there were outtakes included in the pre-show signal—and they were recorded on tape for Rick Davey to view. Segee appeared on-camera in his home, which was decidedly low-rent and sparsely furnished. The old man was wearing an Indian headband and he was holding an Indian rattle. He claimed to be an Indian from Buffalo Jump, Montana rather than a potentially violent arsonist from Portland, Maine. Throughout the initial questioning, he denied having set the circus fire, but the sly smirk on his face suggested that he was enjoying the attention that the crew of a nationally syndicated television program was lavishing on him. His attitude—and his denial—infuriated Rick Davey, who resented the fact that the savvy old man was receiving publicity rather than punishment.

After the publication of the *Courant* article, an investigative reporter for the ABC affiliate station in New Haven contacted Rick's FBI source in Ohio in an effort to obtain additional data on Segee. The agent willingly provided material that found its way into the station's primetime newscast that very night. A day or two after the broadcast, Rick Davey attempted to contact his source, but he was told that the agent was no longer assigned to the FBI office in Ohio.

In the days following the publication of his findings, Rick turned his attention to the possibility of an arrest and prosecution in the circus fire case. He had compiled and presented the evidence, and the Serial Arson and Bomber Research unit had agreed with the results of his investigation. Rick had assumed that, even if there were no prosecution after so many years, the information he had obtained during his inquiry into the Ringling fire would be made available to the people, and that the truth would finally be known. He trusted that Connecticut authorities would speak out once the facts had been reviewed.

Meanwhile, Rick waited for the written confirmation that Gus Gary had promised would come. One week after the Quantico presentation, the agency's silence began to trouble Rick, who had hoped that the approval of his investigation and its findings would have arrived prior to the first conference with Connecticut officials. Reluctant as he was to make contact, Rick placed a call to Gus Gary's office, but there was no response. He placed several more calls the next day, but none of his messages were returned. Rick tried to tell himself that it was simply a matter of timing, but the seeds of doubt had been planted in his mind, making him wonder whether he would ever hear from the NCAVC.

On March 12, a second meeting was held regarding the published findings in the Ringling case. This time, a small cadre of state officials gathered around the conference table. Most important of those who attended were Chief State's Attorney John Bailey, State Medical Examiner Wayne Carver, and Luis Velasco. Dr. Carver asserted his belief that the identity of Eleanor Cook was proven to be of paramount importance to the people of Connecticut, as evidenced by the overwhelming reaction to the *Courant* feature. He went on to state that "the method used in 1944 to dispute the original identity of Eleanor Emily Cook [because] the tooth eruption pattern showed the victim was too young to be Eleanor was consistent with technology [of the time], but is now out of date because x-rays might have shown adult teeth still below the gum line." That statement bolstered Rick, who believed all along that any issues relating to Little Miss 1565's teeth were resolved by the Connecticut State Police report discovered during Rick's re-investigation. As the meeting drew to a close, the undercover ATF agent announced that the FBI VICAP unit had placed Segee under suspicion in a series of recent killings, and he warned that the suspect's identity should not be released during media interviews.

The only official promise made in the glare of the intense media scrutiny triggered by Rick's published findings was that there would be a new state inquiry. On the afternoon of March 12, the State Fire Marshal's Office and the Office of the Chief State's Attorney announced in a joint press conference that they would begin an "investigation into the cause of the fire, but [they would] not investigate the fire itself." Members of the media who had gathered for the press conference that day were not certain they had heard the statement correctly. They found it difficult to comprehend the purpose of the investigation as it had been proposed, so they asked for clarification. Rather than explain their intentions, state officials simply repeated their announcement verbatim, leaving all of its semantic implications intact.

Rick knew instinctively that something had gone wrong. Experience told him that any state investigation, regardless of its scope or intentions, could easily consume two years or more before formal results were published. Even then, there would be no way to predict the outcome. The state's public reaction to Rick's findings suggested that political wounds had been opened, wounds that could take a long time to heal. State investigators were free to dispose of his conclusions in the Ringling case and, if they did, Rick's investigative reputation would be left in limbo. At that moment, he knew that his involvement in the circus fire case had ended forever, and that history would have to judge the value of his work—and his reputation.

Nine years earlier, he had made a promise to the spirit of a little girl, and that was the only promise that mattered to him now. His true goal had been fulfilled: he had restored the identity of Eleanor Emily Cook, and he had sent her home to her family. In the process, Rick had brought emotional resolution to an old woman who had lived with her scars, her memories, and her self-inflicted guilt for too long. All told, those things offered more compensation than most investigators would ever receive in the course of their careers.

The official state reaction to Rick's investigation left him unsettled. Given that the proposed review of his findings could take two years or longer, he turned his attention to the SABR confirmation, which he hoped he would receive at any moment. After three weeks of anxious waiting, Rick placed another call to Gus Gary. Once again, there was no response. With his doubts rising, Rick decided to reach to the heart of the matter. Seeking resolution, regardless of the outcome, he asked Luis Velasco to make a back-channel call to the NCAVC for a declaration of their interest in the Ringling case. Assured that he would have an answer soon, Rick tried his best to be patient—a trait for which he had never been known.

Days later, the letter arrived. Eager as he was to know what the agency had decided, Rick placed the envelope on his desk and stared at it for several minutes before tearing it open. The two-page letter was concise, even terse. Written by an accomplished FBI profiler who would later find additional celebrity as the author of a book that lent support to John and Patsy Ramsey's claims of innocence in the death of their daughter, JonBenet, the letter made it clear that the NCAVC's SABR unit would not participate any further in Rick's investigation, and that they would not fulfill their commitment to recreate a semblance of the circus atmosphere for the purpose of interviewing Segee on suspicion of arson. Rick had hoped for an arrest and conviction on a federal charge of arson murder on behalf of the victims who died in 1944, but any chance that such an action might have been legally possible evaporated with the NCAVC decision. The letter signaled the end of Rick's inquiry, leaving little doubt that there would never be an arrest or prosecution in the Hartford circus fire case. Rick would soon come to accept the fact that Segee would not be prosecuted, but he remained bitter about the fact that the man who had caused the death of 168 people had been allowed to remain free for nearly fifty years.

The next day, Luis called to report what he had learned. Although the information was certain to be anticlimactic, given that Rick had already received the SABR team's decision, he listened carefully. Federal sources were said to have received a call in early March from an unnamed Connecticut official, presumably one whose rank demanded respect. The official requested that all action in the Ringling case, most especially any action related to the investigation or interrogation of Robert Dale Segee, be deferred. The request was interpreted as a signal that state authorities were either opposed or indifferent to Rick Davey's investigative findings, and that further promotion of those findings would somehow embarrass the State of Connecticut. With that in mind, the SABR team tabled its interest in the Ringling case—and in Segee. As difficult as it was for Luis to deliver the message, he believed that Rick would want to know the truth.

There was no way for Rick to deny that he was hurt and disappointed by the decision. He even allowed himself to get angry for a while. Then he came to the conclusion that he had one last chance to change the opinion of the federal agency which he had hoped would assist him as he addressed the ramifications of the Ringling circus fire, a deadly blaze that had changed the lives of generations of people in Hartford. Later that day, Rick wrote a letter to the NCAVC. He requested the opportunity to make a second presentation to the SABR unit, hoping to answer any residual questions or doubts they might have about the re-investigation. As with his prior requests to the agency, his letter went unanswered, leaving Rick no other choice but to accept the finality of their decision. As time went on, he grew used to the idea that all avenues of recourse were closed to him, and he realized that John Vendetta had been right to be skeptical about the likelihood of federal assistance in the circus fire case.

On June 21, the remains of Eleanor Emily Cook were quietly exhumed at dawn from Northwood Cemetery, where she had rested for 47 years. With Rick Davey standing by, Gene Kowalczyk—funeral home manager for the Talarski Maple Hill Chapel—placed the remains into a small white casket that he had provided for the child's journey home. When Eleanor was disinterred, Rick and Gene noticed that an array of permanent teeth were in place within the segments of her jaw, providing corroboration of Dr. Weissenborn's last comments about the child that even he believed was Eleanor. Rick knew that medical forensic specialists had found that the only accurate way to determine the exact number of teeth in any human skull was through a post-mortem extraction of the mandible. Although nature, rather than medical science, had performed this particular extraction, the evidence was the same: Eleanor had eight permanent teeth, the number required to declare once again that she and Little Miss 1565 were the same person. Later that day, Eleanor was taken to Southampton in preparation for a memorial service on Saturday, June 22. When the news of her departure was published, some Hartford residents expressed vigorous opposition, still claiming the child as their own, even after five decades.

The ceremony was intended to be private, a gathering of relatives who had come to Center Cemetery for a service that triggered both sadness and joy. Rick Davey, in dress uniform, stood guard while Mildred and the Parsons family honored the child they had lost so long ago. Fresh flowers covered the surface of the white coffin that lay before them—one of the many gifts and services that Gene Kowalczyk had provided at his own expense. In a brief eulogy, Rev. Robert Gardner addressed the irony of Eleanor's return. "We are here today to do what could not be done 47 years ago, to recognize the death of Eleanor Cook and the joy of her brief life. In this intense moment we say both Goodbye, and Welcome Home. At long last, we have found you." Rick Davey stood erect throughout the service, his silent vigil a statement of the bond he felt with the child whose spirit had become a constant presence in his life. Words could never convey his commitment to Eleanor, a commitment first developed while she was lost, then more firmly sealed in the days after she was found. If tears of sorrow and release had found their way to the rim of Rick's eyes, they were hidden behind reflective sunglasses.

Mildred had begun to prepare herself for the graveside experience the night before the service. As the time approached for the interment ceremony, she kept telling herself "I'm not going to cry, I'm not going to cry," just as she had recited each time she faced adversity as a young girl. When a childhood friend of Eleanor's played *Jesus Loves Me*, Mildred's throat tightened and tears fought their way into her eyes, but she never lost control. As always, no one ever saw her cry.

Standing together after the casket had been lowered into place and the Parsons family had said their goodbyes, Rick Davey, John Vendetta, Gene Kowalczyk and Tom Goodrow took turns spooning dirt from Little Miss 1565's Northwood Cemetery grave into Eleanor's final resting place in Southampton. "It just seemed that a part of Hartford should come with her," Kowalczyk said later. His insight was accurate, in that it suggested a reciprocal exchange that was wholly appropriate to the moment. A part of Hartford had come with Eleanor. And just as surely, a part of her would always remain in the hearts and minds of those she left behind in the city of hope.

Rick wrote his first letter to Mildred on November 14, 1991—eight months after the identification of Eleanor. He groped for a proper beginning for the letter, acknowledging that "the urge to write Dear Mom was overwhelming," and that a "feeling of family closeness was there in [his] head and heart." Rick revealed that he hoped the notoriety that had come from the identification of Eleanor would subside in subsequent months, and he was regretful that interest was still high, bringing attention and scrutiny to Mildred and her family. He went on to express his hope that he had done the right thing, and that he had not caused Mildred "more pain than good" by having brought her daughter home again. He closed with a promise to contact the old woman again as time went on.

In her response dated November 26 (*See Appendix*), Mildred wrote that she "would not have been offended if [Rick] had written Dear Mom" in the opening of his letter to her. "If it weren't for your tirelessness, ingenuity and your own personal feeling for Eleanor, I would not have found my daughter and had the satisfaction of bringing her home to lie next to her brother." Mildred went on to say that she remembered "a thought crossed my mind when I was told of the deaths of my two children [in 1944]: Why Go On? But then I thought of the one son I still had, and it helped to give me the strength to endure. Then I found that one must keep busy, both physically and mentally in order to avoid thoughts of tragedy.

"It would be a great satisfaction to me if that *person* in Ohio could be brought to justice, but at this late date I expect that will be impossible.

"Thank you for all your efforts in bringing this matter to a conclusion, and for keeping me informed of future events. Feel free to keep in touch with our family, whether it's on this matter or not."

Mildred signed the letter just as she had signed thousands of letters throughout her life. Then, in a gesture that revealed her emotional attachment to the man who had found her daughter, she wrote "Mom" below her signature.

A 1943 portrait of Edward, Eleanor and Don Cook.

PHOTO COURTESY OF DON COOK

Epilogue

March 17, 1991   12:03 AM

In the first frigid minutes of this late-winter morning, Rick walks along a well-manicured pathway to a cluster of shrubs surrounding a row of inlaid granite markers. He stands silent and alone, gazing down at the gravestone bearing the inscription "Little Miss 1565." The child who is buried here was born on this day 55 years earlier. Although this sacred site has been a vital part of Rick's life for nearly a decade, this is the first time he has visited.

He and the child had come to each other as numbers. Her gravestone read 1565, and his badge read 539. When added together, each of those sequences equaled 17. Eleanor Emily Cook had been born on March 17, and Robert Dale Segee—the man who admitted that he set the circus fire that claimed this child's life—had been born on September 17, and he had been arrested on May 17. Rick had sometimes wondered about the meaning that might exist in those apparent numerical coincidences, and whether the recurring number suggested that he was somehow bound to both victim and perpetrator by spiritual design. But in the years since he first entered the labyrinth of history, such questions had been washed away, replaced by an emotional commitment to Eleanor that could only be called love.

Standing near her grave for the first time in nine years, alone with his thoughts and her memory, Rick knows he could not love this little girl any more than he does at this moment—even if she were his own flesh and blood. But he is still a sensible man. He knows that, although Eleanor will always be a part of him, she belongs to her family—and to God. This is the time to say goodbye.

When his mission began, Rick had been a dedicated member of the law enforcement community, a man devoted to the legal system of which he was a part. Since that time, he had learned that the system had reneged on its promise to ensure that justice would be obtained on behalf of the victims of the Hartford circus fire. Rick considered his re-investigation of the Ringling case the culmination of his career. He knew that thousands of people had longed for justice in a variety of forms after the tragedy. There were the victims themselves, then the injured and the survivors, then the generations who followed, all of them spiritual inheritors of cultural experience, residents of the same community, all of them entitled to know the full truth about what had happened on a summer afternoon in 1944. Now, the full truth might never be known.

Rick had considered long and hard before making the visit to Eleanor's grave site. As he weighed his options, he became aware of the implications of his symbolic journey of the heart. He soon came to the realization that he had changed profoundly during the quest for Little Miss 1565's true identity. He was no longer a man of the concrete and the absolute. He could still hear a voice, but it was a voice within himself, a voice that said his work was done, and that there was no longer any reason to remain a part of the system to which he had given so much, a system that had kept dark secrets for nearly fifty years.

Hours before his trip to Northwood Cemetery, he wrote a prose poem—a letter, really—and placed it in the pocket of his uniform in preparation for this moment. Standing by the grave, he reads the letter aloud, struggling to contain his emotion. The words are his own, intended as a token of remembrance for a birthday in death, a birthday that should have been enjoyed in life. "Our only gift is the thing you once had—your name. How we all wish it could have been possible to correct a more terrible wrong and bring you back. You may join your other loved ones and members of your family, but you'll never be forgotten. I'll always love you." Rather than signing his name at the end of the poem, Rick had written his badge number instead.

When his reading is complete, Rick places a small, stuffed kitten—meant to symbolize the pets that Eleanor loved most of all—on the edge of the gravestone. Seconds later, he reaches to his heart and removes the shining shield that had been placed there twenty years earlier as an expression of his commitment to the Hartford Fire Department, and to the legal system from which he would achieve his professional identity. His decision made, he kneels at the grave and buries Badge Number 539 with the child he has come to think of as the daughter he will never know. "Happy Birthday, from one number to another."

With this gesture, Rick recognizes that he and Eleanor have been symbolically reborn, restored to the world with new identities and a new purpose. They will remain together in spirit, having become part of each other in a way that would not have been possible in the material world. As he walks from the grave, toward the rest of his life, Rick is comforted by the newfound knowledge that human beings are always more than numbers, that we are all fragile spirits who enter this world for a brief, bright moment, and then we are gone. And he knows that the extent to which we open ourselves to each other while we are here, listening to a voice that calls us to compassion, to commitment, and to love, is always a matter of degree.

PHOTO COURTESY OF RICK DAVEY

AFTERWORD

Although the fiery tragedy in Hartford was a devastating loss for the Ringling circus, the veteran entertainment troupe recovered as quickly as possible, performing under canvas from 1945 through the summer of 1956. During that time, it became clear to circus management that the increasing interest in a new entertainment medium called television would change the destiny of the traveling show. By December 1950, Ringling paid every cent that was due the victims of the circus fire. The City of Hartford, however, was never required to make any payments of any kind to the survivors of the blaze.

On July 6, 1945, Tom Barber and Ed Lowe placed flowers on the grave of Little Miss 1565—their personal commemoration of the tragedy that had claimed her life and her name one year earlier. In a statement to the press, Barber expressed disbelief that "a child like that little one could disappear from her own small world without somebody noticing that she had gone." For the next 47 years, the family that had lost her would long for the means to bring her home.

In August, granite stones were placed over the graves of the six unidentified victims in Northwood Cemetery. In a public ceremony, young Patty Murphy—a circus fire survivor whose burns were so severe she remained hospitalized for nine months after the blaze—was asked to select the stone that would soon mark the grave of Little Miss 1565. Three months later, the keystone monument for all the victims was installed as a centerpiece. Carved into its polished surface was a chalice-shaped inscription that read:

> THIS PLOT OF GROUND
> CONSECRATED BY THE
> CITY OF HARTFORD AS
> A RESTING PLACE
> FOR THREE ADULTS AND
> THREE CHILDREN WHO
> LOST THEIR LIVES IN
> THE CIRCUS FIRE
> JULY 6, 1944
>
> THEIR IDENTITY
> KNOWN BUT TO GOD

Over time, many people would expound theories about why the beautiful young victim of the Hartford circus fire was never identified. In 1946, Police Chief Michael Godfrey asserted that 1565's family had claimed the wrong body at the armory, and that their decision orphaned the child forever. Godfrey's statement implied that the family must have failed in their attempt to identify her. In the course of his investigation, Rick Davey came to believe that such a scenario was logical, even probable, but he rejected the idea that another body had been claimed in error. Instead, he believed that those medical and police personnel who had seen 1565 in the hours and days following her death had tricked themselves into assuming that she looked exactly as she did while she was alive, and that she could have been, and should have been, identified by her family. They had based their assessment on the fact that 1565 was the only unidentified victim of the Ringling circus fire who actually appeared human.

Most bodies on view at the armory had been burned beyond recognition. In contrast, Little Miss 1565 was a beautiful child with a minor char mark on her left cheek. In every other way, the authorities reasoned, she was the same child she was in life. The fact that she was not claimed by anyone led officials such as Godfrey to assume that some other body must have been claimed in her place. In fact, nothing could have been farther from the truth.

Although Little Miss 1565 was judged identifiable by those who had never known her before the fire, the young victim's family—the very people who had raised her and cared for her—found her appearance so changed as to render her unrecognizable. The weight of the evidence led Rick Davey to conclude that Emily Gill and the Parsons family, faced with the responsibility of searching for Mildred's missing daughter, understandably rejected the possibility that 1565 was their niece, Eleanor Emily Cook. In the end, the facts would support Davey's conclusion.

After serving prison sentences in Connecticut, the key circus men returned to their jobs in 1946. By that time, James Haley had become a bitter man, angered and humiliated because of the flawed legal advice that had led to his imprisonment without a reasonable defense against charges of manslaughter. Haley, the senior Ringling Brothers official who received the harshest sentence of all, made no secret of his bitterness toward the officials who had ordered him to spend "the longest eight months of [his] life on the banks of the Connecticut River" in Wethersfield.

Robert Ringling's apparent abandonment of Haley while he was in prison created a serious rift between the two men. In April 1946, Haley voted his wife's stock shares for himself, joining with John Ringling North in a successful challenge to Robert's authority and management. Although Haley and North had previously been enemies, they joined forces in order to wrest control of the circus from Robert and his team. Ironically, the circus became more profitable in the first year of Haley and North's leadership than it had ever been before.

George Smith and Leonard Aylesworth, who were granted a two-month stay of sentence until June 7, 1945 in order to prepare the circus for its summer tour, were released from prison on February 23, 1946. Aylesworth was a broken man after his release. In the years that followed, he spent each of his last days at Circus World Museum, in Baraboo, Wisconsin. He would sit in silence among the remnants of the Ringling circus—the traveling show that had been such an enormous part of his life—staring into the past that had come and gone. Whenever children ventured into the exhibits, his spirits would revive and he would happily answer their questions, or tell an anecdote about circus life. His visits to the museum continued every day until his death.

The Ringling corporation made its first settlement payment to the City of Hartford in 1946, followed by a payment of more than $1 million in January of 1947. In his capacity as receiver, Attorney Edward Rogin fulfilled his responsibility to distribute the money in accordance with the settlement amounts determined through arbitration.

In 1948, John Ringling North—who had become president of the corporation by then—announced that the circus would return to Hartford. However, troubled residents rose up in opposition and refused to let it happen. Their memories of the blaze were still too fresh and painful to allow Ringling to perform in the city. The return of the circus would have meant a return of the tragedy, and it was still too soon to contemplate the extent of their personal and communal loss.

In April 1948, the Ringling corporation made the third of its annual settlement payments. One year later, Rogin engaged in a financial battle with circus management over the license fee paid by producer Cecil B. DeMille for the right to film *The Greatest Show on Earth*, which would go on to win the Academy Award for Best Picture in 1949. Rogin ensured that the fees were paid directly to his office, and that the money was applied against remaining claims.

In December 1950—seven months after Robert Dale Segee confessed to arson—the circus made the final payment to Attorney Rogin, settling all claims in full. Rogin had struggled against the tide of John Ringling North's efforts to force the circus into bankruptcy so as to avoid further payment of claims. North tried to overturn the arbitration agreement in 1945, then he attempted to reduce the length of the summer season in order to diminish circus earnings below $750,000 for the year. His purpose was to defeat the mandatory settlement payments by generating less revenue than the minimum amount stipulated in the agreement. When Rogin learned that Ringling receipts were allegedly decreasing in 1948, he ordered an investigation by the Pinkerton Detective Agency, whose operatives observed the show and counted the gate in Dallas, Houston and San Francisco. The Pinkertons provided Rogin with the details of Ringling earnings, details that North was said to have concealed.

Rogin served as receiver for a total of six and a half years. For his services, he submitted a fee request totaling $175,000. Rogin thought that was a reasonable sum, given the extent of his obligations, but he became infuriated when the court reduced his request to $60,000. Four years later, his old friend Julius Schatz sought and received more than $100,000 for his own services as receiver's counsel, a position that Rogin had helped him obtain. Ironically, Schatz had also filed one of the largest negligence suits against the City of Hartford on behalf of 41 families—despite the fact that he was simultaneously a member of the Bar Committee that enacted the arbitration agreement. Rogin was incensed by the judicial ruling that the receiver's counsel would be paid more than the receiver himself. Rogin asserted that his services had been far more valuable to the receivership plan, and that he had dedicated six years of his professional life to its execution. His irritation was made worse by the cordial working relationship that had developed between Schatz and John Ringling North, Rogin's metaphorical enemy in the settlement battle. Although Rogin later appealed and was awarded additional fees, he and Schatz never reconciled.

As part of the State Fire Marshal's review of Rick Davey's findings, investigators Bill Lewis and Robert Butterworth traveled to Ohio to interview Robert Segee, the man who had become the focus of their inquiry. Segee claimed once again to be a true Indian named Chief Black Raven, and he rambled about having been railroaded in 1950, the year he confessed to the Circleville fires. When asked if he had set the Ringling circus on fire in 1944, Segee denied any involvement at all. Like so many convicts who protested their innocence after having been imprisoned, Segee claimed that he had been interviewed without interruption for twenty four hours, and that exhaustion had led him to confess. He never mentioned that, in the transcript of his confession, he had thanked Ohio authorities for the "friendship" he had been offered while in custody, and he never mentioned that he had expressed his gratitude for the opportunity to be treated for his emotional problems. Whether or not the Connecticut SFMO investigators asked Segee about the contents of his confession is not known, nor is it known whether or not they had ever read either the confession or the psychiatric report. When they returned to Connecticut, they reported that Segee did not appear to be sane, and that he had provided no new information relating to the 1944 Hartford circus fire.

On April 2, 1993—several months before the State Fire Marshal's decision was officially released—Rick Davey ended his 22-year career with the Hartford Fire Department. His decision to retire was a profound choice that required enormous strength. In essence, he was turning his back on the man he once was, acknowledging that he had changed as a result of the Ringling circus fire case. That seemed appropriate, given the role that Eleanor had played in his life for nearly a decade. Subconsciously, Rick always knew that he was searching for something unattainable—a dead child. But in a symbolic sense, he had found her and brought her home again. His quest signified the myth of the fireman, the popular ideal of a courageous man in a turnout coat risking his life by racing into raging flames and returning with a terrified child in his arms. Rick never had much interest in fantasies, but he knew that the fire myth had power. After all, that image was one reason he joined the department when he was a young man. He had always had a desire to contribute something to the world, especially by saving a young life from a fiery death. He had not saved Eleanor, but he had restored something of her life by providing an identification that had been lost in smoke and flames for nearly half a century. He could acknowledge that achievement now. Eleanor had changed him, and he was willing to begin a new life after his nine-year mission of the heart. The quest had come to an end.

On August 10, 1993—more than two years after Rick Davey's findings in the Hartford circus fire case were published—the State Fire Marshal's Office announced that the subsequent investigation had not revealed sufficient evidence to declare the July 6, 1944 fire a deliberate act of arson. However, their investigation did find justifiable grounds to change the officially recorded cause of the blaze from accidental to undetermined—just as Deputy State Fire Marshal Paige had promised two years earlier.

On July 6, 1994, Captain Charles Teale of the Hartford Fire Department organized a memorial service to commemorate the fiftieth anniversary of the Ringling circus fire. Numerous dignitaries were invited to share the stage, and scores of survivors gathered in the stifling auditorium of the Fred Wish School on Barbour Street. On behalf of the city he served, Captain Teale presented a plaque to commemorate the victims. He had written the inscription himself: "In loving memory of those who perished on this location fifty years ago, July 6, 1944, and with heartfelt condolences to their survivors." The plaque would be mounted in the lobby of the school, which had been built on the site where the fire had occurred.

Near the end of the program, Rick Davey offered his own thoughts to the audience: "History was written in flame on July 6, 1944. One hundred and sixty eight lives were taken that day, a staggering loss by any standard. One victim, in particular, stands out in our minds. She was eight years old, blond, and perfectly beautiful, in the way that only children can be. We didn't know her name, but we claimed her as our own. She became the symbol of our communal grief, offering us the means to mourn for a part of ourselves that was lost forever.

"Every life is precious, but most precious of all are the lives of children. They embody our dreams. We see in them the hopes and possibilities for a world we know to be difficult, even cruel, at times. Our instinct to protect them can be defeated by an unpredictable force rising up against them, against us. Fifty years ago today, lives were taken by such a force, a demonic blaze with a will of its own. We will never know what contributions they might have made, or what benefits might have been offered to us, had they lived. All we can do is tell the world that they mattered, and that someone cared. We stand on sacred ground. It is right that we honor the memory of our loved ones here. They will never be forgotten."

Robert Dale Segee died on August 3, 1997. Ironically, his body was cremated by an undertaking firm named Cook & Son. Although Segee was sentenced to prison for various arsons he acknowledged having committed in Ohio, he was never interrogated or prosecuted in Connecticut.

Mildred Parsons Cook died on August 22, 1997—less than three weeks after Segee's death. In the months following Rick Davey's 1991 identification of her daughter, Mildred had occasionally been the object of intense media scrutiny, much of which related to the question of how her little girl could have remained unidentified for so many years. The issue of identification has been addressed within the text of this book. It is sufficient to add that the loss of her only daughter under the most horrific circumstances—without the subsequent benefit of either identification or recovery—was an excruciatingly painful memory that stayed with Mildred for the rest of her life. She had also suffered the loss of her youngest child, Edward, as a result of the circus blaze.

During her prolonged hospitalization and treatment for severe burns, Mildred was forced to accept the deaths of two children, an immense emotional burden. After her recovery, she remembered Edward at his burial site in Massachusetts, and she placed a stone bearing Eleanor's name over an adjacent grave that remained empty until 1991. Mildred's surviving son, Don, guided the close-knit Parsons family in their efforts to protect Mildred from painful memories over the balance of her life.

Rick Davey had the opportunity to meet with Mildred in 1991. She was an articulate, active, vibrant person even in advanced age. Rick has been told repeatedly by Mildred's family that she accepted and appreciated the formal identification and symbolic return of her daughter, a process that afforded peace and certainty after many years of nagging doubt. In a letter to Rick dated nearly three years after Mildred's death, Don Cook wrote:

"My mother thought of you as part of the immediate family after your exhaustive efforts resulted in the identification of Eleanor. My mother reached a sense of closure upon Eleanor's return home to the family cemetery plot in Southampton. I know that you have developed a closeness to our family, and to Eleanor's memory, as well. I appreciate your sensitivity toward so many of my relatives as you completed the final phases of your investigation. I want you to know that I fully support your findings in the identification of my sister."

Attorney Edward Rogin died in December 1999. The authors are indebted to him for his willingness to offer his recollections and insights about the events that took place between 1944 and 1950. In a 1992 meeting held in the law offices of Rogin Nassau, the firm he had founded, Rogin revealed that James Haley was a man of impeccable reputation, a man whose conduct and character had never been questioned prior to the Ringling fire. Haley was so deeply humiliated by his conviction, Rogin stated, that he refused to allow his own family to see him during his imprisonment. Rogin acknowledged that there were some other visitors, although Robert Ringling was not among them. While in prison, Haley retained his position as vice-president of the Ringling corporation, and he continued to cooperate with Rogin on circus business affairs. Haley was even allowed to use the anteroom of the warden's office for business meetings.

The most astonishing fact revealed by Rogin during the interview was that Haley had received one unexpected visitor on the afternoon of December 24, 1945—the day of Haley's release. As he was packing for the trip back home, Haley was told by the warden that someone had come to see him. Haley made the assumption that it was Ed Rogin, whom he expected would pay his respects one last time, but Haley was wrong. His unannounced visitor was Judge William Shea, the man who had sentenced him to prison ten months earlier.

Shocked by this news at first, Haley refused to meet with Shea. Then, after intercession from the warden, he relented. When the judge entered the room, Haley was stunned by his appearance: unkempt, unshaven, and carrying the scent of alcohol. Seconds later, Shea got down on his hands and knees and began to cry. Clearly a guilt-ridden man, he pleaded for absolution from the prisoner whose reputation he had damaged. Because of extreme bitterness and residual humiliation, Haley offered Shea only cursory forgiveness. There would be no melodramatic reconciliation based on a gentleman's understanding of the reasons for Shea's courtroom decision. According to Rogin, the public interest in retribution had to be appeased, and Shea had done what was necessary.

Author's Note

My search for information was very much a secret for most of the nine years required for me to unravel this mystery. During that time, my family was curious about what had drawn my interest, and they were occasionally annoyed with me for having allowed this mission to consume so much of my time and attention. After working up to fourteen hours a day as an investigator, I would work long into the night on the Ringling circus fire, trying to find order in the chaos of conflicting facts. The process of discovery was never easy, and it took a great toll on everyone involved, including those closest to me. Although I made sacrifices along the way in order to complete this project, so did my family, and I want Joan, Rick and Michael to know that my mission would not have been accomplished without their support. I will always appreciate their patience, and their understanding.

Since 1991, Don Massey has been my most stalwart and vocal supporter. Our relationship began as a business contract sealed with a handshake, and it has grown into a friendship that continues to this day. He has protected me from people whose intentions would not have served the best interests of Eleanor Cook's memory, and he has allowed me to maintain my principles in the face of extreme pressure to conform to the demands of those whose concept of the truth differed from my own. Without his friendship, his support, and his gift for the written word, this book would not exist.

Rick Davey

AUTHOR'S NOTE

Nine years gone in the blink of an eye. Hard to believe that so much time could have slipped by without my being fully aware of it. I like to think that I was actively in this world for all that time, but that simply isn't true. Those who are closest to me know that a part of me was missing and unavailable. It is bittersweet to leave this project forever, since traveling back to the tragic past was an important part of my life for nearly a decade. But the journey would not have begun, nor would it have been completed, without the love and support of my family. I cherish my wife and daughters, human beings who have grown more precious to me than ever before, and I am grateful to them for showing me the purity of their souls. I thank them from the bottom of my heart for allowing me to be a part of their lives. I look forward to our future together.

In March of 1991, Rick Davey announced to the world that he had identified Little Miss 1565, a beautiful child who died as a result of the Hartford circus fire. Eleanor Emily Cook's identification provided a historic moment of closure for her family, and for the community that had adopted her as one of its own. Although I had never met Rick Davey, I called him because I was compelled to offer my congratulations for what he had done. In return, he made a personal commitment to the voice on the other end of the line, a commitment from which he has never wavered. I will always be grateful for his belief in me. Rick is a man of honor and loyalty, and I am privileged to call him my friend.

Don Massey

Appendix

A Matter Of Degree

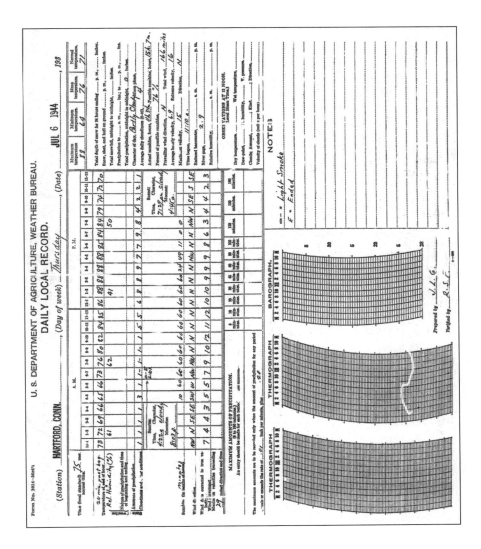

National Weather Service Report (July 6, 1944)

DEATHS, RESIDENT AND NON-RESIDENT, BY AGE, SEX, and RACE, RESULTING FROM THE CIRCUS FIRE WHICH Occurred in Hartford in July 6, 1944

	Total	Under 5 Yrs.	5 - 9 Years	10 - 14 Years	15 - 19 Years	20 - 24 Years	25 - 29 Years	30 - 34 Years	35 - 39 Years	40 - 44 Years	45 - 49 Years	50 - 54 Years	55 - 59 Years	60 - 64 Years	65 - 69 Years	70 - 74 Years	75 Yrs & Over	Age Unknown	Male	Female	Municipal Hospital	Hartford Hospital	St. Francis Hospital	Circus Grounds
Resident																								
Males		5	5				1	3	1		1	1				1	1		18		5			13
Females		5	11	2	2		3	3	4	4	1	1			1	1	1			37	7			30
Total	55																							
Non-Resident																								
Males		3	11	2			1	1	7	8	5		1	1	4	1			23		7	3	3	16
Females		4	16	3	8		3	7	11		5	4	1	2	5	1	1			83	18	3	3	59
Total	106																							
*Unknown																								
Males*			2									2		1					2					2
Females*			3	1																4				4
Age & Sex Unknown																		1						1
Total	7**																							
GRAND TOTAL	168**	17	39	11	4	10	8	13	16	13	8	8	1	7	6	3	3	1	43	124	37	3	3	125

* Age estimated

** Total is one more than sum of males and females because age and sex of one victim, who was crushed and torn to fragmentary remains, is not known.

Note: Of the out-of-state non-residents, 1 was from Massachusetts, 4 from New York, 1 from Pennsylvania, 1 from Rhode Island ---- Total 7

Accurate mortality record compiled by Dr. Milton Fleisch. Note narrative explanation of total victims.

```
                                          STATE OF CONNECTICUT
                                       DEPARTMENT OF STATE POLICE
                                             100 WASHINGTON ST.
                                             HARTFORD, 1, CONN.
```

Address All Departmental Communications to
EDWARD J. HICKEY
COMMISSIONER OF STATE POLICE

STATE BUREAU OF IDENTIFICATION
FRANK V. CHAMEROY
LIEUTENANT IN CHARGE

C O P Y

STATE POLICE CASE
H-25-Z

Submitted at 10:45 A.M. of July 15, 1944, by Officer Mercier, for purposes of comparison, were the following items:

Exhibit 1

Combings from the brush of one Eleanor Cook

Exhibit 2

Hair cut from the head of an unidentified body of a small girl, approximately six years of age

Results of examination: The several strands of thin brown hair, averaging 4" in length and submitted under Exhibit 1, show a great similarity microscopically to those hairs submitted under Exhibit 2. Most of the hairs are lacking in the medulla. A scanty fine linear distribution of dark pigment is confined to the central portion of the light cortex. It may be concluded from this examination only that both specimens may have been derived from the same scalp. Absolute identification is, of course, impossible.

Opper/Sullivan

Lincoln Opper, M. D.
Director of Clinical Laboratories

Results of hair sample analysis performed by the State of Connecticut on July 15, 1944.

```
                    Bureau of                                                OCT 9      Certificate of
                Vital Statistics      CONNECTICUT STATE DEPARTMENT OF HEALTH      1944      Death
    1. Place of Death
        a. County ................................... Hartford ...................................................
        b. City or town .............................. Hartford ...................................................
                                            Note: If outside city or town limits, write rural
        c. Name of Hospital or Institution    Barbour Street Circus Grounds
                                            Note: If not in hosp. or inst., give street No. or location.
        d. Length of stay: in hosp. or inst. ........ - ............ in this community ........ - ........
    2. Usual residence of deceased
        a. State ........................ - ........................ b. County ........ - ........
        c. City or town ................................ - ................................
                                            Note: If outside city or town limits, write rural
        d. Street No. ................................ - ................................
                                            Note: If rural, give location
        e. If foreign-born, how long in U. S. A.? ........ - ........
    3a. Full name ........................... UNKNOWN #1503 ...........................
    3b. Social Security Number ........ - ........
                    PERSONAL AND STATISTICAL PARTICULARS
    4. Sex ... Female ... 5. Race Probably ... 6. Single, widowed, married, divorced - ...
                                    White
    6a. If married, widowed, or divorced, give name of husband or wife ...... - ......
    6b. Age of husband or wife, if alive ............ - ............
    7. Date of death ........................... July           6           1944
                                                month         day         year
    8. Date of birth of deceased ........................... -           -           -
                                                month         day         year
    9. Age ... 9 ... years ... - ... months ... - ... days ...... If less than one day ...... hrs. ...... mins.
    10. Birthplace ... Height 3'11"; approx. weight 55 lbs., slender
                                        City or town              State or foreign country
    11. Usual occupation   build, light brown hair with red glow. Dental
    12. Industry or business     chart at Coroner's office
FATHER  13. Name ...................................................................................
        14. Birthplace ...................................................................................
                                        City or town              State or foreign country
MOTHER  15. Maiden name ...................................................................................
        16. Birthplace ...................................................................................
                                        City or town              State or foreign country
    17a. Informant ...................................................................................
    17b. Address ...................................................................................
    18. Burial, Cremation, or Removal. Date, ... July 10, 1944
        Cemetery ........................... Northwood
        Place ........................... Wilson, Connecticut
    Was Deceased a Veteran? ........ - ........ If so, give War ...................................
    Company ........................... Regiment ........................... Was Body Embalmed? ... No
    If so, Name of Embalmer ........................ - ........................ License No. ...... - ......
                                                                                    Home
    Signature of Licensed Embalmer
        or Licensed Undertaker   Joseph J. Talarski for Talarski Funeral
                    Address   380 Maple Avenue, Hartford, Connecticut
    Form O.V.S. 18 Rev. (9-42) 20M
```

The formal Certificate of Death for Victim 1503

MEDICAL EXAMINER'S REPORT TO CORONER

The undersigned, Medical Examiner, having notice of the death of ....
"An Unknown" #1565

a white ~~colored~~ female, ...6........ years old, late of ....address unknown........

who on ....July 6, 1944 at 6:04 PM........

came to a ~~sudden~~, violent, ~~untimely~~ death, ~~was found dead~~ at ....Municipal Hospital........
in the town of ....Hartford........
and having viewed the body of said deceased, and made immediate inquiry concerning her death,
do hereby certify that said ...."unknown"........
died in the town of ....Hartford........
on ....July 6, 1944........
from* ....Burns, 3rd and 4th degree by fire.........

........While attending the Ringling Bros. Circus on the afternoon of July 6, 1944 the tent and circus equipment became ignited and the child was severely burned. She was taken to the Municipal Hospital where, in spite of supportive treatment, plasma transfusions, etc., she expired. She was then taken to the State Armory which was used as a temporary morgue and then taken to the Hartford Hospital morgue and attempt made to identify her. This was unsuccessful. The outstanding data is: a white female, 6 yrs. of age; blue eyes; shoulder length light brown curly hair; Ht. 3'10"; approximate wt. 40 lbs.; normally developed; 2 permanent lower Incisors; others - deciduous teeth. Her clothing consisted of a flowered dress and brown shoes. These were delivered to the Coroner's office for identification. A dental chart, X-rays of the skull, teeth and sinuses and a picture of the body likewise will be sent to the Coroner's office, the State Police and the City Police. The body had to be interred because it was becoming decomposed.........

I am NOT satisfied that the said death was not caused by the criminal act, omission, or carlessness of any other person or persons, and that an inquest is unnecessary. In accordance with the statute I have delivered the body of said deceased to ....
........Taylor & Modeen........ for burial.

Dated at ....Hartford........ this ....10.... day of ....July.... A.D., 19.44.
                                    ....W. Weissenborn........ Medical Examiner.

FEES:

External examination		$10.00
Travel .....3..... miles @ 15		.45
		10.45

Medical Examiner Dr. Walter Weissenborn's formal examination report on the body of Victim 1565

DEPARTMENT OF STATE POLICE

Case Report. Case No. H-25-Z Station No. K, Colchester July 8, 1944

JUL 18 1944

Number of Pages 1-1

Time	Circus Fire Hartford
8:00 AM to 2:00 PM	Reporting further in my attempt to locate one Eleanor Cook, age 8, who was supposed to have died unidentified, at the Hartford Municipal Hospital and of whom we could find no trace.

At Station "H", I showed the picture of Eleanor, that I had obtained from Mrs. Gill, to several of the officers who had been at the Hartford Armory where the bodies of the unidentified dead had been. Officer John Ring and Officer Charles Casalengo seemed to be positive that this picture resembled a girl whose body had been at the Hartford Armory and since had been removed to the Hartford Hospital morgue. Sgt. Nolan, assigned Off. Ring to accompany me to the Hartford Hospital morgue where I sppke with Dr. Weisenborne, Hartford Medical Examiner. I showed the doctor the picture, and explained the circumstances in this case. He also seemed to feel that the girl that they had at the morgue, was Eleanor Cook.

I contacted Mrs. Brodigan, the Nurses' Aid, who took care of the girl, whose description she said, was that of Eleanor Cook. Mrs. Brodigan is employed by the O.P.A., Allen St., Hartford. She agreed to come to the morgue to see if this was the child that she had reference to. When she arrived, she made positive identification ß the child, as well as the clothes, and stated that this was the girl that she had taken care of the day before. Off. Ring and myself took Mrs. Brodigan back to her office, and then picked up Mrs. Gill and brought her to the morgue. She viewed the body again and said that this was the one that she had looked at at the Hartford Armory with her brother. The only thing that made her say that this was not Eleanor, was the fact that she thought that Eleanor had 8 second upper

Officer *S. E. Freeman* #231

S. E. Freeman #231 State Police

Freeman, S. E. Officer

Connecticut State Police Trooper Samuel Freeman's definitive report on the attempt to identify the body of Eleanor Emily Cook on July 8, 1944 teeth, whereas this body had four second upper teeth and four second lower teeth. She said that if it hadn't been for that, she would say that the child was her neice, Eleanor Cook. She was advised to get a dental chart from the child's dentist as she said there had been some work done on Eleanor's teeth. The Medical Examiner showed Mrs. Gill where there had been work done on the back teeth of the girl that he had at the morgue, but she still stated that because of the teeth she did not think it was Eleanor.

    A later attampt to get a dental chart was not successful as the dentist was on vacation in Canada.

    As I could do nothing further, and Mrs. Gill had looked at the rest of the bodies of children, I returned to Station "K". I was advised later that Mrs. Gill had been declared incompetent to identify the body of Eleanor Cook, by the Medical Examiner, Dr. Weisenborne. I will close this case at this time and if any evidence warrants the reopening of same, I will do so. This of course, only pertains to this particular phase of H-25-Z, as assigned by Commissioner Edward J. Hickey.

    Case Closed.

Page Two of Connecticut State Police Trooper Samuel Freeman's definitive report on 1565's identity

```
                                        15 Tower Lane
                                        Easthampton, Ma. 01027
                                        Nov. 26, 1991

Lt. Rick Davey
Fire Prevention Bureau
275 Pearl St.
Hartford, Ct. 06103

Dear Lt. Davey:

It is difficult to reply to your letter of Nov. 14th as I don't
have the gift of expressing myself as you most certainly do. I
would not have been offended if you had said "Dear Mom". If it
weren't for your tirelessness, ingenuity, and your own personal
feeling for Eleanor, I would not have found my daughter and had
the satisfaction of bringing her home to lie next to her brother.

I remember a thought crossed my mind when I was told of the deaths
of my two children, "Why go on?" But then I thought of the one
son I still had and it helped to give me the strength to endure.
And then I found that one must keep busy both physically and
mentally and I feel that same way now.

As far as the furor is concerned, it has practically died down;
although I did have one call from a local reporter after the Life
Magazine article was out.

It would be a great satisfaction to me if that "person" in Ohio
could be brought to justice, but at this late date, I expect that
it will be impossible.

As I have said before, thank you for all your efforts in bringing
this matter to a conclusion, and for keeping me informed of any
future events. Feel free to keep in touch with our family whether
it's on this matter or not.

                                Sincerely,

                                Mildred Cook

                                Mildred Cook
                                "Mom"
```

Mildred Cook's first letter to Rick Davey, which began an ongoing correspondence between them in the years after Eleanor's identification.

INDEX

A

ABC 275
Abramson, Dr. B. W. 184
Absolution 293
Academy Award 288
Accelerants 154
Achilles heel 135
Adler, Felix 130
Aerial ballet 22
African-American 130
Age discrepancies 258
Albums 263
Alcorn, Hugh Sr. 61, 62
Alcorn, Meade, 62, 86, 98, 105
Allied forces 23
Alligator scarring 130
American flag 37, 53, 63
Anderson, Don 56, 136
Anglo-Saxon 12
Anteroom 293
Arbitration 122, 123, 130, 287-288
Archibald, Rev. Warren 120
Armory 78, 79, 80, 87-88, 91-93, 97, 101, 111, 112-114, 116, 232, 236, 241, 248, 251, 285
Army servicemen 45, 53, 60, 71, 79
Arson 111, 130, 139, 153, 164, 165-166, 167, 169, 173, 185, 186, 195, 197, 261, 262, 264, 270-271, 287

Arson murder 272
Arson squad 166
Arsonist 107, 152, 167, 170, 173, 177, 178, 182, 186, 192, 194, 195, 198, 200, 264, 271, 273, 291
Ashton, Mrs. 156-157
Atonement 142
Attorney General of CT 143
August clown 22
Autopsies 217
Aylesworth, Leonard 26, 86, 95, 98, 100, 105, 125, 137-138, 140, 141, 286

B

Back door 46, 49, 104
Back yard 68
Badge Number 539 5, 282
Bailey, John (Chief State's Attorney) 270, 271, 275
Baldwin, Governor Raymond 62, 75, 76, 77, 78, 82, 122, 128, 129, 136, 140
Baldwin Park, CA 141
Baling rings 56
Bally girl 22
Baltimore, MD 99
Bankruptcy 100, 122, 126, 142, 288

Banshees 62
Bar Committee 245, 289
Baraboo, WI 19, 287
Barber, Detective Thomas 116,
    117, 118, 136-137, 251, 285
    and 1565 grave tradition 136
Barnum & Bailey Circus 20
Barnum, Phineas (P. T.) 19, 20
Basal metabolism test 170
Beal, George Brinton 21
Beast 50, 51, 58, 61, 143, 152-153,
    158
Beckwith, Captain Paul 105, 169,
    175, 178, 179, 182, 196-197,
    200
Benedetti, Ralph 192
Berman Family 239-240
Berman, Judith 239
Bill, Albert S. 205
Blanchfield, David 63, 86, 104-105,
    125, 140, 141-142
Bleacher jacks 129
Blood red moon 38, 107
Blowdowns 110
Blue bleachers 46, 213, 222, 225
Board of Inquiry 126-127, 135, 226
Bond Hotel 98
Bone growth 255
Boston, MA 23, 33, 73, 182
Boston Sunday Post 21
Bracelets, ID 80
Bradley Field 60, 69
Brice, John 44, 49, 86, 95
British 9
Brodigan, Mrs, 241-243
Brophy, Thomas (Fire Marshal)
    218-220, 221, 224, 227
Brown School 77, 81, 90, 91, 97
Brown Thomson 70
Buffalo Jump, MT 274
Building Commission 135
Bull men 50
Bureau of Alcohol, Tobacco
    and Firearms (ATF) 263, 276
Bureau of Identification 247
Burgdorf, Dr. Alfred 116, 127
Burns School 156, 158
Bushnell Park 10, 28
Bushong, Dr. Roy 204

Butler, Dr. Edgar 79, 235
Butler, Roland 109, 110
Butterworth, Robert 289

C

Cage chutes 46, 47, 48, 54, 55, 56,
    64, 71, 84, 85, 116, 133,
    134, 138, 157, 158
Caley, William 44, 138, 140, 141
California 21
Caliper measurements 257
Callan, Harry (Fire Marshal) 168,
    169, 176, 179, 180, 181,
    182, 192, 193-194
Calliope 20, 37, 57, 61
Campbell, Jesse 270, 271
Camphor cream 72
Canada 256
Careless Smoker Theory 44, 111,
    129, 130
Carson, John 86, 98
Cartilage 238
Carver, Dr. Wayne 267, 270, 272,
    275
Casalengo, Charles 243
Case 417A 176
Case H-25-Z 129
Case 91-7600 270
Cat who walks alone 112
Catholic Church 44, 71
Cattle prods 55
Cause and origin 153, 154
CBS 267, 274
CBS *Morning News* 273
Center Cemetery 118, 269, 279
Center poles 59
Central Park 10
Chain of Identifications 255, 261
Chameroy, Lt. Frank 247-248
Chapman, Cliff 56
Chapman, Richard 178, 179, 194
Charter Oak Terrace 149-150, 151,
    152
Cherubs 44
Chief Black Raven 289
Chimney effect 214, 215
Christmas 259

Index

Churchill Park 28
Circleville, OH 165, 166, 167, 176, 181, 196, 197, 200, 204, 289
Circleville Herald 179
Circus Day 39, 44
Circus Fans of America 110, 127, 128
Circus World Museum 287
Cirque d'Hiver 20, 22
City of Hartford 110, 116, 121, 122, 126, 137, 142, 271, 285, 286, 288, 289
City of hope 120, 142, 143, 280
City of New York 220
Clark, Bill 168, 180
Clark, Samuel 140
Cleveland, OH 104
Cline, Guy G. (Ohio Prosecutor) 166, 170, 198, 206, 211
Clothing 256-257, 261
Clown(s) 11, 20, 21, 22, 40, 45, 46, 68, 69
Clown Alley 56
Cocoanut Grove 73
Cole Brothers Circus 22
Collinsville, CT 249
Columbus, OH 166, 169, 170, 175, 176, 184, 188, 197
Columbus Dispatch 207
Columbus State Hospital 209
Coma 73, 135
Comic relief 45
Common Council 120, 126
Concentration camp (Nazi) 65
Confession (Segee) 165, 168, 173, 174, 177, 179, 180, 192, 194, 196, 248, 265, 272, 290
Conn. Medal for Distinguished Civilian War Service 136
Conn. State Library 163, 271
Conspiracy 229
Cook, Don 13, 15, 29, 40-44, 47, 52, 69, 90, 91, 95, 96, 97, 107, 112, 115, 247-250, 252-254, 259-261, 267, 292
Cook, Edward 13, 14, 18, 27-32, 36-38, 40, 41, 43, 47, 52, 57-58, 90, 95, 96, 97, 112, 116, 118, 247-248, 258, 268-270, 292
Cook, Eleanor Emily (Honey) 39, 40, 41, 43, 47, 52, 57-58, 62, 81, 90, 91-92, 93, 96, 108, 112, 113, 114, 118, 129, 136, 232-237, 239-245-247, 249-252, 255-258, 260-261, 267-269, 272-274, 276-280, 282-284, 287, 290, 292, 295-296
Cook, John 138
Cook, Mildred 12, 13-19, 22, 27-34, 38-44, 47, 52, 57-58, 69, 73, 80, 90, 92, 95, 96, 112, 114, 116, 118, 123, 125, 135, 136, 247-248, 250-251, 254-257, 268-269, 273-274, 279-281, 287, 292
Cook, Wesley 12-14, 255, 256
Cooper, Jackie 187
Cortege 119
Cortex 240
Court, Alfred 20
Cover-up 197, 211
Crematoria, Nazi 65
Criminal liability 212, 227
Curlee, Bill 55-56
Curlee, David 55
Cutler, Rosemary 186, 188

D

D-Day 11
Dallas, TX 289
Davey, Bud 148, 152
Davey, Madeline 147, 149
Davey, Mrs. 147-148
Davey, Rick *x*, 148-152, 158, 177-184, 187, 196, 197, 199-201, 203, 205, 208, 211, 217-219, 222, 224, 229, 240, 242, 246-250, 251-258, 260, 271-274, 286-287, 289-292, 295-296
Davey, Steve 147, 151

Death certificate(s) 251, 258, 260-261, 267, 270, 272
Death roster (Fleisch) 111
Deliberate ignition 213, 220, 223, 226
Delinquency, juvenile 208
DeMatteo, Anna 246-251, 257-258
DeMille, Cecil B. 288
Demma, Miss 156
Dental chart 234-236, 245
Department of Agriculture 215
Depth of char 154
Diamond Match Lumber Co. 172
Dillon's 113
DiMartino, Anna 87-88, 121
DiMartino, Sal 87-88, 121
Disaster March 50
Domino 22
Donahue, Linda 65
Dover, New Hampshire 177, 178, 180
Dow, Everett 45, 129
Downeaster 23
Driscoll, Barbara 172, 173, 180, 195
Dunbar, CSP Trooper 148
Dunn, William 94
Dutch lineage 12
Dutch settlers 9
DuVal, Herbert 35, 86, 95

E

Ear lobes 238
East Hartford, CT 163
East St. Louis, IL 166
Eastern authorities 196-197, 211
Eastland Hotel 182
Election of 1950 273
Electroencephalogram 170
Elegant clown 22
Elizabeth Park 10
Ellis, Carlos 133
Ellis, Whitney 133
Emanuel Synagogue 120
Enfield, CT 163
England 22
Erickson, Raymond 71, 89

Erickson, Sophie 89-90
Euclid, OH 55
Europe 11, 20, 22, 123
European villagers 47, 65
Evans, Merle 46, 50, 57, 61, 68, 110
Evanston, IL 111
Eviction 151
Excommunication 44
Extraction, post-mortem 279
Extradition 166, 198, 203, 204, 212, 228

F

Facial features 257, 260
Farley's 113
Fauliso, Joseph 127
FBI 112, 262, 264, 267, 275
FBI profiler 277
FBI VICAP unit 276
Femoral artery 72
Film cartoonist 21
Finnegan, James 94
Fire 152, 153
Fire extinguishers 86, 98, 100, 102, 103, 104, 137
Fire Victims Relief Fund 134
Fireline 153
Fireproofing 99, 111, 125
First Call 45
First Congregational Church 18
Flame growth 223
Flash message 65
Fleisch, Dr. Milton 111, 233
Flowered dress 236, 256
Flying Squadron 34, 133
Flying Wallendas 20, 45
Four Feathers 205, 206
Fourth of July 11, 19, 28
G. Fox & Company 70
France 20, 22, 268
Fred Wish School 291
Free passes 135
Freeman, CSP Trooper Samuel 113, 114, 246, 255, 261
French Child's Song 268

Freud, Sigmund 184
Front yard 51
Full moon 27, 38
Fundamental Orders 16
Funerals 119, 120
Funnels, canvas 56

G

Gaffer 102
Gardner, Rev. Robert 279
Gargantua 44
Gargantua, Mrs. 44
Gargoyles 44
Gary, Agent Gordon (Gus) 263-264, 266, 267, 275, 277
Gasoline and wax 26, 86, 99, 125, 188
Geek show 43
Gentian violet 89
Germany 22, 152, 268
Gill, Emily 69, 80, 81, 90, 91-93, 95, 96, 107, 112-114, 123, 125, 232, 233-234, 239, 241-245, 250, 255-257, 259, 261, 269, 287
Godfrey, Michael (Chief) 59, 60, 62, 97, 135, 169, 286
Goodrow, Detective Thomas 264, 270, 271, 280
Gospel of St. Matthew 120
Graham, William 165, 166, 176, 195
Gratuities 135
Greatest Show on Earth 11, 20, 288
Griebling, Otto 22
Gwinnell, Kenneth 138, 179, 222
Gypsies 22, 46, 107, 110

H

Hackett, Earl 176
Hadden, William 124, 140, 143
Hagenbeck-Wallace 22
Hair analysis 129, 257
Haley, Aubrey Ringling 125-126
Haley, James A. 34, 86, 87, 91-92, 94, 98, 105-106, 125, 130, 139, 140-142, 169, 287, 293
Hallisey, Thomas 35, 49, 50, 51, 59, 62, 86, 124
Harris, Dr. Robert 68
Hartford Circus Fire 1-2
Hartford (City of) 9, 10, 11-12, 15, 17-18, 27-28, 31, 34-35, 38, 39, 44-45, 64-65, 69-70, 77, 78, 80, 86, 94, 100, 103, 104, 107, 109, 110-112, 116, 119, 120-123, 126, 132, 143, 147, 158, 169, 175, 180, 199-200, 203-204, 207-208, 217-218, 220-221, 226-229, 232, 249, 262, 265, 267-268, 271, 274, 278-280, 285, 288-289
Hartford Courant 109, 110, 115, 123, 125, 129, 137, 155, 164, 256, 266, 273
Hartford Hospital 70, 73, 113, 116, 118, 119, 123, 135
Hartford Police Court 98, 115
Hartford Times 65, 115, 125, 134, 143, 164
Hawser ropes 57
Hayes, Joseph 137
Healy, Frank E. (Coroner) 94, 124, 125, 135, 139-140
Height 250, 257-261
Heiser, Jennie 80
Hertford 10
Hertfordshire 9
Hickey, Edward J. 62, 75-76, 78, 82-87, 91-92, 94, 97-100, 102, 105, 111, 113, 116, 122, 124, 128-130, 132-135, 137-140, 164, 168-169, 175-183, 197, 198-203, 205, 208, 210-212, 218-219, 221-230, 232, 240, 241, 248, 273
Higley, Dr. Bernard 170-174, 175, 177, 179, 184, 185-186, 188, 194-197
High wire 11, 47, 49
Hindenburg 66
Hobo 21, 22

Holden, Mrs. John 252
Hollywood, CA 21
Holocaust 65
Homicide 195, 196
Homosexual 195
Honey (Eleanor Emily Cook) 13-15, 18, 27-28, 30-33, 36, 38-41, 43, 47, 52, 57-58, 62, 81, 90, 91-92, 93, 96, 108, 112, 113, 114, 118, 129, 136, 245, 261
Hooker, Thomas 9, 10
Hooper Manufacturing 99
House of hope 9
Houston, TX 289
Huckleberry Finn 10
Human pyramid 47
Hurley, John 127

I

Impulse neurosis 204
Indian 274, 289
Indictment 204, 216-218, 220, 221, 224, 227
Indies 10
Inquest 94, 95, 124, 125, 132, 133, 139
Inside Edition 273, 274
Insurance, certificate of 35, 85, 100, 221
Insurance City 226
Involuntary manslaughter
    See Manslaughter
Iraq 263

J

Jester 22
Jesus Loves Me 31, 280
Jewish religious laws 239
Jinx 27
Jitney bus 110
Journalists 228
Judge, Dan Gordon 106, 122, 123
Jute 26
Juvenile delinquency 208

K

Kaddish 120
Kearney, Inspector 182
Kelley, F. Beverly 110, 128
Kelly, Emmett 20-22, 45, 49, 50, 51, 59, 68-69
Kelly, George (sailmaker) 45
Keney Park 37
Kettle drum 57
King, John (Chief) 35, 61, 109, 115, 121, 137
King, John (Judge) 126
Knott, Edward 178
Kochian, Capt. Edward 178, 182, 183
Kovar, May 20, 47, 49, 54, 55, 110
Kowalczyk, Eugene (Gene) 278, 279, 280
Kurneta, Stanley 71, 89

L

Ladies Agreement 126
LaMonda, Charles R. (Chief) 166, 175, 176-177, 192
Last rites 68, 71
Lavin, Captain Paul 169, 175-177, 178-179, 180, 182-183
Leikind, Burr 62, 84, 85, 86, 98, 100, 105
Letter of commendation 266
Lewis, Bill 289
Liability coverage 86, 100
Liberty Mutual 17, 112
Life Magazine 196, 273
Lima State Hospital 196, 197, 202, 204, 209-210
Lion queen 20
Liquidation 126
Little Miss Fifteen Sixty Five (1565) 117, 118, 120, 123, 125, 132, 136, 137, 150, 155, 157, 160, 161-16, 230-234, 237-245, 246-248, 250-252,

Index   313

254-258, 260-262, 265, 267,
    269-273, 276, 279-280, 282-
    283, 285-287, 296
Lloyds of London 23, 100
Lodge, John 273
Logging industry 147, 149
Looney, Rev. Thomas 120
Los Angeles, CA 102
Lowe, Detective Edward 116, 117,
    118, 136-137, 251, 285
Lowe, Judith 239, 240, 256
Luidens, Dr. Harry 209
Lunch box 253
Lynche, Chief 180

M

MGM 102
M'Naghten Rule 211-212
MacDaniel, Andrew (Chief) 178,
    180, 182
MacDougal, Inspector 182
Mackenzie, William 94
Madden, Frances 77
Madison Square Garden 22
Maine 149, 172, 176, 178, 181,
    182
Manchester, Dickie 187
Mandible 279
Mansfield State Reformatory 108
Manslaughter 105, 106, 111, 124,
    140, 141, 164
Mark Twain 10
Marquee 42, 54, 66
Marshall Street 17
Martin, Katherine 130
Massachusetts Bay Colony 9
McBride, Mona 204
McCarthy, Mary 176, 177
McDonough, Dr. Edward 270
McGovern Granite Company 84,
    91
McLaughlin, Reid 184
Means 168, 184
Medulla 129, 240
Menagerie 104
Mercier, Lester 129
Meriden, CT 272

Middletown, CT 117, 118, 133
Midwest 253
Migraine 264
Mingle, George (Colonel) 176, 199,
    205
Mitchell, Charley 85, 179
Molars, six-year 236, 255
Mole Rahmim 120
Moody, Margaret 241-243
Moors, Guy (Inspector) 202-203
Morale, national 35, 111
Morning Song 67
Morphine 72, 73, 96
Morse, George (Marshal) 180
Mortensen, William (Mayor) 62,
    65, 75, 78, 82, 85, 86, 94,
    97, 116, 119, 120, 121, 122,
    126, 127
Motive 168, 173, 195
Municipal Hospital 70, 71, 72, 73,
    81, 82, 89, 90, 91, 95, 107,
    112, 114, 116, 134, 234,
    241, 242
Municipal negligence 226
Murphy, Patty 130, 285
Mystery Girl 232, 233

N

Napalm 53
Nassau, Louis E. 122
National Anthem 46
National Center for the Analysis of
    Violent Crime (NCAVC)
    263, 277
National Fire Prevention Association
    (NFPA) 214, 217, 224
National Weather Service 215
Native Americans 38
Nautical lines 26
Navy (U.S.) 89
Nazi 65, 70, 111
Nedelsky, Dr. Eugene 209-210
Negligence 39, 140, 142
New England 5, 12, 14, 23, 26,
    108, 165, 174, 181, 183,
    192, 204, 207
New Hampshire 172, 177, 180-182

New Haven, CT 247, 275
New Haven County Home 247
Newington, CT 28, 36
Newkirk's 113
New Orleans, LA 61
Newsweek 273
New York City 10, 106, 124
New York Times 273
Nolo contendere 140
Nook Farm 10
Normandy (D-Day) 23
Norris, Judy 117, 118, 249, 250-251
North, John Ringling 125, 126, 142, 287, 288, 289
North Meadows 127
Northampton, MA 118
Northwood Cemetery 119, 136, 278, 280, 283, 285
Norwich State Hospital (NSH) 129, 240

O

Obsessive-compulsive 204
Ohio Highway Patrol 175, 176, 199, 205, 206
Ohio State University Hospital 170
Olmstead, Frederick 10
Olver, Hal 111
Onderdonk, Dr. Henry 87
Operation Desert Shield 263
Operation Desert Storm 263
Opper, Dr. Lincoln 129, 240, 257
Opportunity 168, 184, 195, 225
Orient 10
Outtakes 274

P

Paige, David (Marshal) 270-271, 272, 291
Paraffin 26, 137
Parsons 12, 14, 16, 38, 96, 110, 118, 249-251, 255-256, 261, 279-280, 287, 292

Parsons, Dorothy 249
Parsons, Marion 36-38, 39, 40, 42, 69, 114,
Parsons, Ted 14, 16, 27, 30, 31, 37, 39, 40, 69, 70, 95, 96, 107, 118, 241
    and Emily Gill 103, 106-108, 119-120
Pearl Harbor 35
Penicillin 72, 74
Performance anxiety 21
Persian Gulf 263
Peterson, Alice 176
Phantom sounds 214
Philadelphia, PA 23, 27, 38, 44
Pickaway County Jail 176, 203, 205, 211
Pied Piper 20
Pinkerton(s) 76, 289
Piscataqua River 172
Pituitary function 260
Plasma 72
Point of origin 163, 177
Pope Park 28
Portland, ME 23-24, 26, 27, 38, 107, 133, 139, 172, 176-180, 182, 274
Portland Evening Express 184
Portland Pier 186
Portland Telegram 182
Portsmouth, NH 24, 172, 180, 184, 206
Pratt's 113
Press corps 142
Priest, unknown 68, 71, 89
Prison sentences 141-143, 164
Probie 152
Progression of flame 154
Prophet Elijah 21
Providence, RI 26, 27, 38, 107, 138, 189, 193
Puritans 9
Pyromaniac 130

Q

Quantico 263, 264, 265, 267, 275
Quarter poles 37, 61

R

Radcliff, Carl (Sheriff) 166-167
Radcliff, William (Judge) 204, 207, 209
Ramsey, John and Patsy 277
Ramsey, JonBenet 277
Reader's Digest 273
Receivership 289
Red Cross 45, 78, 79, 80, 92, 97, 134
Red Man, the (Segee) 166, 171-172, 184-185, 192-193, 195, 198
Reed, Donna 38
Reiff, Lymoine 85
Renaissance 22
Republican 273
Retinal scanning 240
Revolution, American 10
Rickets (disease) 255, 258
Rickett's Equestrian Circus 44
Rimelspach, Dr. 169
Ring, John 243
Ringling band 50, 57, 61
Ringling brothers 19, 20, 135, 139, 188
Ringling Brothers Circus 19, 20, 41, 63, 65
Ringling Bros. and Barnum & Bailey Circus 11, 22, 100, 107
Ringling circus 11, 19, 20, 22, 23, 44, 61, 62, 63, 68, 70, 71, 82, 85, 107, 111, 115, 118, 122, 124, 125
Ringling, Edith 125, 126
Ringling, Otto 20
Ringling, Robert 34, 98, 99, 111, 125, 128, 142
Ringlings 20
Ringling troupe 20, 22, 23
Ritchie, Mildred 22
Roach, Hal (film studio) 102
Rogin, Edward S. 122, 123, 124, 126, 130, 131, 132, 140, 142, 288, 289, 293-294
Rogin Nassau (law firm) 293
Roll call 185
Roughnecks 37

Roustabouts 23, 26, 41, 50, 56, 110, 133, 165, 198, 225
Runaway theory 123
Ryan, Charley 85

S

Sabotage 111, 112
Saboteurs 193
Sacred ground 291
Sage-Allen 70
Sailmaker 45
Salvation Army 97, 173-174
San Francisco, CA 289
Sanborn, Oliver (Chief) 178, 179
Sanitarium 147
Sarasota, FL 133, 141
Satellites x
Satyrs 44
Scarboro, ME 178
Schatz, Julius 289
See Here, Private Hargrove 38
Segee, Eugene 24
Segee, Lewis III 166
Segee, Robert Dale 24, 25, 26, 27, 41, 133, 139, 165-197, 198, 212, 214, 225-229, 248, 265, 271-272, 274-278, 282, 288-290, 292
Segee, Roselyn (Penny) 206
Seidenberg, Dr. Louis 204, 209
Sells-Floto Circus 22
Serial Arson and Bomber Research (SABR) Unit 262, 265-266, 275, 277-278
Seryak, Joseph 176, 177, 178
Sex play 173
Sexual memories 193
Sexuality 195
Shaw, Captain (CSP) 247-248
Shea, Judge William 140, 141-142, 293
Sheldon Academy 118
Shrine Circus 22
Sideshow barkers 19, 37
Silence of the Lambs 264
Silverman, Rabbi Morris 120

Sisal 26
Skin grafts 74, 135
Slapstick artist 21
Smith, George W. 125, 137, 287
Smith, Inspector Russell 166, 174, 177-179, 182, 186, 192, 205, 211, 225
Social Welfare Department 89
Soldiers (U.S.) 45, 69
Sousa, (John Philip) 50
South Congregational Church 120
South Portland, ME 24
Southboro, MA 141
Southampton, MA 12, 14, 18, 19, 27, 69, 112, 114, 118, 136, 258, 259, 260, 269, 279-280, 292
Southern New England Telephone Company (SNET) 77
Spellman, Sergeant 51
Spiel 43
Spirit voice 162, 231
Spreading eagle 188
Springfield, MA 100, 137
St. Michael's Church 120
Stars and Stripes Forever 50
State Fire Marshal's Office 276, 290
Station 7 148, 152
Steam organ (Calliope) 20
Steel, Captain Douglas 178
Stowe, Harriet Beecher 10
Street parade 19, 20
Subjective bias 225
Sullivan, Mary 89
Symmetry 244
Sympathizers, Nazi 111

T

Talarski Maple Hill 113, 279
Tally, William 112, 113, 114
Talmud 21
Tanbark 46, 56, 265
Teale, Captain Charles 291
Teeth 235-236, 244-45
Tetanus 74
Thanksgiving 136

Thomas, Henry (Marshal) 59, 60, 63, 75, 85, 97, 116, 121
Titanic 55, 61
Today Show 273
Todd, Neil 26, 44, 84, 85, 179
Tolson, Mrs. Clarence 69
Tolson, Ron 69, 258
Tom Sawyer 10
Tooth development 255
Tooth eruption pattern 276
Track 46
Traumatic brain injury 148
Travelers Aid Society 176
Triage 73
Tuberculosis 147, 149
Tunnel vision 225
Tuohy, Lynne 266, 272, 273
Twenty Third Psalm 128
Tyszka, Bill 78
Tyszka, Mrs. Thomas 78

U

UPI 168, 169, 180
Upstairs 47

V

Vandalia, IL 21
Velasco, Luis 262, 264, 270, 275, 277
Vendetta, John (Marshal) 155, 267, 268, 270, 271, 272, 278, 280
Versteeg, Edward "Whitey" 23, 26, 34, 41, 86, 95, 98, 100, 102, 103, 104, 105, 140, 141
Victim 001 119, 233
Victim 1503 234, 250
Victory gardens 61, 67
Viet Nam War 152
Virginia Beach, VA 230
Vitamin D (Deficiency) 255

W

WTIC 97
Waif theory 123
Wallenda, Helen 47, 50
Wallenda, Karl 47
Wallendas 45, 47, 49, 110
Walsh, Joe 47
Waltzing Matilda 50
Wanamie, PA 141
War bonds 45
War Council 70, 97, 101, 128
Ward (Deputy Comm.) 169
Watergate 164
Waterproofing 53, 86, 94, 98, 99, 100, 111, 125
Wax-and-gasoline 86, 99, 125
Weary Willie 21
Weissenborn, Dr. Walter 68, 79, 87, 113, 119, 233-234, 236, 243-245, 261, 279
Wells, Dr. Donald 73, 74
West Hartford, CT 163
West Salem, WI 141
Wethersfield, CT 163, 287
Wethersfield State Prison 141
White clown 22
White Tops (CFA newsletter) 128
Willimantic, CT 126
Willson Children's Center 170, 175, 188
Wilson, CT 119
Winsted, CT 242
Wise, Talmer (Chief) 167
Wish School 291
Worcester, MA 20
World War II 9, 11, 22, 44, 70, 73, 143, 149

X

X-rays 170, 235, 276
X-rays, absence of 236

Y

Yankee 12
Yee, Rev. James 114, 118

Z

Zealots (religious) 9